152.1   LeGuerer, Annick

               Scent
               (The Mysterious and
               Essential Powers o

	DATE DUE	Smell)	
7 AUG 1994			
23 FEB 1995			
AUG. 2 2 2009			

SCENT

SCENT

THE MYSTERIOUS AND ESSENTIAL POWERS OF SMELL

▲

Annick Le Guérer

▼

Translated from the French by Richard Miller

Turtle Bay Books
A Division of Random House
New York
1992

Le Guérer, Annick.
[Pouvoirs de l'odeur. English]
Scent, the mysterious and essential powers of smell/Annick Le Guérer;
translated from the French by Richard Miller.
p. cm.
Translation of: Les pouvoirs de l'odeur.
ISBN 0-394-58526-7
1. Odors—History. 2. Odors—Social aspects. 3. Smell—History.
I. Title.
QP458.L4413 1992
152.1'66—dc20   91-51049

Manufactured in the United States of America
24689753
First U.S. Edition

Designed by Oksana Kushnir

To Bernard

CONTENTS

▼

PART THREE
BLOOD AND INCENSE: A SEARCH FOR THE SOURCE
OF PERFUME'S POWER

PART FOUR
THE PHILOSOPHICAL NOSE

PART ONE

FROM PERFUMED PANTHER TO GERMAN BROMIDROSIS: THE POWERS OF SMELL TO REPEL AND ATTRACT

1

SMELL AND CAPTURE

▼

You left three years ago. Still your perfume
haunts my solitude. Even now my room is filled
with it, but where are you, my Beloved?

Li Po, *The Absent Lover*

Perfumes . . . calme and soothe all mindes and
drawe them as the magnet draws iron.

H. C. Agrippa, *Occult Philosophy*

ODOR, MAGIC, POSSESSION,
AND PROTECTION

Texts on magic and sorcery make constant reference to the
attractive, bewitching power of smell. Since antiquity perfumes
and unguents have been a part of the witch's arsenal. The satirist
Lucian and the philosopher Apuleius both record Greek and
Roman superstitions with regard to the use of odors. For example, in order to transform herself into a bird, the sorceress must
stand naked before a brazier of burning coals into which she has
thrown some incense, and recite several formulas. She then
smears her body with an unguent, which transforms her and
enables her to fly away.[1] However, used by an outsider who

might attempt to penetrate the mystery, the levitating balm could have a strange effect. In a tale by Lucian, the protagonist Lucius was changed into an ass when he disastrously selected the wrong vial of potion, and was condemned to perform as a trained animal until he was lucky enough to happen upon the correct magical antidote: "At that moment a man went by carrying some flowers; among them, I espied some fresh-picked roses; without a moment's hesitation I jumped to my feet: everyone thought I was about to dance, but instead I dashed to the flowers, I picked out the roses and devoured them. To the great amazement of the spectators my animal shape collapsed as if in a swoon, the ass disappeared, and there stood I, Lucius, stark naked."[2]

The mysterious power of odors is also evident in cases of those possessed by evil spirits. The famous seventeenth-century demonic-possession trials held at Loudun that ended with the execution of Father Urbain Grandier are a prime example. At the public hearings the odor of musk roses brought on hysterical attacks among the victims and their exorcists, to the vast delight of the spectators. Less fortunate than Lucian's ass, the nuns fell into fits after sniffing at an accursed bouquet: "On the very day that Sister Agnes, an Ursuline novice, made her profession (11 October 1632) she was possessed by the Devil, as the Reverend Mother herself told me. The charm was a bouquet of musk roses that was found lying on a dormitory staircase. The Reverend Mother picked it up and sniffed at it and others followed suit, whereupon all were seized with possession."[3] By casting a spell that affects both body and spirit, perfume, in this case, is actually a tool of Satan.

Although sorcery draws upon the powers inherent in both pleasant and unpleasant odors, witches and their minions emit nauseating smells that are redolent of their satanic natures. A sixteenth- and seventeenth-century myrmidon of the Devil who devoted her perfume-making talents to ravishing men's bodies and souls would follow a strict regimen that resulted in her stench. From her melancholic blood and humors, grown sickly with wrath and cupidity, there arose poisonous vapors that infected both man and beast. The witch's vegetarian diet of onions, cabbages, and legumens and her copulations with the "Obscene Goat"[4] gave her body a truly deadly odor, which she used as a weapon. "Tender young children"[5] and other weak creatures were the first victims of her evil breath, but she had only to blow to flatten even the strongest.[6] In her dark and miserable hovel she brewed up noxious mixtures with which she could bring down the plague, transform herself into a wolf,[7] or take to the skies on a broomstick to travel to her Sabbath.

She combined medicinal herbs, plants that are poisonous (hemlock) and/or narcotic and hallucinogenic (belladonna, henbane), the fat of a newborn child, human and bat blood, cat brain, snake, pitch, and the droppings of toads and crows, with mandragora—the mandrake root. This root, found in loamy and fetid soil that had been fertilized by the fat and sperm exuded by hanged men, vaguely resembled the human body in shape and was believed to possess (among its other unusual powers) the ability to fortify weakened seminal fluid and to cure impotence. Made as it was, according to the apothecary Laurent Catelan, "wholly of virile sperm consumed, digested and enriched within the earth by nature alone, the root must surely connect, intermingle and join with the natural sperm of him who takes it into his mouth . . . eventually reaching the womb and therein combined, engendering and producing a man."[8]

Since the collection of the ingredients she needed forced the sorceress to rob graves and haunt gallows, she developed a repulsive stench that was, according to the physician Pierre de Lancre, "hardly surprising,"[9] and that inevitably recalled the emanations produced by the Devil and the plague, other "vessels of infection, corruption and putrefaction."[10] Thus, when political philosopher Jean Bodin reported the complaint made by Abel de la Ruë, "a worker in old leather," against one such demoniacal creature, the reek of "sulphur and cannon powder and stinking flesh all intermingled" was noted for posterity.[11]

The same olfactory ambivalence is also evident in formulas for capturing or summoning up spirits or demons according to planetary conjunctions and the signs of the zodiac. An "evil action," like the one designed to bring down wrath and misfortune upon a person, required, according to the theologian Agrippa, a perfume that was at once "impure, ill-smelling and inexpensive."[12] On the other hand, a "good action" designed to inspire benevolence and affection, to bring luck, and to ward off the "evil eye" called for precious ingredients and a pleasant smell.

Present-day writing on astral magic also emphasizes perfumes. According to one theory, odors created by the volatilization of particles of matter emit vibrations that have a profound effect on the behavior of all living creatures and on one's astral twin. A perfume adapted to a person's astral sign will therefore tend to maintain his native humoral balance and autoimmune reactions through the unconscious reactions it provokes in the organism. It thereby acts as a charm that will enable the individual to improve his natural abilities and avoid imbalances. Each sign of the zodiac and each day of the month correspond to specific propitious aromas.[13]

Even today, in very diverse societies, a similar concern underlies many of the practices that accompany important milestones in a person's life. Birth, for instance, a precarious moment in human existence, is assisted by the properties believed to be inherent in various effluvia: sachets of perfume in France's Aquitaine region and in China, a garlic clove hung round the neck of the newborn in Mexico.[14] In North Africa the baby is protected from *djinns,* or evil spirits, by scented fumigations and with balms made of saffron oil and henna. Similarly, marriage in North Africa, an important rite of passage for the female, calls for a variety of aromatic precautions. Prior to the ceremony, the bride, who is particularly vulnerable to any jealous *djinn,* must undergo a whole series of purifications and perfumings. The perfuming of her hair alone requires several days. She also protects herself with incense and scented jewelry, particularly a necklace consisting of tiny black balls of saffron, orris, musk, and benjamin. The use of perfumed ornaments to appease the spirits is widespread in black Africa and Asia.

ODOR AND SEDUCTION

Bodily Odors and Sexuality

The emissions that play a part in animal sexual activity are produced by the sebaceous, anal, and genital glands. Some species—the civet cat, the musk deer, the muskrat, and the beaver, for example—are prized for their abundant secretions, which are collected and used in the perfume industry. The odorous corporeal emissions of ants are produced by their cephalic glands, and butterflies produce theirs in organs that are located along the edge of the wings in the male and at the tip of the abdomen in the female. Jean-Henry Fabre, the great French naturalist, demonstrated the importance of the sense of smell in butterflies. The female butterfly in captivity can, thanks to the odorous substance she produces, attract countless males at a distance of several miles; however, if the female is confined under a glass bell, the males lose all interest in her, thereby demonstrating the essential role smell plays in sexual attraction. Many other experiments have been based on Fabre's work, all of which affirm the olfactory nature of sexual stimulation in butterflies,[15] and countless other experiments have produced similar results with regard to a wide variety of animal species.

The discovery of pheromones—from the Greek *pherein,* "to carry," and *hormon,* "to excite"—some fifteen years ago has led to a better understanding of the importance of smell in animal communication and behavior. These odorous body secretions and/or emissions have no effect on the producer but act on other members of the same species and have been shown to be determining factors in sexual, parental, and social conduct. In vertebrates, chemical signals, sent either directly or indirectly (by a process known as "marking"), can be perceived by both the olfactory and the vomeronasal organs. First identified in mammals by the Dane Ludwig Levin Jacobson in 1909, the vomeronasal organ, which is present in the early stage of the human fetus and disappears (save in exceptional cases) as the fetus develops, has only recently begun to be examined. Located at the base of the nasal septum and consisting of a pair of long, narrow sacs lined with an epithelium similar to that of the olfactory apparatus, the vomeronasal organ is much smaller and was long believed (incorrectly, as it turns out) to be an additional and secondary olfactory organ in human beings. In fact, the organ may play a role in affecting a wide range of animal behaviors.[16]

Pheromones that trigger sexual attraction can be found in insects, crustaceans, fish, salamanders, and snakes. In mammals, many pheromones have yet to be identified owing to their complex compositions, but they, too, apparently play a role in reproduction and behavior. Through the action of pheromones, a canine bitch in heat is able to attract males over a radius of some three miles, and the boar's (male pig's) breath attracts a sow in heat. Today's veterinarians use a boar's odor to select those sows suited to artificial insemination by using aerosols containing androsterone, the agent that gives noncastrated swine their characteristic odor of musk and urine and the scent that the female in heat requires to assume the proper position for copulation.[17] The recent discovery of the presence of a swine sex pheromone in truffles has furnished an explanation for that fungus's appeal to pigs, who are able to detect truffles even when they are buried as much as a meter underground. Needless to say, the delicacy also has an age-old reputation for possessing formidable aphrodisiac powers.

Like the pheromones of the he-goat and ram, which influence their progeny during puberty, the odor of the boar accelerates the pubertal development of the young pig.[18] In mammal groups, physiologist Yveline Leroy tells us, the most odorous males can often perform a kind of physiological castration on their rivals through the action of pheromones. The dominant members of the group are not the strongest, but the ones that emit the greatest quantity of odor signals. Thus, when lemurs vie with each other, they do so "not so much by blows or biting as by 'blasts of scent,' each male rhythmically striking his head with his tail and each stroke releasing a cloud or carpet of odorous substances. The stakes are high, since the effect of the odor's impact on the rival is inevitably—i.e., physiologically—castrative."[19]

Pheromones that induce copulation have been isolated in the vaginal secretions of monkeys and consist of short-chain acid lipids that stimulate the olfactory centers. When these compounds are applied to the genitalia of a surgically sterilized female monkey, they provoke copulation in the male.[20] A similar substance has been discovered in the vaginal secretions of the human female. Thus, the fundamental question: Do humans produce sex pheromones? Some scientists believe that they do. One of the sex pheromones of the sow, *an-alpha,* which is also present in human urine and in the underarm sweat of the human male, may therefore also be a human sex pheromone.[21] According to the scientist Pierrette Langley-Danysz, the supposition is corroborated by various observations and anecdotal evidence. In the course of folk dances in some Mediterranean countries the male dancer stimulate his partner's ardor by fluttering a handkerchief imbued with underarm sweat under her nose. An experiment performed in the psychology department of the University of Birmingham in 1978 tends to support this: To verify that *an-alpha* is a human sex pheromone, volunteers who had been made to sniff a sample of it were asked to assign an "attractiveness grade" to a series of photographs of women. The marks handed out by the sniffers were far higher than those given by the nonsniffing members of a control group.[22]

The biologist Ernest Schoffeniels suggests that "chemical communication must play a considerable role in our human behavior just as it does in other mammals," and expresses regret that such problems have not yet attracted the attention of psychiatrists and psychologists. However, the real significance of such experiments has been questioned by scientists unwilling to agree that human pheromones exist or that man can emit chemical substances that act as triggers for various kinds of sexual, parental, and social behavior. They insist that, unlike many other vertebrates (and especially mammals), the adult male has no secondary olfactory (or so-called vomeronasal) organ designed to detect the female menses. Others, who have adopted a middle position, maintain that the absence of a contact chemoreceptor like the vomeronasal organ does not necessarily rule out the possible existence of substances able to act like pheromones. According to Professor Hubert Montagner, it is "not utopian to suppose that sexual relationships and aggressive behavior can be modified by molecules similar to pheromones secreted by the sebaceous, sudoriparious, mammary or sexual glands." Zoologist Michael Stoddardt asserts that, even though there is no odor capable of inducing a systematic behavior in man, "it is nevertheless possible that we are still subconsciously manipulated by odors."[23]

Long before the discovery of pheromones, however, the link had been established between human sexual behavior and human odors. In 1886 Auguste Galopin, a physician, inspired by biologist Gustav Jaeger's theory that odor plays a part in human sexuality, wrote: "The purest union that can exist between a man and a women is that created by the sense of smell and sanctioned by the brain's normal assimilation of the animate molecules emitted by the secretions produced by two bodies in contact and in sympathy and in their subsequent evaporation."[24] A few years later Freud's mentor and colleague Wilhelm Fliess affirmed the existence of a close and reciprocal relationship between the nose and the genitalia. During menstruation, copulation, and pregnancy, nasal changes occur in the inferior turbinate bones (the *tuberculum septi*); Fliess described these changes as "genital localizations." Swelling, increased sensitivity, and nosebleeds also occur at such times. In addition, "Sympathetic nosebleed resembles menstruation not only because it often accompanies uterine bleeding but also because it often does not occur when such bleeding cannot occur, in those circumstances in which normal uterine menstrual bleeding ceases, i.e., during pregnancy."[25] The relationship between the nose and the genitalia is therefore particularly noticeable in the female. The erectile bodies in the sensitive genital areas, with their spongy tissue, are similar to those of the clitoris and connected to the sympathetic nervous system. Fliess based his theses on gynecological observations made in the course of operations on the nose or during the subjects' inhalation of cocaine. In his treatment of dysmenorrhea he attempted to alter the length of the menstrual cycle by using nasal therapy, on occasion going so far as to destroy certain olfactory zones completely. His results made him even more sure that the importance of the nose is due not only to its respiratory and olfactory capabilities but also to its link with the genitalia.

Moving beyond this simple relationship, the physicians Collet (in 1904), Robert Jouet (in 1912), and Sigmund Freud (in 1929) posited a close connection between the sense of smell and sexuality.[26] Freud saw a connection between the sublimation of the sense of smell and sexual repression. He went on to note that "notwithstanding the undeniable deprecation of the sensations created by the sense of smell, there still exist, even in Europe, peoples who are highly appreciative of the strong odor of genitalia as a sexual stimulant and who are unwilling to forgo it."[27] These precursors have paved the way for contemporary investigations of the role played by the sense of smell in sexual activity and particularly for experiments such as those undertaken by the biologist Jacques Le Magnen, which have demonstrated the functional correlation between the olfactory organs and the sexual hormonal system in humans.[28]

While some body odors affect sexuality, they obviously do not always act as sexual stimulants. Some can have an inciting effect, but others can repulse. In *The Cities of the Plain* Swann finds Madame de Surgis's body odor intoxicating: "His nostrils, drugged by her perfume, quivered like the wings of a butterfly about to alight upon a half-glimpsed flower."[29] However, in Petronius's *Satyricon,* when Encolpius fails to satisfy Circe after his shipwreck, the Sorceress wonders: "Does my breath smell through not eating? Have I neglected to wash under my arms?"[30] The Greek myth of the Lemnian women illustrates this ambivalence. Inflicted with a repulsive odor for having neglected Aphrodite, the women of Lemnos are avoided by their husbands, who take slaves as concubines. The wrathful abandoned wives get rid of their men once and for all by slitting their throats. They turn into stinking and savage fighters, and they do not manage to get rid of their fetidness until desire springs up between them and the Argonauts. Aphrodite's favor regained, they revert to being sweet-smelling, desirable women.[31]

As in literature, examples in real life of the repellent power of smell and the disruptive role it can play in interpersonal relations in modern societies have emerged from the study of olfactory hallucinations. As in Freud's case of Lucy R., there are patients who complain of being subjected to smells of burning, gas, sulfur, smoke, and poisonous exhalations. Such fantasies are frequently encountered in schizophrenics, sometimes with tragic effect. Psychiatrist Harold Himwich reports the case of a man who killed both of his sisters because he was being persecuted by a smell of death.[32] Given the intimate relationship between smell and the sexual act, it is hardly surprising that such "extrinsic" olfactory illusions often accompany delusions about sexual change.[33]

It is also known that olfactory hypersensitivity—or hyperosmia—can be a symptom in certain obsessional and hysterical neuroses. Freud reports the case of one of his patients, the famous Rat Man, who was especially preoccupied with olfactory sensations. As a child he was able, like a dog, to recognize people from their odor and manifested very clear coprophilic (the use of feces for sexual excitement) tendencies. (Indeed, according to Freud, the supression of the intense pleasures derived in infancy from the smell of excreta plays a part in the formation of many neuroses.) Psychoanalyst Karl Abraham's observations led him to stress the specific role played by the sublimation of coprophilic enjoyment in the developement of foot fetishism: the passion displayed by one of his patients for elegant, high-heeled women's shoes was rooted in forbidden olfactory pleasure. According to Harry Wiener, who established a relationship between schizophrenia and a hypersensitivity to external chemical or pheromonal messages, schizophrenic children often possess extraordinary olfactory acuity.[34]

"Intrinsic" olfactory illusions also occur in various acute pathological states. Patients become obsessed with the notion that their bodies are slowly rotting and giving off infectious emanations. A belief that there is some relationship between sin or error and disease, and the feeling that wherever they go in today's ever more deodorized world their body odor will betray them, combine to exacerbate their disease and can completely alter their relations with other people. Tortured by their impotent shame at imposing their decay on others, the sufferers of this syndrome regard their "bad smell as the results of an illness, as a punishment, as a burden, a horrible drawback, the instrument of their total isolation and a pressure upon them to avoid contact with the community."[35]

In a related condition described by psychiatrist Pryse-Phillips in 1975 as an "olfactory reference syndrome," the subjects, who were nonschizophrenic and as a rule reserved and sensible young men, also believed that they constantly gave off highly unpleasant smells. Convinced that they were objects of disgust to all around them, they used great quantities of deodorants, washed constantly, frequently changed their clothing, and avoided bodily contact. If not diagnosed in time, such comparatively minor problems can sometimes eventually lead to suicide.[36] Similar delusions, located somewhere between melancholia and actual odor paranoia, are said to be especially prevalent in Japan, where contact neuroses are being replaced to an increasing degree by odor phobias, "a mysterious change in the expression of shame," in the words of the contemporary philosopher Hubertus Tellenbach.[37]

Perfumes and Seduction
Throughout history there has been a link between perfumes and desire. When Circe sets out to seduce Ulysses, she employs powerful aromatic philters. When the Queen of Sheba travels to

Jerusalem, she seeks help in her campaign to win Solomon's heart from the precious gums and spices of Araby she brings with her in her great caravan: "And she gave the king . . . of spices very great store . . . there came no more such abundance of spices as these which the queen of Sheba gave to king Solomon."[38] In this linkage of perfumes to sexuality and seduction we can discern two functions, both of which lead to a single result: the encouragement of sexual union.

First, pleasant odors can neutralize body odors (or attenuate them if they are too strong) while accentuating certain components. Here, for example, is how sarghine is used by Tunisian Bedouins:

Sarghine is burned for its sweet and evanescent odor; an intimate perfume used by cottage and nomadic Bedouins. The bridal couple incense themselves with it by carrying the burner under their clothing, the shift or the *melhafa,* before they first bed together. The smoke of the sarghine has the property of neutralizing those genital odors—of the female genitalia in particular—that tend to repulse or to hinder the full expression of desire. Thus, the warmth of the bed causes the nostrils to be afflicted by only the lightest of emanations and, among the vapors distilled by the flesh, only those that are both the least harsh and the most provocative.[39]

The unique attributes of aromas can be used as more than aids; they can actually become the basic agents for amorous conquest. In the Old Testament story, before going to Ahasuerus, Esther had been massaged for "six months with oil of myrrh, and six months with sweet odours, and with other things for the purifying of the women."[40] In another Old Testament story, Judith anointed her body with precious ointment to seduce Holophernes.[41] Shakespeare tells us that, setting forth to meet Mark Antony, Cleopatra did not spare the perfume:

The Barge she sat in, like a burnisht Throne
Burnt on the water: the Poope was beaten Gold,
Purple the Sailes: and so perfumed that
The windes were Love-Sicke.[42]

In some traditional societies the process of seduction assumes ritual form through the intensive and refined use of perfumes. The women of the tiny Micronesian island of Nauru perfume themselves both internally and externally. They take perfumed steam baths and rub their bodies and hair with coconut milk and various floral oils. They also use mixtures of odorous leaves and aromatic potions to "perfume themselves within." The latter preparations are reputed to have a devastating effect: " 'All men will come to you,' the Nauran women say, 'all men will be attracted to you, so many will come that you will be exhausted.' "[43] Several of these rites, like the dakare-bark★ steam bath, also entail alimentary taboos and are performed outside the village, in secret—another indication of the connection between perfume and magic. In Nauru, perfumes are love philters as well.

SMELL, HUNTING, AND FISHING

The first guide the primitive hunter had was the smell of his game. Eventually, man turned to the dog, which had an olfactory sense that was superior to his own, and then he began to

★A kind of bark the Nauruans gather on the shore following a storm. Ground into a powder and burned with coconuts, it gives off a penetrating odor.

develop the animal's natural qualities through breeding and training. Sociologist Lucien Lévy-Bruhl reports that dogs used in New Guinea to hunt boar are excited by having onion juice sprayed into their nostrils.[44] Some animal behaviorists believe that the dog's domestication is related to the animal's marked propensity for the odors of human waste. Might this oft-noted trait have led to a process of self-domestication?[45]

Smell is important in both hunting and fishing—more so in primitive societies than in industrialized ones, where technology has considerably diminished the importance of the arts of stalking and trapping. There are many hunting techniques that rely on attracting prey by appealing to the sense of smell. The animal's capture often involves some kind of bait containing its favorite food, but there are also examples in which the trap itself, properly scented, acts as the element of attraction.

In New Guinea, aromatic wood is burned around pit traps to attract the prey into them and is so effective, according to the natives, that animals find it impossible to keep away.

On Nauru, where, according to ethnologist Solange Petit-Skinner, the sense of smell is very highly developed, even fishing makes use of the prey's sense of smell. The Nauruans, who have very precise knowledge of many aquatic species, can select the bait most suited to each. When engaged in net or pot fishing they can bait the trap with such a lasting scent that they can continue to use it indefinitely without having to replenish it.[46]

Although the prey's sense of smell serves the hunter, his own odor can betray him; thus, he attempts to camouflage it beneath other scents. In Melanesia, the natives collect, dry, and preserve the nidorian glands of certain marsupials, which give off a strong, clinging odor. Before setting out on a hunt the men moisten the dried glands and rub them on their bodies, covering their human odor with the stronger, more feral scent, and the game, misled by this ploy, is then more easily approached.[47]

Melanesians also rub a salve on the bodies of young initiates that is designed to attract the "generosity" of the "guardian spirits of the hunt." When the Ngbaka pygmies set out their traps in the forest, they first prepare themselves by acquiring a special smell. Bathing is avoided, as are clean garments. They rub their bodies with an odorous bark procured from the medicine man. Next they sprinkle their bodies with a special aromatic powder and fasten on a belt made of aromatic bark. The resulting complex odor, they believe, has the power to attract the forest spirits, or "Mimbo," who will in turn guide the game into the traps. Before returning to the village the hunters rid themselves of their dual-purpose odor, since it would be unbearable to others. They thrash their bodies with branches to release the forest spirits and make them return to their domain.[48]

In such practices it may be difficult for us to distinguish between the actual hunting techniques (keeping the prey from smelling the hunter) and the rituals relating to "primitive" or superstitious societies. These examples do, however, demonstrate the ritualistic use of odor and its connection to religion and magic.

THE MYTH OF THE PERFUMED PANTHER

The link between smell and capture is reflected in the old Greek myth of the perfumed panther, or leopard (the two terms were—and are—interchangeable). In folklore the panther for some mysterious reason is the only beast to have a naturally pleasing smell. "Wherefore is it," Aristotle wonders, "that no animal save the leopard has a pleasant odor, pleasing even to animals, for it is said that wild beasts smell it with delight?"[49] The beast's delightful smell is involved in the arts of venery, magic, and amorous seduction, and it has also, in an odd transmutation, become a motif in Christian symbolism, the panther's capture representing the effect of Christ's words upon the soul.

The panther, which has no natural enemies (save for man, who can trap the panther with the odor of wine, for which it has a fondness),[50] is prudent, intelligent, and cunning. According to the Greeks the panther employs its scent to attract and seize its prey. Theophrastus tells us: "The panther emits an odor agreeable to all other animals, and thus it can hunt by remaining in hiding and attracting animals to it by its smell."[51] The Roman author Aelian wrote about the panther's death-dealing instrument of seduction:

> They say that the Leopard has a marvellous fragrance about it. To us it is imperceptible, though the Leopard is aware of the advantage it possesses, and other animals besides share with it this knowledge, and the Leopard catches them in the following manner. When the Leopard needs food it conceals itself in a dense thicket or in deep foliage and is invisible; it only breathes. And so fawns and gazelles and wild goats and suchlike animals are drawn by the spell, as it were, of its fragrance and come close up. Whereat the Leopard springs out and seizes its prey.[52]

The Loeb Classics' English translator's "as it were" gets around the problem of the original text's use of the Greek word *iunx,*★ or "jynx," an odd descriptive word for the trance or spell cast by the beast. Aelian's use of it here is unusual, giving the leopard myth a new dimension: that of magic.

Usually a small pierced wheel attached to a string, the jynx

★The word *iunx*, which is both a proper and a common noun, has three meanings in Greek: the torcol, a bird with a rapid, darting flight; a twirling disc or wheel used in magic and hypnotism; and a sorceress who manufactures love potions and philters.

is an instrument that, when whirled, produces a humming sound that can have hypnotic power. Its connection with the panther's smell is even more significant when we know that the jynx is used particularly in erotic magic. Mythology scholar Marcel Detienne has masterfully shown the connection between the jynx, eroticism, magic, and the appeal of perfume.[53] For the Greeks the panther (or leopard) symbolized the beautiful courtesan, and the same word, *párdalis,* was used to designate both the feline and the hetaera. The latter's aromatic spells, also compared to the magic whirligig, echo those worked by the panther's sweet smell, which becomes the symbol of all capture and seduction.

Christianity adapted this belief and, in a daring transposition, made it part of its symbolism. The perfumed panther became the image of Christ himself. The transformation went through several stages, as seen, among other things, in the various versions of the *Physiologus*—dating as far back as the fifth century—that have come down to us. The first version drew a parallel between the cry of the leopard upon awakening from its three-day slumber, an aromatic cry that charms the other beasts, and that of Christ awakening three days after his death and spreading to all mankind his exquisite perfume: "When it has eaten and is replete, it sleeps in its lair and awakens from its slumber on the third day, and cries out with a loud voice, and the beasts, drawn by this perfumed cry, draw near to the leopard. In such wise, too, Our Lord Jesus Christ, risen from the dead on the third day, cried: 'Today is the world saved, the visible and the invisible,' and his utterly good odor spread out for us all, both near and far, and peace, as the Apostle saith."[54]

In the third version of the *Physiologus* the comparison is more explicit and the panther's sweet-scented breath symbolizes the guiding and comforting words of Christ: "The panther assumes the visage and shape of Our Lord Jesus Christ. Since once our Father and Lord Jesus Christ had come and revealed himself as a man among men, from the teachings of his lips came a good odor and, drawn by the perfumes of his breath, prophets, apostles and martyrs came unto him, and all the choir of saints, and thence they returned to their own dwellings.'"⁵⁵ This identi- fication invokes a metamorphosis of the feline, which is no longer a formidable, solitary, and ferocious beast but a creature sociable and kind: "There is an animal known as leopard. The *Physiologus* relates that it is by far the most handsome of all the beasts and the most worthy of affection. As it sleeps a perfume issues from the leopard's mouth, and because of that perfume all other beasts gather in a circle around it, taking pleasure from it and, when they have partaken of their fill, each of them then goes forth joyfully and gaily and returns to the woods and fields.'"⁵⁶ A total inversion has occurred: The leopard's perfume is no longer a mortal trap but has become a generous gift to the other animals. The savage beast now brings well-being and happiness, not death.

However, in the medieval bestiaries, which drew so many of their elements from the *Physiologus,* we find the symbol in its most finished form. In *The Ashmolean Bestiary,* for example,⁵⁷ it is seen to include three essential points: The feline's beauty is an incarnation of the Divine splendor, and its spots, like "golden eyes," represent the many facets of that perfection:

> The panther's spotted coat symbolizes the words Sol-
> omon spake of Our Lord Jesus Christ, who is the Wis-
> dom of God the Father, Spirit of Intelligence, Unique,
> Multiple, True, Sweet, Perfect, Clement, Firm, Stable,
> Sure, Omnipotent Mind, Omniscient. The leopard is
> beautiful, as David says of Christ: He is the most beauti-
> ful of all the sons of man. His sweetness is the image of
> divine goodness. The panther is gentle, and Isaiah saith:

Rejoice and be glad, O daughter of Zion, and proclaim,
O daughter of Jerusalem, behold thy king cometh unto
thee, his heart filled with sweetness.

The comparison with the panther's sweet-smelling breath
and Christ's Word is clear, but the accent is on their instinctive,
irresistible quality: "Thus at the sweet smell that issues from the
leopard's mouth all beasts, from near and far, rush to him and
follow him: thus the Jews, sharing the instincts of the beasts who
were nearby, through their faith, and thus the Gentiles from afar,
devoid of religion, yet all hearkened to the word of Christ and
followed Him, saying: How sweet are Thy words to my lips,
sweeter than honey; from Thy lips falls grace, and thus hath God
blessed Thee forever."

Like Christ, the panther also triumphs over the forces of
evil. Its scent causes the dragon to flee, just as Christ's word
forces Satan to withdraw: " . . . the dragon doth tremble with
fear and doth flee back unto its lair beneath the earth; unable to
bear the panther's breath, he withdraws and falls senseless in his
cave, unmoving as though dead. Thus too the true Panther our
Lord Jesus Christ came down from Heaven to wrest us from the
clutches of the Devil." Like a triptych, the perfumed panther of
the medieval bestiaries illustrates Christ's splendor and the two
aspects of His earthly mission: to bring men to the light of truth
and to save them from the spirit of darkness.

2

SMELL AND DISCRIMINATION

▾

The human element is a delicate fragrance which
spreads itself over every action.

Hegel, *Lectures on the Philosophy of Religion*

Ah, poesie is harde, cast as I am amongst
hirsute hordes, defened by the stryfe of the German tonge,
forced to laud the songes of a noisome Borgundian
with rancid fatte in his hair when all I
feel is disgust. Happy thine eyes, happy thine ears,
and even thy nose . . . for it is not forced
to sniffe the stench of garlic or
onions ten times each morn.

Apollinaris Sidonius, *Letters*

Idiomatic speech often uses olfactory terms to express aversion
and repugnance. We say that someone is a "stinker" or that
something "smells" (sometimes "to high heaven"), that a person
or thing "in bad odor" is to be avoided, that someone "reeks of
hypocrisy"; when suspicious, something "doesn't smell right,"
or we "smell a rat." "Smells fishy to me," we say.

Humans produce a characteristic odor in the air around
them that reflects their diet and/or health, their age, their sex,
occupation, race. It can be argued that because of the physiology
of the olfactory apparatus, the most direct and profound impression we can have of another person is his (or her) smell. Indeed,
smell bypasses the thalamus in the brain and penetrates directly
to that organ's oldest part, the rhinencephalon, known to the

Greeks as the "olfactory brain,"[1] where it produces, willy-nilly, pleasure or repugnance. Sartre wrote: "When we smell another's body, it is that body itself that we are breathing in through our mouth and nose, that we possess instantly, as it were in its most secret substance, its very nature. Once inhaled, the smell is the fusion of the other's body and my own. But it is a disincarnate body, a vaporised body that remains whole and entire of itself while at the same time becoming a volatile spirit."[2] Its inhalation provokes a spontaneous and instinctive reaction that can be either positive or negative, one of acceptance or refusal. The olfactory sense is the prime means we employ for discriminating between the pleasant and the unpleasant, the known and the unknown. It can inspire either recognition or rejection.

SMELL AND RECOGNITION
OF THE OTHER

Many studies have demonstrated the importance of olfactory signals in maternal behavior and in the relationship between the baby and its mother. Animal behavioralist Frank Beach's experiments on rats showed that mothers identify their young through smell and that they can pick out their own in another litter.[3] It is this sense of smell that keeps the young animal close to its mother and serves to protect it from danger. It has now been established that odor plays a prime role in the early stages of human relations. Experiments have demonstrated that human mothers can recognize the bodily odor of their own child as early as the second day following childbirth. The child itself is capable of identifying the odor of its mother's breast and bosom from the third day. It is possible that the olfactory-gustatory data absorbed by the fetus through the amniotic fluid facilitate this postnatal recognition, which can be observed in most other mammals as well. According to Hubert Montagner, much of an infant's behavior can be explained by olfactory bonding, which he describes as "one of the instruments that enables the baby to practice its scales, as it were, via the succouring contact of its mother's body."[4] Essential to the nursling's emotional and intellectual development, "pleasant" maternal odors have a soothing power. On the other hand, a repulsive odor emanating from the mother's breast or bosom can result in rejection of the breast, crying, and repeated regurgitation during and after feeding.

The role odor plays in the mother-offspring relationship is also evident in individual/group relationships in both animal and human societies. In bees, for example, the biological odors emitted by glands located at various sites on their bodies, particularly the abdomen, enable them to recognize members of the swarm and to repulse invaders.[5] Physiologist Henri Piéron's observations of ants confirm the part odor plays in peaceful or hostile relations. If an ant is introduced into a colony of ants of another species, the colony will not recognize it and will attack it. Conversely, if a foreign ant is swabbed with the odor of another species, its members will accept it as one of them. When an ant scents an enemy, it goes into a frenzy and bites the ground. However, if its antennae are amputated, it becomes anosmic—it loses its sense of smell—and indiscriminately aggressive toward both foreigners and members of its own colony.[6]

Similar behavior can be found in human groups. At the end of the nineteenth century, British sociologist Herbert Spencer described the greeting rituals of such ethnic groups as Eskimos, Samoans, Maoris, and Filipinos, in all of which the sense of smell plays a predominant role. Members of those groups rub noses or sniff each other's face in recognition.[7] The Arab custom of blowing in one's interlocutor's face—it is considered an insult to avoid the other person's breath—is based on the same principle.[8] Life-style, diet, exercise, occupation, and hygiene, varying as they do from one culture or group to another, all have an effect on the body and its emissions and provide individuals with guides and points of reference.

In addition to its function as identifier, odor actually seems to determine social behavior. The nineteenth-century physician Auguste Galopin went so far as to maintain that socioprofessional emanations are an essential element in one's choice of partner:

> Working-class marriages most often occur between two persons in the same profession. One of the principal reasons is that the woman's scent harmonizes with that of the man; hairdressers fall in love with perfumers and the draper's assistant with the department-store salesgirl. Sewer workers, tanners, dairymen, butchers, delicatessen workers, lard renderers, etc., often marry the daughters of their co-workers. Maids and domestic servants marry other servants or stablemen who smell of horses and manure. A woman in Marseilles adores the odor of her husband, who reeks of garlic and onions; men who manufacture matches and work with phosphorous almost always marry women in the same profession. One may say that this is because of the daily contact between them—and, indeed, that is quite likely—but something else is also involved: the scent of such men or women pleases their co-workers and drives alien lovers away. It isn't everyone who can love the smell of matches, onions, garlic or unbleached muslin![9]

SMELL AND REJECTION
OF THE OTHER

An odor that denotes an individual's membership in a group and serves to promote that group's cohesion can also mark an individual as alien to other groups and erect a barrier between him or her and the others. It thus becomes an instrument and justification for—or the sign of—a racial, social, and, in the end, moral rejection.

There is some anecdotal evidence that emanations secreted by the skin or carried on the breath often trigger racist behavior. In his 1890 novel *Lalka,* Boleslaw Prus describes how garlic can reflect anti-Semitism in Poland: "The new worker set to work at once, and within half an hour Mr. Lisiecki was whispering to Mr. Klein: 'Where's that smell of garlic coming from?' And after another few minutes: 'When you think that the Jewish scum are starting to push their way into the Cracow suburbs! The damned Jews, why can't they stay in Nalevski or Saint George Street?' Schlangbaum was silent, but his reddened eyes blinked rapidly."[10]

In 1912 sociologist Georg Simmel wrote that the races were prevented from coming together because of olfactory intolerance: "It would appear impossible for the Negro ever to be accepted into high society in North America because of his bodily odor, and the frequent and profound mutual aversion that has existed between Germans and Jews has been attributed to the same cause."[11] In the latter instance hatred and contempt have been expressed in terms of fetidness. Philosopher Ernst Bloch countered the Nazi belief in a "Jewish smell" by riposting: "The Nazi doesn't just emit the odor of blood—he gives off the reek of urine in a chamberpot as well—the stinking chamberpot of his morality, his horrors, his crimes, his ideology; he is a filthy, hell-hound of a beast. . . . And to that smell of the blood of his past bestialities must be added the obscene odor of repression, the typically Nazi smell of stale, unaired bedclothes, a fitting accompaniment to the stench of urine."[12]

Casting olfactory opprobrium on one's enemy is nothing new. In 1916 the *Bulletin et mèmoires de la Société de médecine de Paris* unhesitatingly awarded the Germans the world record for fetidness. In a book written in the previous year, a Dr. Bérillon called upon all his scientific knowledge to come up with a "logical" explanation of German smelly feet:

> The urotoxic coefficient is at least a fourth higher in Germans than in French. Thus, if 45 cubic centimeters of French urine per kilo are sufficient to kill a guinea-pig, the same result can be achieved with only 30 cubic centimeters of German urine. . . . The present-day German's principal organic peculiarity is the fact that his overworked renal apparatus is unable to evacuate all the uric matter from his body and that some of it must be voided through the plantar region. There is thus a physical and factual basis for the saying that the German pisses through the soles of his feet.[13]

So malodorous were the feet of the German soldier that, following the French capitulation at Sedan in 1870 (according to the testimony of one Dr. Deschamps), everyone in Metz had to hold his nose whenever one of the occupying German regiments marched past. Many natives of Alsace-Lorraine took the only course open to them and fled to France to escape the daily torture of forced proximity to the German barracks. The origin of the German people's stench, which also spread to their animals, was attributed to that people's "endemic and chronic guzzling."[14] At an autopsy on a foot soldier dead of suspected poisoning, held in Pouilly in the Côte d'Or, the Teuton's extraordinary bulimia was all too obvious: He had been "distended and swollen to death" by ingesting eleven pounds of raw lard and his abdominal wall had burst. "And to think that had he not swallowed down the whole of it without chewing he might even have managed to digest it!" observed the horrified Deschamps. Such alimentary excess, which forced the skin to perform the functions of a third kidney to eliminate all the repugnant fluids, quite naturally entailed "a truly prodigious excremental output."[15]

It took an entire week for a team of workers to clean out the fecal material of five hundred German cavalrymen who had occupied the Chenevières paper manufactory in Meurthe-et-Moselle for three weeks: There were thirty tons of it! The gargantuan intestinal dejecta of the German troops was confirmed by Dr. Petrovich, a delegate from the International Health Office in Serbia: "In some areas the corridors of the houses, the courtyards, the alleyways and even the houses themselves were filled with it to the height of a meter."[16]

While odors were barriers erected between races and peoples, they also created walls between different sectors of society. Exhalations connected to the exercise of certain professions have sometimes led to ostracism. Such was the case in ancien régime France, for example, with all its tanners, curriers, fellmongers, and tallow chandlers, all trades entailing malodorous processes. However, the distaste could extend to the lower class as a whole. Georg Simmel, expanding on Kant's *Critique,* categorized the sense of smell as "highly displeasing or antisocial" and stated that the "effluvia" of the working class posed a threat to social solidarity:

> It may be true that if social interests should so dictate many members of the upper classes would be prepared to make considerable sacrifices in their personal comfort

and forgo many privileges on behalf of the less-fortunate. . . . Indeed, such privations and sacrifices would be accepted far more readily than would any direct contact with the populace, smelling as it does of the "sacred sweat of its brow." The social question is not simply a moral question; it is a question of the sense of smell.[17]

The introduction of domestic hygiene, at least in the early days, only heightened the contrast. When indoor plumbing was available to the bourgeoisie, it served to bolster that class and its attitudes. According to Somerset Maugham, as late as 1930 the daily morning bath still divided people more effectively than did birth, wealth, or education. The invention of domestic plumbing was nearly as responsible for class hatred as was monopoly capital. It might even be said that plumbing is more essential to democracy than parliamentary institutions!

Repellent odors, in addition to reinforcing class divisions, also carry a moral stigma. The notion of sin is associated with stench. An Egyptian hieroglyphic inscription flatly states: "He whose odor is unpleasant shall be punished and ostracized."[18] Job's stench cut him off from his family and was viewed as a sign of divine displeasure: "My breath is strange to my wife. . . . Yea, young children despised me."[19] In the Middle Ages Jews were regarded as having a nauseating smell, a flaw that seemed to disappear miraculously when they converted.[20] The olfactory intolerance of Jews, prostitutes, and, in the nineteenth century, of the entire working class, has deep social implications: The supposed fetidness of such groups, a sign of their moral inferiority, serves to justify the exclusionary practices of bigotry.

In the fifteenth century lepers and Jews had been accused of poisoning wells, fountains, and rivers by casting fetid objects into them. The *Chronicle* of historian Guillaume de Nangis mentions such criminal acts, which are blamed for spreading disease.[22] Similar accusations led to the massacre of thousands of Jews and lepers at the same period in many towns in Germany as well as in France and Switzerland.

Such recriminations increased in the sixteenth century but, by then, the usual scapegoats no longer served to dispel the fear of contagion. The passions aroused by Jews and lepers were nothing compared to the fears aroused by certain kinds of effluvia. The change in thinking is evident in the measures adopted by the authorities in the Provençal town of Gap. Public whores (the French, *putain publique,* from the Latin *putida,* meaning "stinking," is both more euphonious and, if possible, more contemptuous), who were exemplars of stench and moral corruption, were to quit the town or face flogging. Having adopted that morally symbolic measure the authorities turned to more concrete examples of fetidness: Because of their nauseating activities, the town's workers in leather, skins, and wool were to be relegated to the outskirts and were told to stay there if they wanted to avoid being fined and having their goods confiscated. Olfactory intolerance and social and moral disgust went hand in hand.

In the seventeenth century, the responsibility borne by the lowest social classes for the outbreak and spread of plague was accepted as fact. In 1606, Paris's guild of master surgeons declared that "Large gatherings are dangerous, especially when the poorer classes are involved."[23] In 1617, Angelus Sala, a physician, wrote that "nothing in the world so drawes downe the plague as illnesse and stinke . . . For when plague comes into a land, it begins with poore and dirty folke who live crammed all together like pigges in narrow styes and whose lives, pastimes and converse are like those of wilde beestes."[24]

Such a view of the poorer classes as degraded, subhuman, and threatening in their fetidness served to justify segregating and keeping a close eye on them. In 1649, at Nîmes, the poor were herded together and walled up in the town's famous Roman Arena until the epidemic ravaging the population had run its course.[25] Punishments were fixed for anyone so bold as to protest against such a "wise" order.[26] At the time of the epidemic, few public figures condemned the measures, although Philippe Hecquet, another physician, was an exception: "Another kind of slavery, and one still being practised in time of plague, is embodied in the hovels in which the poor are confined,"[27] he wrote in 1722, while, at the same time, he admitted that such persons might well corrupt a town's atmosphere by their careless negligence, their bad food, and their general uncleanliness.

It is but a short step from physical contamination to moral contamination. A brief treatise published in 1841 serves as a perfect illustration. The existence of particularly repellent foul odors at the very gates of Paris, in its most heavily populated neighborhoods, constituted a twofold threat. The loathsome fetor of sewer catchments and the even more unbearable stench of the knacker's yards, where some ten thousand starved and broken-down horses were cruelly slaughtered every year, had turned the district called Montfaucon into "a horrible sewer," a "monstrosity"[28] that, affecting working-class health and morality as it did, was now posing a threat to society as a whole.

Looming above its insalubrious stockyards, its "disgusting sea of pus,"[29] its heaps of carcasses and innards rotting in the open air, one saw not only the specter of the plague but the equally terrifying shadow cast by the district's notorious "Boulevard of Crime." Aside from the noxious vapors that hung heavily over this urban cesspool, this hotbed of infection attracted not only hordes of rats but a multitude of human fauna as well, many of whom closely resembled their rodent coinhabitants. The ragpickers, who came to the area by day to steal bits of meat, at night gave way to bands of "caitiffs," lowlife criminals, sure of finding there a refuge where the police would not dare follow them. Already perverted by "all the scenes of horror in the cheap theatricals" that had inured them to the sight of blood and death, these criminals thought nothing of murdering someone if he refused to roast them a piece of their favorite horsemeat. The knacker himself was a fearsome figure: Areek with the odor of his victims (which seemed to render him immune from the diseases that teemed in the surrounding filth), dirty, cynical, obscene, ill-mannered, and rowdy, "he personified the stink of Montfaucon."[30]

The filth of the area threatened to poison everything around it. The so-called "fast set," the "gilded and perfumed youth of the city," were also at risk of infection: "All the disgusting evils we see in Paris, all the barbarous symptoms evident in the language and habits of the working classes . . . all this comes from Montfaucon, from its disorder and its contagion, which creep out of it and spread to those classes once deemed well mannered."[31] Thus, Paris could not be considered a civilized city until this source of epidemic disease and proletarian subversion was eradicated.

To the extent that odors contribute to racial or social divisions, deodorization would seem to be a natural step toward achieving integration. For a foreigner to gain acceptance he must dissimilate—lose the things that denote his foreignness and conform to the olfactory norm. This process underlies some of the Arab aspersion (cleansing) rituals, which are designed to abolish symbolically the "differentness" of the foreigner, often referred to as "he who stinks." The smell of "the other" has unknown and uncontrollable elements. Assimilation into Arabic culture implies acquiring the odor of the group: "The household furniture of every family, rich or poor, necessarily includes one or more of the aspergilla used to sprinkle perfumed water on the heads, faces and hands of guests. The cheap ceramic sprinkler and the gold *mras* are both used for the dual function of welcoming and purification: the scented water neutralizes the odor— i.e., the impurity—of the stranger and allows him to enter the community."[32]

However, breaking down olfactory barriers is not always easy. In their attempts to overcome the discrimination to which they are subjected, persons of modest means tend to buy cheap perfume products that are generally considered "vulgar" by the upper classes, whose members use expensive perfumes as status symbols. Psychology professor John Dollard tells us that to counter racist notions about themselves American blacks developed a tendency to wear exaggerated amounts of perfume, thereby only reinforcing white prejudices: If the blacks must wear so much perfume, it's because they really do stink.[33]

According to William Brink and Louis Harris, one of the most common stereotypical notions held by whites is that black Americans eager to move up the social ladder even take pills to counteract their odor.[34] The real and the purported practices combine to form the stigma of racial smell, and the result has had a profoundly destructive effect on people then forced to cope with the social sanctions placed upon them. Rejection of one's own odor is tantamount to a denial of one's existence.

So, identifiable bodily smells play an active part in various kinds of discrimination by setting up subtle distinctions and degrees of taste and distaste. Their emotional charge has made them one of the surest guardians of social and racial bastions. Sometimes, as Simmel has observed, the moral ideal of harmony and equality between the different classes and races runs up against the brick wall of an invincible disgust inspired by the sense of smell."[35]

PART TWO

THE
STENCH
OF PESTILENCE

▼

Smelle alone amongst the senses can
Either destroye or quite remake a man.

Jerome Cardan, *De subtilitate rerum*, 1550

The plague has always been the archetypal evil of all the great evils that befall mankind. The scope of its destruction, the terror and upheavals that have always followed in its wake, have led men to regard plagues as the apocalypse itself.[1]

In antiquity the Greek and Latin terms *loïmos* and *pestis* were used to designate any widespread scourge or calamity. The famous Athens plague, whose true nature is still in doubt, may well have been an epidemic of typhus. However, the theories that sprang up concerning these various epidemic or "common" diseases were quite naturally adapted to explain the epidemics of buboes, carbuncles, and blood spitting that devastated Western Europe, the most terrible of which were the plague of Justinian, which raged from 541 to 580, and the great "Black Plague," which reached its peak in France in 1348 and went on to wipe out a quarter of Europe's population in a few short years.[2] As a synonym for any terrible death, the plague has left its mark on all the European languages: *pestilent empestation* in English dates to the Conquest; in French, the word *empester* has lost its veiled reference to death but has come to mean "to infect with bad smells, to make stink."

Prior to the dissemination of Pasteur's research on microorganisms (around 1880), unpleasant smells were viewed in Europe as having a direct effect on health and life. Nauseating exhalations from sewers, charnel houses, cemeteries, cesspools, and marshes were believed to cause many fatal diseases. Does the double meaning of the French word *empester,* establishing as it does an absolute equivalent between stench and death, mean that the plague was actually believed to *be* an odor? The notion seems surprising because it is so foreign to our present-day ideas about epidemics. However, we must remember that the discovery of the plague bacillus and the role of fleas and rats in propagating the disease did not occur until the very last years of the nineteenth century. There are countless studies on the disease and an abundance of data on the history of plagues including their demographic, economic, and sociological aspects. But the relationship between the plague and odor has attracted very little attention, and when it is mentioned, it is basically in connection with the various methods that were employed to combat the scourge.[3]

In fact, however, the relationship goes much deeper. For centuries it had been at the crux of popular beliefs and gave rise to many medical theories about the etiology and propagation of plague. Prevention and cure by means of odors are merely the logical consequence of such beliefs. The same applies to a whole gamut of measures accessory to deodorization, including the evolution of public and private health practices and the development of various societal isolations and quarantines. Thus, the plague is an especially good indicator of the deadly, prophylactic, and curative powers that smell has been deemed to possess.

1

THE DEADLY POWERS OF SMELL

▼

THE ORIGINS OF PLAGUE

From antiquity to the nineteenth century the plague was believed to be a disorder caused by various kinds of breakdowns:
a spiritual breakdown in the relations between man and the
Divinity; a breakdown in the balance between the elements of
nature, particularly those of the air; a breakdown within the
body itself. These disorders were linked to notions of corruption, death, decay, and pestilence. Thus, it is because corrupt
men so offend God with the cadaverous stench of their souls that
they draw down His wrath upon themselves. It is because the
atmosphere, after long years of storms, loses its integrity, that it
undergoes a change, and becomes a source of infection. Lastly,

it is because the organism, subjected to man's gluttony and excess, has been damaged that it contracts—and also, of course, engenders—the plague.

The respective importance accorded these various causes varied throughout the ages. References to moral stain, already present in the Bible, were also rife during the Moscow plague of 1771. The idea of bodily putrefaction took different forms, but was always present. Notions about instability of the air—although increasingly contested starting in the sixteenth century—remained prevalent until the nineteenth.

Hippocrates and Galen

When he attempted to dispel the "plague" that ravaged Athens in the fifth century B.C. with the help of aromatic wood fires, Acron of Agrigento was acting on the belief that the epidemic had been caused by the air.[1] An essential but dangerous element, the air (according to Hippocrates and his disciples) influenced the physical and psychic constitution of all living things and was the cause of all diseases. The beneficent or harmful effect of the atmosphere, which varied with the climate, was basically determined by what Aristotle called elementary "qualities" (temperature, consistency, dryness, humidity). However, it was also linked to the presence or absence of pollutant and pathogenic emanations. Thus, the exhalations of sloughs and swamps brought on diseases. Epidemic or pestilential fevers were caused by air that had been infected with lethal emanations, with "miasmas" (from the Greek word *miasma:* impurity[2]). As a result, the origin of plagues has been attached to corruption and fetidness.

The historian Thucydides, a keen observer of the Athens epidemic (of which he himself was to fall victim), reports conflicting rumors of its having been brought from Ethiopia or having arisen from wells poisoned by the Peloponnesians. He, however, was the first to posit its contagious character.

Influenced by Hippocrates's atmospheric theories and Epicurus's atomism, Lucretius, fifty years before Christ, attributes the origin of all infections to germs of disease and death. Thought of as "atoms," such germs can foul the sky should they happen to combine. And when we breathe in such contaminated air, we are also "allowing these pernicious principles to penetrate into our bodies."[3] The part a corrupt climate can play in the genesis of epidemics led Lucretius to impute the contagious disease that had befallen Athens to "a deadly breeze" from lower Egypt.

Stench, an indication of rottenness and poison—two terms that tend to be interchangeable in both Greek and Latin—can be deadly. Seneca believed lightning contained a pestilential and venomous element, a smell of "naturally poisonous" sulphur that spoils whatever it touches and gives a nauseating smell to unguents and perfumes.[4] Deep in the bowels of the earth there exist fires and marshes that also exhale poisoned miasmas. When this corrupt air finds release, during violent earthquakes, for example, it spreads disease and death so long as the strength of the virus it contains is not dissipated by the wind. Seneca holds such emanations responsible for having killed a flock of six hundred sheep that breathed the lethal vapors while peacefully feeding in the fields of Campania. Birds unfortunate enough to encounter such exhalations are struck down in full flight: "Their bodies assume a ghastly hue and their throats swell as if they had been strangled."[5] First-century physician Rufus of Ephesus believed such deaths, revealing as they did the presence of miasmas in the atmosphere or the ground, were one of the predecessor signals of plague.[6]

Air was considered a homogeneous but unstable element and therefore susceptible to pollution or impairment. Writing at the beginning of the first century, the philosopher Philo of Alexandria believed "it was in its very nature to be diseased, to become corrupt, to die, as it were." The origin of epidemics must therefore be sought in the breakdown of the air, since "plague is nothing other than the death of the air, which spreads its own sickness for the corruption of even the smallest living thing."[7]

In the second century A.D. Galen advanced an important notion that departed from commonly held belief. It stated that there had to be a conjunction of two putrefactions, two disequilibriums, in order for the plague to strike: An atmosphere "excessively different from the norm" had to be complemented by a body no longer guided by temperance, by the "just mean."[8] According to Galen, plague could not occur unless the air's putridness and disturbed state were accompanied by corresponding changes within the organism. The notion of disorder is present in both cases. However, only "plethoric" or full-blooded people, those with an overabundance of blood and other "humors" owing to their unhealthy way of life (immoderate indulgence in erotic pleasure or the delights of the table, laziness or overactivity, emotional upset) were contaminated by unhealthy air. On the other hand, anyone who led a well-balanced life would escape.

The Middle Ages and the Renaissance

Pressed by the French king Philippe VI to pronounce on the origin of the great "Black Plague" that decimated Europe in 1348, the faculty of the Paris medical school issued an *Opinion* that was to have great influence all over Europe. "The deadly corruption of the air" was due essentially to an ill-omened conjunction of the stars when vast amounts of disease-bearing and poisoned vapors arose out of the earth and the waters and infected the very substance of the air. Through the act of respiration this corrupt atmosphere penetrated into and tainted organisms that were already predisposed to putridness by overeating, intemperance, and excess of passions—factors already mentioned in antiquity—as well as from hot baths, which relaxed and moistened the body.[9] Through this pronouncement a direct relationship was drawn in the public's mind between the putrefaction of the body and the putrefaction of the atmosphere. In France, from the thirteenth century on, the term *peste* or *pestilence* was used for both the disease and the revolting stench associated with it.

Polemics about the Role Played by the Atmosphere
In the seventeenth century most medical men were still attributing the origins of disease to atmospheric and humoral putrefaction. Still, some physicians attempted to distance themselves from theories involving the air. One by the name of Rainssant exemplified this trend when, in 1668, he declared that the plague that was then ravaging Soissons and its environs was not due to any atmospheric contamination at all. He noted that on this occasion none of the signs that were commonly believed to indicate the air's corruption—unseasonal weather, storms, earthquakes—had appeared.[10] In 1685 Thomas Sydenham, known as the "English Hippocrates," dragged traditional etiology into the modern era, breaking completely with the old school of thought. It was obvious, he maintained, that the atmosphere did have a "certain temperature or disposition" of unknown nature, which could "in certain instances, produce various diseases."[11] For example, the plague that decimated the population of London in 1665–1666 had followed a very cold winter and had reached its height at the time of the autumnal equinox. However, a morbid atmospheric condition was not enough, in and of itself, to generate the plague. It could only create favorable conditions for its emergence. Making a promising amalgam of

the plague's origins and its mode of propagation, Sydenham posited the existence of a second, "particular" cause via the spread of a "miasma," a "virus," from some infected site.

Around that same time fear of foul smells reached a peak in London. Danger was perceived to be everywhere: All the inhabitants were assaulted and contaminated by the stench of unburied bodies; pedestrians attempted to avoid the miasmas from infected dwellings by keeping to the middle of the street; pestilential vapors were caught in the fur and hair of animals; the deadly breath of the sick was carried by the servants who shopped and ran errands for bourgeois households; the air teemed with the effluvia of plague victims and of those who were infected although apparently healthy, "but are all that while carrying death with them into all companies which they come into."[12] To avoid all these death-dealing smells, people immured themselves in their homes. The performance of religious rites and attendance at them became acts of heroism. One armed oneself with a myriad of odorous substances that could give off even stronger smells than could be procured from the apothecary or the druggist. Author Daniel Defoe reported that at religious services during the London plague, "the whole church was like a smelling-bottle."[13] Perfumes, aromatics, pungent substances, and a variety of other drugs and herbs, salts, and spirits were all blended together to produce tonic and protective aromas. However, one whiff of mustiness, an odor identified with the plague, was enough to empty the premises: "Once, on a public day . . . in Aldgate Church, in a pew full of people, on a sudden one fancied she smelt an ill smell. Immediately she fancies the plague was in the pew, whispers her notion or suspicion to the next, then rises and goes out of the pew. It immediately took with the next, and so to them all; and every one of them, and of the two or three adjoining pews, got up and went out of the church, nobody knowing what it was offended them, or from whom."[14]

Of all morbid emanations, however, the breath was the most terrifying. Some scientists maintained that the breath of the plague-stricken could kill a bird, "not only a small bird, but even a cock or hen," and that "it might be distinguished by the party's breathing upon a piece of glass, where, the breath condensing, there might living creatures be seen by a microscope, of strange, monstrous, and frightful shapes, such as dragons, snakes, serpents, and devils, horrible to behold."[15]

In the eighteenth century the medical profession still grappled with the etiology of plague. The role played by corrupt air in the genesis of the disease was central to the ongoing doctrinal debate in which partisans and adversaries of the contagion theory found themselves engaged. The argument peaked during the 1720 Marseilles plague and continued throughout the century, despite the discoveries being made in lung function and chemistry.

Dispatched to Marseilles by order of the French regent, the members of the "Commission" identified what they described as a simple and noncontagious–not airborne—epidemic fever. Their opinion was greeted with favor and great satisfaction by the authorities, who were loath to take coercive measures and who feared an outbreak of panic and public unrest. Unable to determine the real nature of the "common" or "primitive" cause for the present plague, the Commission dwelt on such contributing factors as poor diet, unfavorable weather conditions, and, most important, fear and terror.

Jean Fournier, a young and inexperienced physician, was a member of this Commission but was in no position at the time to question what he regarded as its faulty conclusions. He was later to denounce his colleagues' blind desire to curry favor with those in power. "Posterity will find it almost incredible that three of the four physicians dispatched from Montpellier were bent on incorporating into their report the

deluded notion that perturbations in the weather, poverty, and
fear were the sole causes of the Marseilles plague when those
very things were contradicted by the general opinion and
unanimous testimony of all in that city and throughout the
surrounding countryside. . . . "[16]

The strongest criticism was leveled by the Marseilles physician Jean-Baptiste Bertrand. A careful observer of the dreadful
disease that was decimating his city's population, Bertrand accused those who were attempting to prove that the sickness did
not originate in the air or in foodstuffs but was merely another
ordinary epidemic of going too far in excluding any noncontagious origin at all. His argument, which held that a contagious
venom was brought in in the cargo hold of the *Grand-Saint-
Antoine,* was designed for the most part to refute the atmospheric
theories.

When the *Grand-Saint-Antoine* sailed into the port of Marseilles on May 25, 1720, the plague was an unlisted item on the
manifest of its rich cargo. Upon docking, Captain Chataud had
presented the health inspectors with a certificate from the physician and surgeon of the infirmary at Leghorn that mentioned, in
passing, that several sailors had perished of a "malignant fever."
Such strong presumptions should have caused the inspectors to
prevent the disembarkation of all those on board, but greed
prevailed over prudence: The interests of the largest importers,
who were expecting to reap huge profits at the annual Beaucaire
trade fair, were respected. The crew, the passengers, and the
deadly bales of goods were welcomed with "as much trust and
security as that of the Trojans who escorted into their city the
fatal steed that would set them ablaze and destroy them."[17]

In Marseilles and its environs there were no swamps, no
open pits, no charnel houses, or underground caverns capable of
producing so-called pernicious exhalations. There was no stench
in the port itself and there was no filth on the public streets,

which were washed down with water from the town's abundant system of public fountains. The Marseilles air could not be healthier: Scented with thyme, rosemary, and the many other aromatic plants that grew on the surrounding hills, its purity was above reproach. "To what, then, are we to attribute this infection of the air and the strange disease we are trying to impute to it?" he exclaimed.[18] To miasmas from distant lands borne on some deadly breeze? If so, it must first be shown that such miasmas would not be broken down in the course of so long a voyage. And even less could such imaginary atmospheric corruption be related to any purported physical "predisposition" to the epidemic, or to the fateful passage of some comet or meteor.

Exotic Etiologies

Although common epidemics began in Europe, the origin of pestilential fevers had to be found in other climes. Europe's temperate skies harbored no putrefaction capable of acquiring the necessary power to generate plague—such was the opinion expressed by English physician Richard Mead in 1720. Where the air was concerned, "it is certain that in our northern climates it can never be so polluted as to produce plague of itself."[19] The outbreak of the disease required the "atmospheric combinatives" proper to hot countries, such as Ethiopia, Egypt, Persia, India, and China. Ethiopia and Egypt were the most notorious "nurseries" of plague.[20] In Ethiopia, it was believed to be produced by the torrid climate and excessive humidity caused by four months of continual rain combined with a monstrous quantity of dead grasshoppers. In Cairo, the rays of the sun and the "silence of the winds" served to concentrate the decay and filth that fed the disease. Mead's picture of Cairo is picturesque propaganda: His teeming city is traversed by a wide canal that receives the Nile's floodwaters and into which the filthy and poverty-stricken inhabitants cast refuse of all kinds. The result is "a slough with an extraordinary stench and highly dangerous to the health."[21]

Discovery of the Pollution of the Atmosphere through Breathing
The scientific understanding of a phenomenon does not, of course, dissipate—indeed, it sometimes nourishes—fantastic notions. The eighteenth-century discovery that the atmospheric "fluid" is not a single homogenous substance but a mixture of partly breathable and partly mephitic gases[22] caused a revolution in chemistry, and it must also have indirectly shaken many age-old etiological beliefs. If respiration alone can alter the vital atmosphere of an enclosed space, how much greater must be the putrefaction of the air by the fetid exhalations of swamps and corpses? Far from giving rise to a radical questioning of all such antique theories, the chemists' revolutionary discoveries only piled new anxieties on top of millennial fears.

In 1781 physician Ménuret de Chambaud's essay about the relationship between air movement and contagious diseases, a work praised by the Société Royale de Médecine, reflects the confrontation between modern chemistry and old notions about epidemics. The fruitless attempts made by certain scientists to trace the sources of the miasma led many of them to conclude that the atmosphere was "inalterable." "Many of the chemists who have subjected the air to very subtle and precise analyses have maintained that that element is inalterable, that nothing can be extracted from it but air itself."[23] Despite numerous experiments, Ménuret laments, it has never been possible to discover in it any of the miasmas the physicians and practitioners have posited. To safeguard the air, he urges his colleagues to eschew "the feeble and uncertain support of experimentation"[24] and to adhere to the facts as reported in the writings of eyewitnesses! He sets the example himself by going back to Hippocrates. The Father of Medicine was correct, he claimed, in considering that the air was "the true author and sole progenitor," of epidemic and contagious diseases. The atmospheric fluid absorbed the foreign molecules emanated from deadly exhalations "like a sponge." Indeed, in some parts of the atmosphere there were virtual "storehouses" of such life-threatening matter, just waiting to reproduce. Writing at the very height of the Enlightenment Ménuret de Chambaud even dared maintain that the plague was always preceded by the appearance of fetid and toxic meteors.

In later work, in which he again praised the correctness of the views expressed by the "Divine Forebear,"[25] his "model" and "guide," Ménuret attempted to bring the miasmatic theory into line with recent discoveries in chemistry. He maintained that although it did not necessarily unite chemically with the air, matter exhaled by bodies can still remain a part of it for varying lengths of time through "simple confusion."

Even though they were advanced by a recognized "expert" in contagious diseases, such notions were met with cries of outrage from other contagion experts of the day: Polluted air might well bring on some highly contagious epidemics, but it was incapable of producing plague. "That it may corrupt—well and good, I am perfectly willing to go along with him on that; but that such corruption can give rise to plague . . . that seems to me to go against all truth, *prima facie,*" protested the Russian physician Danilo Samoïlowitz in 1783.[26] Stench could only bring on swamp fever, prison fever, hospital fever. And as for the old superstitions about celestial phenomena and the malign influence of stars and comets, such things were all products of "astrological delusions." How, he asks, can anyone today believe Forestus, who thought the pestilential miasma was caused by fiery stars raining down on houses? How can anyone have faith in Schreiber's assertions that birds flee corrupted air and will not fly into pestiferous regions? Samoilowitz indignantly rejected air as the source of the plague . . . nor was it responsible for the scourges in Ethiopia or Egypt. Indeed, the air was not even capable of lessening or increasing its force.

HOTBEDS OF INFECTION

In 1785 Jean-Noël Hallé, a member of the Société Royale de Médecine, attempted to sound a new note in this cacophony of opinions. Writing on sewerman's ophthalmia and lead colic, diseases that attacked cesspool cleaners, he railed against confusing stench and noxiousness. "The most revolting cesspits are not the most dangerous,"[27] he stated peremptorily. Nevertheless, his keen distinctions and the new discoveries about the nature of the air failed to weaken traditional etiological beliefs. There are many reports by the Académie des Sciences and the Société Royale de Médecine, some of which the founder of modern chemistry, Antoine-Laurent Lavoisier, helped to draw up, that attest to their persistence. Areas with a highly concentrated population—prisons, hospitals, barracks, ships, theaters, and concert halls—that had "drawn the attention of hygienists" for nearly forty years were all subject to the two-pronged threat of exhaled air and fetid exhalations.[28]

Prisons, where ill-kempt men wallowed in filth, were the cradles of many of the contagious diseases that decimated villages, towns, and armies and that spread desolation as far away as the colonies. Stinking latrines, the ground covered with spittle, urine, and excrement, overcrowding and defective ventilation and hygiene, clothing reeking with fetid and putrid odors, all combined to make the royal prisons a threat to the general populace. There was an outcry to contain and neutralize the infection. Proposals were made to pave courtyards, to install windows that could be left partially open allowing the air to circulate and earthenware conduits to allow it to rise, to provide clothing made out of blue cloth to screen out miasmas, to provide individual—or at least double—beds and areas that would be set aside for disinfection and for bathing all reflect long-standing and contemporary concerns. Although the major goals were air circulation and an end to overcrowding, the stench of excrement continued to cause great concern and was reflected in an extraordinarily bold proposal to install privies with seats. To reduce the emanations from fecal matter built up on the inner surfaces of sewer pipes and allow it to fall directly into the cesspool, the pans should be "shaped like truncated cones, narrow end down. . . . The openings could be made of cast iron, but they must be made thick enough and strong enough so the prisoners cannot break them."[29]

The hospital, where overcrowding was acute, also drew the attention of hygienists. Paris's Hôtel-Dieu was a particular focus of their indignation. The frightful uncleanliness that prevailed there had earned it the sorry distinction of having the highest mortality rate of any hospital in Europe. The ravages created by its stench are described with particular zest. The whole complex of buildings was one vast open sewer, with crowded rooms, filthy beds in which the sick were bundled together, latrines that were too small and in which the filth "rose to the doorsill," floors covered with the blood and pus of the wounded, repugnant smells from the operating room or the morgue, and fetid and windowless stairwells up which wafted a polluted air that one "could not breathe without pain and disgust." There were lethal miasmas emitted by unclean bodies and mattresses, acrid and nauseating vapors "that made the eyes burn and that were so thick you could part them and wave them aside with your hands" seeping from the sheets of the sick and wafting into wards where pregnant women were lying, killer smells that carried off women in childbirth. "The air that circulates through the Hôtel Dieu from one end to the other and from the ground floor to the third and even the fourth floor, is nothing but one huge mass of corruption."[30] The building's defective construction and insufficient number of windows, before which damp, badly washed bed linens were often hung, made ventilation difficult. Polluted air had to travel a considerable and contorted path before it could be expelled. The outside air, too, had a difficult time entering the building; by the time it reached the innermost rooms it had already picked up the contamination of all the others through which it had passed. And how could the "vital air," which was believed to represent the overall content of the atmosphere, be renewed to support life? A hotbed of foul emanations that continually spewed forth the filth of numerous cadavers, piles of infected straw and bloody feathers located in the very heart of Paris, the Hôtel-Dieu was a hell hole for the needy it took in and a danger to the entire population.

Ventilators and various other pieces of apparatus were constructed in an attempt to cleanse such reservoirs of infection. In 1796 the physician Pierre Garros was singing the praises of an "astonishing and highly efficient machine" that could freshen or heat the air at will, purify it, and instill it with "salubrious and nourishing elements." However, he deplored the fact that in a "transport of folly" the use of his "pyrorefrigerant" had been vetoed, thus destroying a wonderful new opportunity to cleanse ships, hospitals, theaters, and "other public places so noisome as to be actually morbiferous and mortiferous"[31]—not to mention any hope of preserving and improving health.

The city foundered in a paroxysm of filth and overcrowding. Those with weak or delicate lungs could not withstand the sooty emanations of its coal fires and its garbage. Even the weakest reacted immediately to the benefits of good country air and experienced "a kind of euphory due to easier respiration," as physiologist Stephen Hales noted in 1735.[32] Urgent warnings were issued. All citizens were urged to fill their lungs with oxygen:

> Flee the stultifying air of the cities, fill your brains with a healthy dose of country air; stop living like automatons; let the universe know you have a soul, however infrequently it be uplifted. If you constantly breathe in the city's air your throat should be swept just as you sweep your chimneys. The fish that lives in muddy waters takes on a slimy taste; the same holds true for men who breathe in only coal smoke and the emanations of the incense offered up to the Goddess Cloacina, whose many altars are constantly areek with it. The brains and lungs of such persons must be impregnated with those vapors . . .[33]

The purest air of all, as praised by dramatist Joseph Pott in 1782, was unquestionably mountain air. The higher up one went, the better it became. Owing to its high altitude, Switzerland was indubitably the healthiest country in Europe, and it was believed that for the same reason Quito in South America had never been prey to pestilential infections. All European mountain dwellers, whether Swiss, Scotch, or from the Pyrenees, lived longer, and when they descended into the plains they suffered from the heavier atmosphere and became prone to circulatory problems and to "a tormenting melancholy that produces a sadness, a hypochondriacal 'humor' and a burning desire to return to their native land which is commonly called . . . homesickness."[34]

The notion that the physician must now rely on the chemist was forcefully expressed. According to Jean-Baptiste T. Baumes, a physician, his profession would forever be grateful for Lavoisier's genius: "The discernment of different kinds of air, the air that of mountains, plains, stables; the medical use of gaseous fluids like carbonic gas, nitrogen, oxygen; methods for cleansing diseased or weakened areas with a gas formed by combining common salt with concentrated muriatic acid—these are all the happy results of chemical knowledge applied to the materia medica, which, as a result, are now becoming less ostentatious and redundant."[35]

Such new notions, however, did not divert the attention of important scientists from the usual hotbeds of infection. In 1789 a commission (of which Lavoisier was a member) entrusted by the Académie des Sciences with examining the dangers posed to the citizens of Paris by the slaughterhouses that still existed in the city's center was cautiously prudent: The infection arising from the districts in which such establishments operated had not yet been the subject of "direct experiments" and "in-depth research" to establish their harmful effects. However, although contemporary physics could not precisely evaluate the effects of their putrid emanations, "the experience of all nations and of time immemorial" led to the conclusion that "the places where animals are butchered or their skins dried or where their fat is rendered into tallow, or where their midden intermingles with blood and flesh, must perforce be unhealthy, and that the influence of such exhalations corrupts the air."[36] And indeed, if proof were needed, one had but to recall the wan complexions of the women who lived around the perimeter of the Cemetery of the Innocents, the fevers that rose from swamps and battlefields, or the annual plague in Constantinople that was caused by the great filth and the many dead animals that decayed rapidly with the return of the warm spring air.

Furthermore, neither the failure of the recently invented eudiometer, constructed to track the miasma and measure the purity of the air, nor the discoveries of atmospheric or "pneumatic" chemistry succeeded in dispelling old beliefs about the "constitutions" of the air and its corruption by all sorts of emanations. Although newly acquired knowledge about the air made regarding it as an element subject to "decay" difficult, many still viewed it as a gaseous mixture that could act as a receptacle for and carrier of pernicious emanations that were capable of propagating and spreading epidemics.* Even Lavoisier, who had conducted basic experiments on the changes that occur during respiration, fell back on traditional concepts when invited to explain the origin of the Constantinople plague.

The conflict that had been dividing the European medical profession since 1720 came to a head in 1846. At the behest of the Ministry of Agriculture and Commerce, a Commission appointed by the Académie Royale de Médecine to report on plague quarantine measures, drew up an unwieldy and voluminous report of over a thousand pages. Out of its confused and conflicting mass of opinions two noteworthy, etiologically oriented concepts emerged: One was set forth by Prus, the Commission's rapporteur, and the other by Pariset, a member of the Commission who expressed dissent with that body's overall conclusions.

Prus agreed with the Commission, which supported the noncontagionist thesis that the origin of the plague was not to be found in some fanciful germ, but in a "concatenation of causes": local unhygienic conditions, the constituents of the air, physical (and moral) degradation. Egypt, Syria, and Turkey headed the list of plague-prone and plague-producing countries. However, contrary to eighteenth-century beliefs, Prus held that the disease itself was the product of man, not nature. A victim of governmental ignorance and neglect, the Egyptian villager led a subhuman and nearly bestial existence. His dwelling was a hovel built of mud and animal bones, low ceilinged, dark, and

---

*In this connection Jacques Guillerme has noted that "in the guise of mephitism a confusion persists between air polluted by the respiratory process and its contamination by other kinds of emanations."[37]

dank. The doorway was so narrow that inhabitants were forced to enter on all fours. In these squalid and unventilated huts men, women, and children slept on mats of decaying rushes laid on the bare ground. As if he were purposely trying to provide and acquire every element needed for his own destruction, the "fellah" surrounded his shanty with piles of garbage and debris. Wallowing in filth and decay, he seemed eager to "avoid any ventilation that might cleanse the locale where he dwelled." And the food he ate was just as disastrous as the stagnant water he drank and the air he breathed. His bread, only partially cooked over feeble embers, was too underdone to be food truly fit for humans. The meat his master deigned to allow him came from diseased animals. His usual diet consisted of aged, worm-infested cheese and rotten fish. His fuel, which was a mixture of human excrement and animal dung, added a sorry note to this picture of a human feeding on waste matter and cadavers. To the excremental reek of his dwelling was added the stench of the adjacent "gaping tombs, which emit a cadaverous odor that Europeans find difficult to bear."[38] How could such extraordinarily unhealthy living conditions fail to give rise to the cruelest of diseases?

Deprived of the effective sanitary system once enjoyed by the ancient Egyptians, the city dweller was little better off. In Cairo the narrow, dark, and winding streets were unpaved. They passed before buildings that were asymmetrical (albeit beautiful) and skirted ruins teeming with putrid stagnation and wild dogs. The filthy and anarchic city was traversed by a polluted canal into which all the sewers emptied. It distributed a turbid water drunk by the poor from which mephitic vapors rose, producing headaches and stomach cramps. Cairo's thirty-five cemeteries added to the general infection.

Pariset, however, highly disapproved of the report's etiological conclusions. In his opinion, the true cause of the plague could not be imputed to the condition of the atmosphere or to swamp miasmas, nor was it caused by uncleanliness or poverty. "Yes, of course," he admits, "I would be the first to concede all the ills that can befall men because of an unconcerned and uncaring government . . . over-fond of the notion that Europe, with its forceful precepts of hygiene and conservation, is merely indulging in vain speculations and puerilities."[39] The plague, he states, is caused by emanations from cadavers containing animal poisons. The "hidden evil" from which Egypt is suffering is caused by its abundance of such rotting matter: Cemeteries are built so close to inhabited areas that the "dead seem to mingle with the living"—dark, dank, and airless districts, where the houses vomit corpses; whole neighborhoods "built of carrion and mud," veritable "hotbeds of mortality." The abandonment of the old salubrious embalming practices has turned modern Egypt into the cradle of the plague. The decaying corpse, no longer prepared, salted, dried, covered in tar and scented cloths, laid in stone tombs in coffins of sycamore, or stacked in thousands upon thousands of terra-cotta urns and buried in deep holes, is today "thrown all unprepared and incorporated raw, as it were, into the earth," and the practice has transformed the country into one vast cemetery, a "distillery for cadavers."

Both Prus's and Pariset's theories, however, share the same constant: namely, stench. Whether exhaled by animal decomposition or vegetable decay, miasma occupies a central place in all etiological descriptions of the plague.

Similar debates occurred elsewhere in Europe. In England, social reformer Sir Edwin Chadwick, writing in 1844, established a relationship between the "impurities" of the air and the evils of overpopulation. On the other hand, physician William Budd, taking the extreme case of the stench in London, which had become "thrice that of the Augean stables," set out in 1858 to demonstrate that despite all the sinister prophecies there had been no increase in either mortality or putrid diseases.

Early Awareness of Industrial Pollution

In that same year of 1858, a man named Laurent wrote to the Emperor Napoleon III complaining that the well-being of fish appeared to be receiving greater attention than that of man: "The lawmaker has been more diligent in dealing with the hygienic conditions of water-dwelling creatures than he has in dealing with the hygiene of those who breathe the air."[40] Although laws protecting the waters were already on the books, there was no law to protect the integrity of this other vital and "very fragile" fluid. The shortcomings of the law contributed to a deterioration that could well generate many kinds of epidemics, such as the 1854 cholera epidemic. Coke ovens, smokestacks, foundries, and soda works all spewed out an enormous quantity of deleterious miasmas, and no law existed to stop them. Indeed, wrote the indignant author, it often seemed they were actually being encouraged to do so! He proposed various methods to remedy the state of affairs, including one to modify the system for evacuating the vapors emitted by large industrial firms: "If . . . rather than having tall chimneys reaching to the clouds and belching unclean exhalations into the atmosphere, they could be made curved so that their fumes would be directed down, we might achieve a maximum decomposition of their gaseous components."[41] The picture the text conjures up makes us smile today; nevertheless, the author was attempting to deal with a problem that still exists: the treatment of noxious industrial fumes. Although it had been a subject of concern for several centuries, the purity of the air could still awaken antiquated fears in 1880, when an unusual number of bad smells wafted over Paris. It was not until pioneer bacteriologist Robert Koch's discovery of the cholera vibrio in 1833 and Georg Gaffky's isolation of the typhus bacillus in 1884 that the age-old link between fetidness and noxiousness began to weaken.

The Smell of Rats

Perceptions of the etiology, nature, and spread of the plague were to remain linked to smell until the end of the nineteenth century. The force and durability of the notion are surprising until we remember that the conviction was indeed almost universal. Chinese medicine, for example, which had made a thorough study of various forms of the plague and had long recognized a correlation between rats and human plague, gave an important place to smell in its explanations of the etiology and spread of the scourge: "Rats died because they took on the foul odor of the earth, and men then caught the plague because they took on the foul odor of the rats."[42]

Despite the efforts made by physicians to promulgate the microbe theory, perceptions in which smell plays a decisive part in both sickness and health still persist today in certain traditional societies. For the Sereer-ndut of Senegal, for example, inhaling the odor of the brush genies along with the mist causes fevers, influenza, and malaria, and the smell of the sick (especially their underarm perspiration) transmits the disease.[43] Similar beliefs are still present among the Andean peoples. When a person dies of tuberculosis, he "emits a kind of vapor that can penetrate the weakest persons."[44] As a logical result of such notions, there are Andean practices against epidemic that employ counterodors. To combat the harmfulness of a sick person's breath, "like the air that seeps from fissures in the earth, from tombs and from crevasses,"[45] the healer's breath must be made impregnable with alcohol and tobacco. The body of the sick person is massaged with a vegetable paste mixed with urine to cleanse and neutralize the malignant emanations.

A STENCH FROM HELL

An evil smell—like the stench rising from fields and bodies of water—is so much a part of the plague that it was regarded as one of its earliest symptoms. Thucydides noted its fetid breath, and Lucretius and the physician Diemerbroeck both mentioned the odor of "corrupt cadavers,"[46] of "rotten flesh,"[47] given off by the breath of plague victims.

There was something unnatural and nonhuman about the unbearable nature of this death-dealing fetor that caused it to be regarded as a kind of demonic emanation that rose from the underworld to spread over the surface of the earth. "A supernatural disease wrought by the wrath of God,"[48] the plague had an odor unlike any other: It offered a glimpse of supreme punishment to unheeding and rebellious mankind. It was likened to being borne off to hell. Even for the ancients, there was something unnaturally violent about the fever that wasted the dying, as evidenced by Lucretius's memorable words: "The innards are burnt away to the bones, a fire flames in the stomach as in the belly of a forge."[49] In their desperate search to cool their fever, not able to bear the contact of even the lightest garments, victims would throw themselves into the icy waters of rushing streams and down wells. "The unslakable thirst devouring their burning bodies made them unable to distinguish between a few droplets of water and an abundant flow. There was no respite for their sufferings."[50] Fiery, burning fever, despair, and an infection that repulsed even vultures—is it surprising that the plague should have been perceived as a diabolical stench? Were not the torments of the plague-ridden like those of the damned?

In 1585, Montaigne recorded the "strange effects" produced by the epidemic. Besides its hellish effects on the flesh, the venomous air poisoned the tenderest of relationships and dissolved the most affectionate ties. Fleeing the plague with his family and seeking some refuge, he learned what it was to wander from place to place, to find friendly doors closed to him. He witnessed the terror he and his family inspired and that even crept slyly between the family members themselves: "I, who am so hospitable, had a great deal of trouble finding a retreat for my family: a family astray, a source of fear to their friends and themselves, and of horror wherever they sought to settle, having to shift their abode as soon as one of the group began to feel pain at the end of his finger."[51]

During the Marseilles plague of 1720 Fournier reported that fathers and mothers drove their children without pity into the streets and, with unimaginable cruelty, left them there to their unhappy fates, abandoning them with nothing but a bowl and a jug of water. The children, for their part, "meted out the same barbarous and cruel fate to those who had brought them into this life; the calls of blood, tenderness and affection were totally stifled."[52] And the bishop of Marseilles raised his voice to cry out: "All France and all Europe has armed itself against thy unfortunate inhabitants, who have become hateful to all men."[53]

As the stinking flesh of rotting bodies was eroded, shred by shred, the social fabric, too, putrified and dissolved. Duties and functions were cast aside. Terror-stricken physicians and judges fled the city, abandoning the sick without care and leaving the looters to their base pursuits. Since, to avoid contagion, trade of any kind was forbidden, the inhabitants had nothing, and famine, accompanied by the twin scourges of poverty and disease, created an atmosphere of nearly total dismay and devastation. All feelings of solidarity were destroyed by the fear of contamination; selfish interests moved to the fore and people cared only to avoid their fellow men. All mankind was in disorder. Barbarism and terror replaced sympathy and pity. Men reverted to a "state of nature" and, like lone wolves, ran away or fought amongst themselves: "Everyone flees in fear and disarray; the bewildered citizens wander the streets aimlessly, not knowing where they go; they avoid each other and dare not draw near: a few barricade themselves within their houses, heedless of the risks they are running, and others withdraw to their farms. . . . All of them, with inexpressible concern and dismay, seek some dwelling place, some retreat where they can live cut off from the human race."[54]

And the delicate scent of the incense that was "wafted up like a prayer" to God, sealing the sacred bond, was replaced by a pestilential stench, symbol of the breach that had opened up between Heaven and man. The "smell of death"[55] emanating from the souls of sinners disrupted and severed that unity and brought down the Divine wrath.

The stench of the plague corrupted not only the body but the mind and the heart as well; it destroyed the bonds between men, who could no longer bear each other's sight, each other's smell. It seemed truly to be a hellish exhalation straight from the Devil's lair where, in the words of Saint Teresa of Ávila, "it stinks, and there is no love."[56]

2

THE CURATIVE POWERS OF SMELL

▼

Where are they now, the days of
aromatic warmth and hot-scented remedies!

Gaston Bachelard, *The Psychoanalysis of Fire*

Ever since antiquity, the prevention and treatment of illness have
involved a constant concern to maintain the proper balance of
the atmosphere and the body fluids, which were believed to be
subject to all kinds of disturbances—from malign movements of
the stars and planets, to thunder, lightning, and even transports
of passion. Since the causes of organic putrification were
thought to be analogous to those of atmospheric pollution, it is
hardly surprising that recommendations aimed at preserving
bodily health should have a great deal in common with those
aimed at preserving the purity of the air. The essential role of
odors in purification was due not only to perceptions of how
plagues were spread, but also to the link that had been established between smells and the principle of incorruptibility as far

back in time as ancient Egypt. There was also a third reason: Certain odors had the power to open up or facilitate communication between men and the gods and to calm the latter's wrath.

THE HIPPOCRATIC FIRES AND THERIAC
(VENICE TREACLE)

Long before the theories of Aristotle, Theophrastus, and Lucretius about the hot, dry, fiery, and incorruptible nature of pleasant odors and their beneficial effects, perfumes had already been associated with fire in combatting diseases. According to the Greek physician Galen, the only therapeutic method used by Hippocrates had consisted of cleansing polluted air with aromatic fires. Bonfires of scented wood and flowers permeated with perfumed unguents were lit in the streets of Athens. And Galen himself prescribed theriac,★ or Venice treacle, for both the prevention and cure of plague because it was believed to cleanse the malignant air "like a refiner's fire."[1]

Theriac was a sovereign remedy against all sorts of poisonous substances, including those in the atmosphere. It was therefore regarded as the antidote par excellence to the poison of the plague. Drunk as a preventive measure, it made for a stable temperature and healthy constitution, absorbed superfluous humid residues, warmed chilled members, strengthened the organism's resistance, and protected it against disease. It could even

★This remedy owes its name to its property of combating the effects of the bites of wild animals (in Greek, *therion* has, since Homer, been used to designate any kind of ferocious or wild animal). It was purportedly invented by Mithradates and was widely employed by Andromacus, Nero's physician. Galen gives a recipe that was later to undergo many modifications but that always included snake skin and an electuary composed of some sixty different plants. During the Renaissance its preparation was often the occasion of public ceremonies. Theriac was considered to be a panacea up until the nineteenth century.

bring about a complete cure in persons who had already succumbed. Galen tells us that the compound was used with success during one of the epidemics of the plague that raged through Italy. However, theriac was not the only odorous compound employed against illness in antiquity. For example, Rufus of Ephesus recommends a pharmaceutical mixture of aloes, myrrh, and incense: "I know of no sick person," he says, "who has failed to recover with this potion."[2]

In addition to the perfumes and aromatic products that played an essential role in plague prevention and treatment, Greek and Roman physicians used other remedies whose objectives were always cleansing. Indeed, the threat of putridity was a central medical concern. Galen stated that all his therapeutic methods were derived from that perception,[3] and he recommended bleedings, purges, and emetics, all techniques inherited directly from Hippocrates. Phlebotomy and other purgative treatments were widely used to combat overindulgence. Having contracted the plague, Rufus of Ephesus reportedly escaped death by opening a vein in his leg and losing a large quantity of blood.

THE SPICE AGE

In the Middle Ages pleasant smells were the principal weapons against bodily and atmospheric pollution. After the Greeks, Arab physicians played an important role in the prophylactic and therapeutic use of odors. The prophet Mohammed had a pronounced liking for pleasant smells. Born in Mecca, a center of the spice trade, Mohammed had granted great hygienic and medicinal virtues to perfumes and had viewed the use of cosmetics as one way by which Moslems could set themselves apart from Jews and Christians.[4] In the eleventh century, Avicenna, a

Persian, invented the apparatus and process of alembic distillation by which essential volatile oils could be extracted from flowers. Quoting the Prophet ("In your world, three things are dear to me: perfumes, women and, my greatest joy, prayer"[5]), Avicenna promoted the life-giving virtues of aromas and their effects on "good morals" and "perfect acts": "For the Prophet—may God grant him His blessing and His peace!—the interest in using excellent odors is that they fortify the senses. And when the senses are strong, the thoughts are precise and their conclusions upright. When, on the other hand, the senses become weak, thoughts become unbalanced and their conclusions confused."

The convergence between antique and Arab concepts influenced physicians to employ odors for their decay-preventing, purifying, restorative, and revivifying capabilities. Used in many forms, they combated the baser passions like fear and sorrow, which altered the organism's natural disposition and contributed to disease. By comforting, repairing, rectifying, refreshing, warming, or desiccating, they ensured both the salubrity of the air and the health of the body. In order that the primal qualities of the air and body should remain stable, care had to be taken that neither would become too damp, too hot, too dry, or too cold. Although a cold, dry temperature made the body susceptible to pollution because it closed the pores of the skin and prevented the evacuation of body fluids, heat and humidity were considered even more dangerous because they opened the emunctories to the poisoned air.

Scents began to be classified in relation to climate. According to the season, they provided the air and the body with the elements needed to maintain their balance. During the 1348 plague, the collegium of the Faculté de Paris prescribed breathing in the summertime "cold aromatics like roses, sandalwood, nenuphar, vinegar, rose-water, camphor lozenges that comfort the heart, and chilled apples," and in winter, "hot aromatics like aloe wood, amber or sweet gum, nutmeg and pomander."[6]

A second classification, this one social in nature and one that was to remain operative over the years, was also established. Owing to their cost, musk, ambergris, aloes, and cinnamon were reserved for the "rich and powerful."[7] The "comfortably off"[8] used storax, costus, frankincense, marjoram, and mastic. As for the poor man,

> *Qui, en yver ne en esté*
> *Ne peut mie ces choses faire,*
>
> (Who, in wynter nor in sommertime
> Maye of such thinges have nonne,)

his only recourse was

> *Que prier Dieu, le débonnaire,*
> *A lui faire bonne défense*
> *En tout temps de mal et d'offense.*
>
> (To pray unto his goodlie God,
> For to protect him straight
> In days of sicknesse and of sinne.)[9]

To cleanse and freshen the air in patrician dwellings, the floor was sprinkled with rose water or covered with "cool-hued" flowers. In wintertime rooms were warmed with fumigations of musk, sweet gum, and ambergris, aloes, and "lozenges," for which the Faculté de Médecine de Paris provided recipes and instructions for use.[10] People burned "fistics," "tamara," juniper berries, quince, and something called "ase." In warm weather, vinegar water was used, and the floor was strewn with vine leaves and plants to alleviate the heat and humidity:

> *Jonchier la chambre druement,*
> *Et l'arrouser légiérement,*
> *D'eau très froide et de vinaigre,*
> *Fort odorant, poignant et maigre,*
> *Et dessus semer volentiers*
> *Des roses et fleurs d'aiglentiers*
> *O feuilles d'ongle cabaline,*
> *Qui est herbe moult froide et digne,*
> *Et de choses autres bien fresches,*
> *Bien odorans, plaisans et sèches.*

(Strewe well the room and sprinkle it lightly with very cold water and strong tart vinegar, atop that strewe a deal of flowres, roses and eglantine or caballine aloes, a most cooling and worthie plant, as well as other fresh thinges whose fragrances are strong, pleasant and dry.)[11]

Measures to cleanse the "breath" of the house were accompanied by suggestions for urban hygiene. Fetid and muddy areas were to be avoided, and polluted air kept out by glazing the windows or covering them with waxed cloth. The medieval poet Olivier de La Haye also stressed the importance of living in healthy areas away from the effluvia of swamps, mines, and cemeteries and even in locales that were well protected and surrounded by trees. He counselled against living near certain plants that were believed to give off unhealthy emanations:

> *Pour éviter l'infection*
> *Aussi est bon certainement*
> *Quérir un tel hébergement*
> *Où n'ai prez noyers, ne sénes*

Figuiers, jusquiame, cicues,
N'autres choses, portant encombre
Par leur oudeur ne par leur ombre.

(To avoid infection it is also surely good to seek to dwell there where is neither walnut tree nor senna, fig-tree, henbane, hemlock nor any other thing that can create cumbrance by smell or shadow.)[12]

Pomanders and scent boxes, electuaries and lozenges, lotions and syrups could purify polluted air before it entered the lungs and could build up the organism's resistance. Some products acted as a both a protective screen and a tonic, while others were merely medicaments—substances used in therapy.

Pomanders, which originated in the East, were hollow spheres of gold or silver, often set with pearls and precious stones. The height of fashion up until the eighteenth century, they inspired magnificent examples of the goldsmith's art, some being given a variety of highly imaginative shapes. They were worn at the belt, around the neck, and even as rings, and contained solid perfumes made from such rare and extremely costly animal bases as musk and ambergris. Their presence in Europe far predates the fifteenth century: In 1174, the Emperor Frederick Barbarossa is recorded as having received from the king of Jerusalem several golden apples filled with musk.[13] The amber or ambergris pomander, filled with a fragrant substance derived from the waxy secretion of the alimentary canal of the cachalot, or sperm whale, was prized in the Middle Ages as a sovereign protection against plague. Thanks to its powerful odor it possessed to a very high degree "the property of pleasing the senses and toning the body,"[14] of soothing the temper, and of facilitating respiration:

> Car l'ambre pure et excellente
> A propriété véhémente
> A donner confort et léesce,
> Et à tollir toute tristesce.

(For pure and estimable ambergris is strong in its power to make comfortable and gay and to assuage all sorrow.)[15]

Because of its cost, however, this remedy was available only to the extremely wealthy. As a result, other diluted and less-expensive remedies were created, many of which contained not a trace of the true ambergris whose fragrance was so highly praised.

Some famous compounds, such as the ones offered by the Arab philosophers Messoué and Avicenna, contained many other aromatic ingredients that were pulverized, sifted, and mixed with water to form a paste that was then made into a ball and hardened. Here is one of the many recipes for a pomander ball from the members of the Faculté de Médecine in Paris:

Take a very pure gem of two ounces; storax, calamite, gum Arabic, myrrh, incense, aloes, of each three gross; choice red roses, one gross; sandalwood, musk, two gross; nutmeg, cloves and mace, of each a gross; ben-nut, the upper and lower shells of a Byzantine oyster, karabé, aromatic calamus, the seed of basil, marjoram, savory, dried mint, gillyflower root, of each substance half a gross; aloe wood, a half ounce; ambergris, one ounce; musk, one and a half gross; camphor, a half scruple; oil of spikenard, oil of muscatel, enough to give fragrance; add a small piece of white wax.[16]

Scent boxes abounded as well, containing either solid perfumes or a piece of cloth or sponge imbued with vinegar, which, although inexpensive, was reputed to be an effective shield against putrefaction because of its "cold and dry" nature. Sponges, which surgeon Ambroise Paré considered the substance best able to retain "the virtues and spirit of aromatic and odorous things," were still being used for that purpose in the eighteenth century.[17]

Lotions, syrups, pills, and lozenges were all part of the medieval arsenal against the plague: "The heart must be eased by external bathing and internally with syrups and other medicines; all such preparations must contain some perfume and some aroma, like the fragrance of the lemon tree, syrup of apples and lemons and the acid pomegranate."[18]

The Greek and Arab sources of some of these compounds are reflected by the use of substances supposed to possess antivenomous properties—precious stones, pearls, gold, ivory, and hart's (red deer's) horn, which were found in formulas used to treat the fever and buboes of plague.

Odor also played a large part in the purification of linens, clothing, and food. Galen believed that malodorous sheets, mattresses, and blankets could accelerate the pollution of the body fluids, and the Italian writer Giovanni Boccaccio reported that the clothes of plague victims were hotbeds of contamination. It was advisable to scent linens and clothing (silk and the color scarlet were thought to create the best screen against poisonous effluvia).

The agreeable smells of spices were supposed to arrest the corruption of food. Boiled meats and fish were seasoned with ginger, cloves, cubeb pepper, cardamom, nutmeg, mace, saffron, and cinnamon. However, the costive properties of many spices also opened the pores of the skin to the pestilent air, and, as a result, their use was usually restricted to the wintertime.

In the fifteenth century fragrant substances and antidotes systematically went hand in hand in both the prevention and the treatment of plague. There were many varieties of antidotes, beginning with precious and semiprecious stones: jacinth, topaz, garnet, ruby, coral, and diamond, among others, whose powers were constantly being stressed. The emerald, for example, was so powerful that it could actually blind vipers and toads.[19] And such precious substances were not the only compounds with "the property and ability to dispel venom." There were many others, precious and nonprecious, real or mythical, that actually were shields against death: gold, silk, the horn of a unicorn, or simply wood from an ash tree.

The antidote par excellence was the hard material known as bezoar, a word that actually means "antidote" in the original Persian. Bezoar is not stone, but rather a concretion found in the alimentary organs of such animals as camels, sheep, deer, and giraffes. Of Eastern origin, it came in three different colors: dark blue, blue and green, and bluish white. Its immunizing powers were so great that should a scorpion happen to come into contact with it, the venomous creature would instantly be rendered harmless. Crushed and inserted into a serpent's mouth, bezoar would result in the creature's instant death. This rare substance could be worn around the neck or set in a ring. It was advisable to augment its protective powers by having it engraved with the figure of a snake or scorpion. It was also used in the compounding of various aromatic medicines: Incense stamped with a signet ring of bezoar would protect against poison as well as the substance itself.

Less valuable and easier to procure, ash wood was also combined with fragrances to combat pestilence: "For the ash has

such a strong ability to prevent any poisonous creature from
entering into its shadow or smelling of it that the beast would
rather cast itself into the flames than approach that tree."[20] One
could protect oneself from the air by breathing through a sponge
"attached to a piece of ash" and impregnated with "that salutary
fragrance," combined with rose water, rose vinegar, malmsey
wine, and zedoary root or lemon peel.

Fragrant substances and antidotes frequently figure in prescriptions of the time. In addition to theriac, which the philosopher Marsile Ficin deemed the "Queene of all the compounds
vouchsafed by Heav'n to Man" and into which one dipped
one's handkerchief, there were all sorts of other pleasant fragrances (incense, myrrh, violets, mint, melissa balm, rue, or a
"cedar apple" made of storax, sandalwood, camphor, and roses).
One could also carry a citrus fruit, flowers, or a sweet-smelling
plant; one could wear a unicorn's horn, a jacinth, a topaz, or an
emerald around one's neck or hold one in the mouth. Pills and
electuaries were compounded of aloes, myrrh, saffron, and other
ingredients "to accentuate their virtue and strength": precious
stones, pearls, "scrapings of hivorie," roasted unicorn horn, and
hart's horn or "a bone of that creature's hearte." For the wealthy
there were several recipes for pills to desiccate the body fluids,
fortify the heart, and contract the vessels to prevent poison from
entering. Powders made of precious stones and incense were
highly recommended. People drank and ate decoctions of
flowers to dry out "poisonous humidities"; antitoxic plants like
wild horseradish, "so powerful against venom that it can kill the
scorpion that touches it"; waters of melissa, rose, or scabious; or
scorpion oil, which was made by boiling that dangerous creature
in fifty-year-old olive oil. Perfumed sachets to be worn close to
the heart to strengthen it were made of red roses, aloe wood,
sandalwood, and coral. Epithema, or poultices, made of sandalwood, camphor, and roses, as well as coral and ivory, were worn

on the stomach or under the arm. To make the compounds more effective, highly toxic substances were often added to poultices and sticking plasters—arsenic, hemlock, and vitriol, as well as quicklime, orpiment, borax, ammoniac salts, and pitch, which worked on the poison contained in buboes. These medicines were thought to be "powerful in drawing venom from the body."

The search for antidotes also led Ficin to mix precious substances with the spices usually used in food preparation in order to counterbalance the effects of their hot and diuretic qualities, which could "prepare and ready man more easily to receive the venom."

Comparing the plague to a dragon "enveloping man with its poisonous breath," Marsile Ficin contributed to the widespread fear of the plague and made people more aware of the need for greater hygiene. To protect themselves from poison that could adhere to the skin, clothing, objects, and even to the walls of houses, men must above all "keep dwelling and bodie clean."[21]

For the house, Ficin promulgated methods that went back to antiquity and the Middle Ages, especially the use of fragrances and aromatic fires. The house must be clean, ventilated, and "perfumed with good smells," the rooms sprinkled with vinegar and filled with flowers and fragrant plants: "So let vine leafs, sweet rushes, willow and osier, smalle plantes and leafs of the lemon-tree and all other greene things like flowres and sweet-smelling pommes be strewne throughout and placed in the corners and on the walls of the chambers."

As for bodily cleanliness, along with traditional techniques for internal purging there were instructions for new methods—which did not, however, include any increased recourse to bathing. On the contrary, that practice was deemed dangerous insofar as it opened the pores of the skin and allowed pestilential air to enter the body more easily. Although some physicians during past plagues had advised against hot baths only, Ficin believed that any bathing was dangerous.[22] (Indeed, the fear of bathing led in the sixteenth century to the closing of public baths.) The practices he did recommend tended to avoid the use of water altogether. The hands and face were to be cleansed with aromatic lotions. Physicians and others who had contact with the sick were to be even more watchful and to cleanse their entire bodies twice a day with tepid vinegar. Frequent changes of clothing and the abundant use of perfumes were regarded as indispensable precautions.

Advice on hygiene was accompanied by urgings to adopt a different attitude toward the use of bed linens and dishes that reflected a new trend toward individualization: "In time of plague one should utilize separate vessels for drinking and eating and for the dressing of beds, and should separate bedsheets and other needful thinges not be available, then should they be well cleansed with washings and perfumes."[23]

Similar preventive measures were also applied to the problem of sickroom care, and when contagion appeared, it was to be combated according to similar principles. Recommendations for bodily hygiene were especially applicable to the sick: "One must see to it above all that the shirt and all sheets, linens and perfumes of the sick be changed often, as well as the vessels in which the perfumes are made up."[24] As for methods of cleansing with perfumes, they were directly inspired by those used to disinfect.[25] No clear distinction is made between preventive hygiene and curative methods, for both derive from the same concept. However, Ficin's regulations would continue to influence methods of disinfection that would be developed and practiced systematically in later centuries.

. . .

Whatever the principle behind their power, throughout the sixteenth century odors continued to be the surest allies of all who cared for the sick. Physician Ogier Ferrier's advice to his colleagues in 1548 illustrates how important the whole array of aromatic substances was to contemporary physicians. Before the attending doctor would enter the house of a plague victim, doors and windows had to be opened to aerate it and a fragrant fire lit to disinfect it. Preceded by a "censer box" in which incense, myrrh, aloes, roses, gum benzoin, labdanum, styrax, and cloves burned on a bed of hot coals, and bearing in one hand a juniper branch and in the other a pomander ball, the practicioner would then proceed to the patient's side. Once he had reached the fumigated bedchamber, the consultation could begin. This procedure demanded the combined talents of juggler and tightrope walker and called for great diagnostic perspicacity, since the physician's auscultations could be performed only from a distance, gropingly, as he moved back and forth near the bed:

> Thus, holding a bit of your massapa in your mouth, and holding the hand with the aforementioned fragrances under the nose and in the other the aforementioned branche of burning juniper, you must look upon your patient from a certain distance away and enquire into his sicknesse and his symptoms and whether he be in paine, or if he hath any tumor anywhere, and so converse with him. And then, approaching him, and with your backe turned upon him, you will hand your branche of wood to someone who will continue to hold it before your face and, reaching behind you with your hand, you will take the patient's pulse and feele his forehead and the region of his harte, always maintaining some fragrance beneath your nose.[26]

Finally, the courageous physician, still equipped with all his aromatic accessories, was to perform his last and most dangerous task: the examination of the patient's urine and fecal matter, but with the proviso that this be done only "should the condition of the patient demand it."

DISINFECTING BY CANNON FIRE

Pleasant odors, however, did not have the hoped-for effects, and concern and anxiety about the plague continued to grow. The notion then began to spread that it might perhaps be possible to combat it with *stronger* smells. There were two possible options: Fight stench with stench or augment the action of familiar fragrances with more pungent odors.

In 1634, the physician Henri de la Cointe suggested neutralizing pestilential odors with even more objectionable ones—the stench of goats, for example, or the smell of dead bodies. In support of his proposal he cited the ancient practices reported by his colleagues Thomas Jordanus, Alexander Benedictus, and Palmarius. The first had written that "It is the custom to raise goats, which are stinking creatures, where there is pestilential air, so that all the bad or unpleasant smells can coalesce around them or so that their stench will overcome all the others and destroy in such wise that barely a trace remains."[27] The others testified that during a cruel plague that had ravaged Poland and Scythia the population had been asked to kill all dogs and cats and leave them to rot in the streets "so that such malign and stinking vapor might waft up into the air and pervade it, either to alter the pestilent air or to absorb it and consume it utterly."[28] The same notion underlay the advice given in 1628 by Alvarus, the Toulouse physician, who thought that drinking one's own urine each morning was far too filthy a suggestion: "Better the frequent smelling of goat urine and of the goat itself, one of which might be kept in the house for such purposes."[29] This custom was not without some basis in fact: The odor of the goat, as well as that of other animals (cattle, horses, sheep, and camels), repels the fleas and lice that spread bubonic plague. The same is true of the odor of some kinds of oils made from olives, walnuts, peanuts.

Henri de la Cointe found confirmation of the principle that one bad smell can eradicate another in the fact that certain kinds of laborers who are avoided because they work with "base and stinking objects" are less subject to the epidemic: The nauseating stench of skins protects those who dress leather, just as cesspool cleaners are mithridatized, or made immune, by the excremental emanations that are inherent to their work. As for hospital personnel, who must perforce breathe pestilential air, they are apparently not unduly threatened by the disease. Fetidity, therefore, was no longer synonymous with danger, and a new aromatic credo slowly began to develop: "It would be precipitate and foolhardy to undertake to state and promulgate as an eternal verity the premise that none but pleasant fragrances should be used to perfume infected bedchambers and never those that are disagreeable and displeasant."[30] Indeed, pleasant smells seemed now to be responsible for abetting disease: "In truth, when it comes to sweet and pleasant smells, they would rather appear to be a vehicle for transporting plague-ridden air into the heart, for the heart, making no attempt at defence and following its natural penchant for fragrance and good odors, embraces them forthwith: just as, contrariwise, it retracts and protects itself against displeasant ones."

However, not all of Henri de la Cointe's contemporaries favored so complete a reversal of olfactory values. The majority preferred a system in which violent odors and pleasant smells were commingled. The purifying and reinvigorating virtues of the latter had to be supported and augmented by "reinforcements" adapted to the enemy's terrifying nature. In disinfecting houses, clothing, and persons, aromatic fumigations were fortified with toxic products that gave off acrid effluvia (sulphur, arsenic, antimony, gunpowder, pitch). From the seventeenth century on, however, specific attention began to be paid to the powers inherent in the irritating smells of such additives and to making their use more widespread. No longer, as Angelus Sala noted in 1617, was it a question of "correcting a particular stench in the air" through the use of fragrances, but of combatting a "very subtle" poisonous vapor, something that could not be accomplished with violent and antidotal perfumes alone.[31] The epidemic was "such a malignant and vehement infection that it cannot be quelled by the scent of roses, of violets, of orange-blossom, orris, storax, sandalwood, cinnamom, musk, ambergris, civet or other fragrant things." And, just as the "strength of a lion cannot be overcome by that of a lamb," or the power of "the great poison of arsenic reversed with sugar candy," one could not fight the air's pestilence by using only such things that pleased the sense of smell. Despite the disagreeable side effects of unpleasant smells, Sala recommended their use because "one cannot preserve one's health by keeping one's nose forever buried in a bouquet of roses." The new trend was illustrated by the appearance of pomander balls containing sulphur, pitch, and castoreum (made from the dried perineal glands of the beaver and their secretion)[32] as well as various "fetid and pestilential pills."[33]

The triumph of a "hawkish" medicine of violent smells over a "dovish" medicine of pleasant ones was won over mighty obstacles. Any argument served in the quarrel between groups of specialists. Supporters of traditional aromatherapy, unwilling to seem less progressive than their opponents, backed up their theory by proposing new and sometimes ingenious methods.

Representative of the confrontation between new trends and old methods is the polemical contest waged in 1622 by physicians Jean de Lampérière, author of *Le Traité de la peste, de ses moyens et de sa cure,* and David Jouysse, who published his rebuttal *Examen du livre de Lampérière sur le sujet de la peste.*

A leader in the fight waged by the old guard (he remained a partisan of gold, pearls, precious stones, and bezoar salts), Lampérière went on to dream up new fragrant compounds, all of which bear witness to his vivid imagination and make him an almost comic figure. At any cost, he stubbornly continued his campaign to bring aroma back into fashion by wrapping it in mystery and creating links between it and "modern" medical practices. His writings on the use of perfumed substances oscillate between received opinion, common sense, and sheer fiction. On the surface his aim was to pique the curiosity of a public that had begun to lose faith in the virtues of aromatic products, and to refurbish their once-prestigious reputation. To do so, he went back to the secret practices of alchemy, the customs of distant cultures, and even imaginary ingredients—anything, in short, that might serve to burnish up the once-shining halo with which aromatics had earlier been crowned.

According to Lampérière, there were some "universal perfumes" that furnished very effective protection because their hearty, dark, and sooty odors could penetrate the pores of the skin and block the entry of unclear air. Giving them a touch of the occult, he told of having seen a Jewish physician in Paris, a "great naturalist and chemist," who, assisted by a Dr. Cayer in the Abbaye de Saint-Martin, had employed a similar antidote during the 1596 plague in Paris. Twice a day, morning and evening, the two alchemists had exposed their totally naked bodies to fumigations so strong they had blackened their skin. Afterwards, however, they had been able to have contact with sick persons of all kinds without fear or danger. This odoriferous preparation, which, in David Jouysse's jeering words, "stank to something higher than heaven," must have indeed had a unique bouquet, given some of its ingredients, which included goat urine and dried peacock dung.[34]

Recalling the Sicilian custom of rubbing the entire body with black lead (graphite) to block the pores of the skin and prevent its being penetrated by pestilential emanations, Lampérière also praised an aromatic laundry soap that produced the same results. Thanks to its astringent and desiccative qualities, one could wash oneself without danger. In reality, this compound, which enabled a person to enjoy a mild "sponge-bath" without injury to the skin and without the use of water (which "relaxes and softens" the skin), was nothing but a mixture of well-known odorous products.

Lampérière tried to make aromatic products fashionable again by suggesting improved formulas and new materials. He maintained that the energies inherent in perfumes had never been fully exploited. His campaign was notable for such innovative concoctions as "weasel powder," an "adhesive cordial," a "protective shirt," and a "medicated cloth for the burial of plague victims," all designed to combine odors with the latest developments in prophylaxis.

Obtaining "weasel powder," however, was not the simplest of tasks. First, the animal had to be poked at with sticks until it became enraged, at which point it was tossed into a pot of boiling wine and aromatic plants. It was then simmered until all the liquid had evaporated. Dried and "rinsed in petifite water," a heart-fortifying salt was obtained from the residue. Other more or less fanciful products were used in other concoctions in the same vein, all with links to the supernatural and serving to support the good doctor's fantasy.

In his rebuttal Jouysse noted that some of these extravagant recipes had no smell at all: "When you prescribe the fragrances of weasel powder and powder from a stag's tear bag, tell me how the ashes can burn and what odor they can possibly emit, given that they have no perfume at all? Stag's tear bag must be fairly common, since you prescribe burning a whole gram of it. . . . "[35] Why not also recommend some other products equally easy to obtain? he asks with heavy irony: "the blood of beasts born with more than four legs, the sperm of the first ejaculation of a hermaphrodite flea and the furots [hooves] of Phoebus' steeds, which might be just as—if not more—effective."[36]

Lampérière's "adhesive cordial" was the scented or vinegar-drenched handkerchief carried to extremes. Its novelty consisted in macerating the bandage with various plants until it was completely permeated. Cloth so treated acquired a perfumed substratum and became almost a different substance, like a piece of petrified wood. Physicians were advised to use it for treating diverse maladies and to wear it themselves, making it into perfumed gloves without fingers to be worn when taking the patient's pulse. So equipped, and having perfumed their own bed linens and clothing, bathed their hands and faces with lotion, smeared their nostrils, temples, and lips with balms, and taken perfumed substances into their mouths, physicians were then able to resist the effluvia of the plague.

The "protective shirt" used perfumes to "fortify" the clothing used in hospital work. Lampérière reports that at the Hôtel-Dieu and in many other places he had witnessed the staff wearing "a kind of uniform like an ecclesiastical rochet, dipped and 'poached' in various protective liquids."[37] It was made by putting the fabric into a bath of essences or liquids that were mixed with melted wax and stirred frequently so that the cloth became completely impregnated. It was then dried and made up into clothing. The shirt, with its complex combination of aromas, was supposed to preserve "the flamme of life and protect from the rigours of any inimical draught of air."[38]

"Impermeable cloth for the burial of plague victims" was made into a shroud impregnated with aromatic substances like aloes, which were mixed with stronger-smelling materials such as sulphur.

Jouysse's criticism was focused on the stubborn determination to rely on odors at all costs. He denied their therapeutic properties and even held them to be injurious. They exacerbated female hysterics, and they had a libidinous effect on males, he maintained. Far from possessing strengthening and disinfectant virtues, they actually weakened the body. Jouysse met aromatic prescriptions with an indignant cry: "By Hippocrates' ashes, stand I not on ceremony when I answer my own calls, I have opened up beds without observing the same, oft have I come upon patients over the basin or using the stool. There were too the stinks and smells of the public infirmary, and thanks to God we are still here, we who have oft handled dead bodies and stomached their ejected wastes and . . . I had nor bandage nor censer."[39]

In the seventeenth century, the profession of perfumer—whose job it was to disinfect and cleanse homes and build-ings—was an honorable one. A perfumer employed assistants who performed nearly all the work under their master's orders and supervision. To avoid theft, which was easy to carry out in deserted houses, it was recommended that the assistants' uni-forms not include pockets. Sobriety was also a requisite, given the constant risk of fires. Here, according to Arnaud Baric writing in 1646, is the way in which the disinfection of a dwelling and its occupants was to be performed in those days:

Led by the "health captain,"* who carried a white baton to

*The health captain saw to the implementation of the orders handed down by the Health Council created in 1577 to control the epidemic by setting up a whole series of procedures. He was in command of lieutenants and soldiers and directed commissioners and "dizainiers" entrusted with closing up infected dwellings and isolating the sick. Each warn passersby of the danger of contagion, the perfumers, followed by the scrivener, entrusted with administrative and record-keeping duties, would make their way to the plague-stricken dwelling: "Two perfumers will each wear around his neck a pan of coals, one will lead an horse to bear the belongings to the furnaces and the dirtied linen to be washed; others will carry pans of coal, broomes, and the common, strong and sweet-smelling perfumes in three small leathern bagges, in order to avoid any mixturing of them beforetimes."[40] While the captain procured the keys from the district watchman, the perfumers would light a fire in front of the house, shut the windows, block up any holes, and open all the interior doors and any chests or containers so that the "perfuming" would destroy all the miasmas. The head perfumer—who entered first—would then melt some ordinary perfume in a pan and set forth to "cook out the accursed plague sprung from the hellish deep."

Once inside the house, it was his task to see that the perfume burned constantly and to guard against setting fire to the beds, the straw, or any paper. "Trailing the burner along the ground and lifting it gradually higher and higher, without undue haste, and finally holding it as high as he can without spilling the melted perfume within," he was to pass through every room, taking care not to miss any corner in which pestilential air might linger. Before leaving, he was to set the burner in the middle of the lower room, where the remainder of the perfume would be left to burn itself out.

Following that preliminary disinfection the other perfumers and the scribe, who had been waiting outside, entered and continued the cleansing process. They collected the dirty linen, which would be dealt with elsewhere by "washerwomen," and

---

dizainier supervised ten houses and every morning would order the inhabitants to "fall out" to make sure that none was absent and thus a victim of the plague.

all clothing, which was put into very hot ovens by "oven-keepers" to rid it of putrid exhalations. They also emptied the mattresses and burned the straw contents in the courtyard or in the street, swept out all the rooms, wiped down all the furniture and utensils with vinegar or good wine, washed the dishes, removed the bed linens from their chests and spread them over benches or between lines, and, finally, dipped any silverware or jewelry in boiling water. Wheat and flour were also purified; the perfumers were instructed to sift through them with a scoop while "common perfume" was burned in the granary and the storeroom. The scribe was to oversee all these activities, carefully keeping a list of all the objects taken from the house and taking care that the perfumers did not converse with strangers. The rooms in which the sick had been treated were subjected to intensive disinfection with a "strong, harsh perfume" that was burned in a large pot of hot coals.

The perfumers were then to move on to the "steaming room," where they were joined by other specialists aptly known as "steamers." Cloth tents were erected, inside which the perfumers could stand as they themselves were disinfected with fumes of the common perfume, which was allowed to boil away in a pot. Their clothing was also disinfected. The washerwomen and clothes collectors were subjected to the same treatment. Even the horse that had transported the linen and the clothing was cleansed with common perfume. The disinfection of the house's inhabitants was to be carried out at the same time as that of the house, using various perfumes adapted to their ages and constitutions.

A distinction had to be made between grown-ups, children, the strong, the weak, and those in delicate health: for "like treatment for all could well end in disaster."[41] To avoid asphyxiation children under five were spared the steaming room and merely passed several times over a mixture of pleasant and common perfumes. The perfuming of pregnant women and of children from six to nine years of age, however, was done in steaming rooms filled with emanations of pleasant perfumes and eau-de-vie. The hardier members of the household were treated in a similar way, but with common perfume mixed with salt and vinegar.

Once out of the steaming rooms, the perfumers, still supervised by the scribe, were to return the clean linen and clothing, laying it over bars or lines and treating it with a mixture of common and strong perfumes. The same mixture was then carried through all the rooms to eradicate any lingering putrid exhalations. A day after the last of the fumigations had evaporated, they were to burn "sweet perfume" or aromatic wood throughout the house. Their work was then concluded, and the perfumers returned the keys to the neighborhood watchman.

Still, the physical disinfection of humans was a novelty: "The disinfection of persons is a new invention, the Ancients having been content to prescribe quarantines for them, leaving those infected to the weather, the air and the wind, cut off from society and communication." However, as Ranchin, Chancellor of the Montpellier Faculty of Medicine, wrote in 1640, "Today a way has been found to shorten quarantine and to permit communication between infected persons immediately following their purification."[42] Peasants were to use their ovens, in which they were to "sweat out the infected and then introduce their clothing and then perfume them." Ranchin did note that the "public steamrooms," "well-equipped and laid out, and with the necessary attendants, are much more suitable." Up to thirty persons could be treated per day at a low cost; the poor received treatment free. The practice was also used for domestic animals. Before being perfumed, cats, dogs, donkeys, horses, and mules were to be scrubbed down with soap and water or put to swim in the river for a few hours. Packs and saddles were cleansed with strong perfume.

Cannon fire was also used to cleanse urban environs. The sharp odor of gunpowder had great purifying powers. Ranchin deplored the fact that this practice had certain unpleasant side effects:

> I am well aware that following the disinfection of houses there are those who bring small or medium-sized cannon into the streets and fire them off at crossings and in doorways and even in the center of principal streets in order that the smoke may dispell the infection that may linger in the woodwork or on the outer street walls of buildings. I highly approve of the smoke, but experience has taught me that setting off cannons can cause great expense and great inconveniences in cities.

He went on to note the destructive effects in Montpellier: broken windows, damaged walls that were cracking and about to crumble, shops broken open and prey to thieves and, worst of all, wines that "turn and spoil in the cask."[43]

THE DISAPPEARANCE OF MUMMY

Recourse to "perfumes" in the fight against the plague had a final resurgence during the two great plagues that raged across Europe in 1720 and 1771. Throughout Europe, perfumery was living through its last hours of glory. In Marseilles, disinfection was mandated by ordinance, and commissioners were appointed to supervise it. It was practiced intensively and carried out in both private and public buildings, especially churches, as well as aboard ships. Contaminated buildings were marked with red crosses, a practice that created considerable consternation: "Then one truly sees the extent to which the plague has ravaged the city. It has not spared a single street, and there are few that can boast a single healthy house. In all the other streets it had ravaged one after the other, and all the red crosses remain to mark out for us all the horrors of that cruellest of all massacres."[44]

In the late eighteenth century, chemical advances helped to discredit the use of perfumes in combating the epidemic. Attention was focused on the search for a product to neutralize the deadly exhalations from cesspools and other fetid places, which were believed to cause the plague and many other ills. The fight against stench became a crusade. The ravages thought to be caused by noxious odors, which were a source of public affliction and responsible for the countless deaths that were devastating whole towns and provinces, could no longer be tolerated. Emboldened by the positive results of his experiments in deodorizing sewers, Janin de la Combe-Blanche, a physician, announced the arrival of a new day when cleaning a cesspool would no longer pose a threat to an entire neighborhood, polluting streets and alleyways, or "dishonor" the countryside, a day when the lives of cesspool cleaners would no longer be endangered or cut short. The discovery of the "sovereign" antimephitic agent might even herald an era of real "social peace": "Every class of Citizen will bless the Supreme Being for having put into their hands and vouchsafed them knowledge of this formidable enemy capable of destroying and annihilating every kind of fetidness."[45]

Along with the emergence of hygienic concerns in the eighteenth century came the abandonment of a medieval and macabre drug widely recommended in the treatment of disease, including the plague. "Mummy" or "mommie," thought to be derived from the Persian word *mūm,* meaning "wax," and the

Arabic *mūmiyah,* "pitch," and used throughout the Middle Ages to refer both to the embalmed bodies of ancient Egypt and to the matter that resulted from such embalming, must be one of the greatest oddities in all antique pharmacopoeia. Bizarre as it seems to us today, however, the ancient remedy, as writer François Dagognet has pointed out, was actually based on a kind of logic. The centuries-long success of this "human" medication was due not only to the antiputrid and energizing virtues attributed to all aromatic herbs, but also to the belief that the process of decomposition could *create* life as well.

The genesis of the substance's use is obscure and riddled with gaps. According to pharmacologist Jean de Renou, "a few centuries" after the outbreak of the Egyptian war, most likely in the seventh century A.D.,[46] the Arab invaders who were ravaging the countryside managed to find entry into the tombs where the pharaohs lay embalmed with precious aromatic substances. They discovered in their sarcophagi "a certain odorous liquid elixir having the consistency of honey therein distilled."[47] They collected it and sold to the physicians of the land, who knew its use and value. Driven by their desire for gain and the therapeutic powers imputed to the new drug, they then began to bypass the newly discovered royal and princely sepulchers and turned to robbing the tombs of the common people and the poor. Although well aware that the exudate from bodies other than those embalmed with scented ointments was far less valuable, the physicians administered it to their patients nevertheless.

Another version places the emergence of mummy in the more recent past. In 1003 or 1100 A.D., "a clever Jew named Elmagar, a native of Alexandria, and reputed to be an expert physician well-versed in the Arab teachings,"[48] is said to have prescribed mummified flesh to the Christians and Moslems "who were in those days warring in the East for possession of Palestine." According to historian Louis Guyon, medical men of all nationalities then followed suit and prescribed the substance for "chills and bruises." Owing to their rarity, their price, and the difficulty of procuring them, rich mummies, which had been eviscerated, anointed, and "stuffed" with costly aromatic substances according to age-old rules, rapidly became unobtainable, and the apothecaries' pestles began to grind down the bodies of the poor.

In the twelfth century or perhaps even earlier, Alexandrian Jews, following the erroneous teachings of Diodorus of Sicily and of Strabo, who had maintained that true pitch had been used in the preparation of mummies,[49] began to peel off the resin with which the dead had been covered. Given the belief that this "human" pitch was the most effective, similar powers began to be imputed to the embalmed body itself, whereupon it began to be used in the manufacture of the drug: "Alas, poor Egypt! After having known civilization at its zenith, after having sacrificed its all to respect its dead, it was now forced to see the eternal dwellings of its venerated kings despoiled, profaned and violated and the bodies of its sons turned into drugs for foreigners."[50]

In any event, rich mummy or poor, the substance became wildly popular in the sixteenth century—a time that saw a huge increase in the number of animal and human medicines in general. In 1553, naturalist Pierre Belon reported that "the employ of said embalmed bodyes in Egypt—our Mummie, in fine—is so grately prized in France"[51] that the king, François I, never went out without some of it about his person. Eventually the real source of the products being offered consumers became increasingly dubious. In 1579, the surgeon Ambroise Paré attempted to shatter the illusions of those naïve enough still to be using it: How could anyone believe that the powerful in ancient Egypt had gone to such lengths to preserve members of their family and friends with costly substances solely that they might later be served up "as food and drink for the living"?[52] How could anyone believe that they would have approved the violation of their tombs and removal of the bodies in them "far from their landes to be devoured by some Christian folke"? The only mummies (if any) that had really come from Egypt were those "of the ordinary folk, who were embalmed with common asphalt or with the pitch used for caulking the hulls of ships."

Fakery was rampant. Since a ban had been put on the exportation of mummies[53] and the demand for them was continuing to grow, traffickers had recourse to substitutes of all kinds. In 1550, physician Jerome Cardan declared the ersatz material made from cadavers that had been dried in the heat of the desert sands to be a "fetid," "sorrie" and "horrid kind of mummie."[54] But, according to trustworthy accounts, far worse counterfeits were to appear on the market. Guy de La Fontaine, the famous physician to the king of Navarre, told Ambroise Paré that in 1564 he had paid a call on a Jew who trafficked in mummies from Alexandria. Without further ado, his host had led him into a storeroom in which thirty or forty "mummied corpses" were stacked in a disorderly heap.[55] When La Fontaine ventured to ask if they had really been taken from Egyptian tombs, however, the trafficker burst out laughing and informed him that he had embalmed them himself. La Fontaine complained about such trickery, whereupon the Jew reminded him how incredible it was to think that Egypt, where the practice of embalming had been abandoned for centuries, could possibly provide the Christians with so many mummies. When pressed further about the origin of the deceased and the cause of their deaths, he replied that "it mattered not to him whence they came nor what the manner of their dyeing, or whether they be olde or young, manne or woman, so long as they could be acquired and so long that they could not be recognised once having beene embalmed."[56] As for the process used, La Fontaine was informed that the brain and entrails were first removed, after which long, deep incisions were made in the muscles and then filled with Jew's pitch and rags that had been impregnated with the same substance; each part of the body was then wrapped separately, after which the entire corpse was swathed in a sheet imbued with pitch and "left to pickle" for two or three months. The dealer even expressed—not without a certain irony—his surprise that the Christians always seemed to be so taken with anything to do with some kind of cadaver.

According to Paré some people maintained that mummies were being made in France and that certain bold and greedy apothecaries were even going so far as to steal bodies off gibbets at night. Once eviscerated, dried in an oven, and soaked in pitch, the hanged were then sold as bona fide mummy imported from Egypt. Paré says that he himself had seen on the premises of certain apothecaries limbs and other bits of cadavers and even whole bodies embalmed with tar pitch and emitting a repulsive odor. All of which proved, he concluded, "we are with crueltie and greate rudenesse being made to swallow down the stinking and diseased carrion of hanged men, or that of the lowest scum of the Egyptian populace, or that of those dead of the pox, the plague, leprosie."[57]

Condemnation of the practice was not at the outset based on its immorality, but on its noxiousness. The Church's attitude appears to have been ambiguous. Although some ecclesiastics rejected the "despoiling of human bodies created in the image of God,"[58] others were more accommodating.

Counterfeit mummies continued to flood the market well into the next century. Upon his return to France an apprentice barber known as La Martinière, who had been captured by pirates and sold into slavery, revealed to his countrymen the arcane workings of mummy trafficking in Algiers.[59] In 1626, Jean de Renou observed that the use of fake mummy had become so common that people had come to look upon it as the real thing, and he gave an example to illustrate this pernicious belief. Engaged one day in conversation with some cultivated persons who were discussing the admirable qualities of "true" mummy—i.e., the "odorous and aromatic"[60] Egyptian kind— he heard a man (who was very intelligent but totally ignorant of medical matters) maintain that true mummy was nothing but ordinary dried cadaver.

> Thus one sees how this impious and barbarous opinion has gradually overtaken the feeble mindes of some who care not if they be gulled and persuaded by atheistic and lost persons into thinking that the horrid stench and corruption that emanate from man's bodye be fitte for the curing of alle and of many other sicknesses. Now, far from having true mummie as was once to be found in the graves of the Kings of Egypt (the which existed in very smalle amounts and which lasted very little time) nor even that of Avicenna nor other Arabs, albeit it was only rotted human flesh and tar–pitch; in place of those we have onlie a thicke liquor presst from cadavers and today administered to the lasting shame of physicians and the aweful horror of the sicke.[61]

Apothecaries and physicians tried to educate consumers as best they could and to see that the most dangerous products were avoided. Powerless to "prevent all the abuses"[62] or to dissuade true mummy afficionados, the herbalists Pomet and Lémery urged that only fine, very black, shiny, bone-free, dust-free, and sweet-smelling specimens be used.

According to Pénicher, the former leader of the Paris Apothecary's Guild, the sense of smell should be the guide in all purchases of mummy. However, there was an even surer method of controlling the quality of the product: One could make one's own. This daring notion was not a new one. In the preceding century the famous Swiss physician who could boast of the resounding name Philippus Aureolus Theophrastus Bombastus Paracelsus had produced several interesting recipes. Addressing his colleagues, "asses"[63] ignorant of chemistry and ignorant of nature's mysteries, the great innovator informed them that the thing they sought so far afield in the deserts or among the "Barbarians" could be found much more cheaply closer to home. Paracelsus believed that it was possible to prepare three kinds of mummy by using the chemical process of distillation: "fresh" mummy, dried mummy, and liquid mummy. Here is his recipe for fresh mummy: Cut the flesh from a healthy corpse into small pieces; place these in a glass container having a medium-sized opening; cover with olive oil; swathe the container in thick cloth; dig a wide, deep hole in a garden apart from any dwellings; fill it with fresh horse manure, tamped down so that it will continue to emit heat for several weeks; bury the container in it so that it is completely covered save for two to three fingers of the neck; pour three or four *'sapinées'** onto the manure to activate the heating process; leave for a month or more until the flesh, having putrified and released its ill-smelling aquosity, has become nothing but olive oil, salts, and oil of mummy; decant the contents into a retort and place it on the coals in an oven; distill.[64]

The formula for dried mummy is far less complex and also quicker, but it calls for one ingredient not always easy to come by—"liquor" from an embalmed body. Place the roughly powdered exudate from an embalmed body in a glass container and add nonalkaline spirits of wine; cover; after twenty-four hours, draw off the spirits and replace with fresh; repeat the preceding

*A measure based on the pine (*sapin*) container that was used.

step; distill; allow the extract to congeal. This mummy can either be used "straight" or mixed with other components.

To produce the third, liquid, variety of mummy, a silver or glass container filled with the blood of a young, healthy person must be set out of the sun and the wind until the serum separates out of the blood; the container should then be tilted to drain off the serous fluid; replace the fluid with an equal amount of salt water; allow the contents to ripen. When so prepared, the vital fluid will not decay and will remain red. This "balm of balms" or "secret of the blood" was believed to protect the blood from all corruption as well as be extraordinarily effective in the treatment of leprosy and epilepsy.

In the recipes for these three mummies derived by "extraction" Paracelsus's followers were particularly struck by the need to obtain a young and healthy cadaver. To find the very best quality one should use—for lack of a "living man"—a condemned person. The just-executed were highly desirable, since the increase in blood pressure due to fear prevented the body's decomposition.[65] Redheads were preferred, their blood being thinner and their skin, owing to its sulphur and balsamic salt content, more easily impregnated with "aromatics."[66] The recipe of iatrochemist Oswald Crollius, which was much prized in the seventeenth century, links these new requirements with methods derived more from meat-drying techniques than from Egyptian embalming processes: Procure a young, redheaded executed prisoner and reserve the thighs and buttocks; remove the ducts, veins, arteries, nerves, and fat; wash thoroughly with spirits of wine; expose to the rays of sun and moon for two days in fine mild weather so that the principles concentrated in the flesh are exhaled; rub with true balm; dredge in myrrh, amber styrax, aloes, and saffron; macerate in a tightly closed container with good-quality spirits of wine and salt for twelve or fifteen days; open, drain, and dry in the sun; macerate a second time; expose the contents to the sun or to heat "as with beef or pork tongue and hams that are hung in the chimney, which, far from acquiring unpleasant odor and toughness, are turned into an exquisite and highly agreeable food."[67]

During this period, unbelievably complex formulas became the basis for still other compounds. Gabriel Clauder, a physician from Saxony, came up with an "absolutely extraordinary"[68] mixture that included soot and gold leaf. "Mummied" tinctures, extracts, and elixirs proliferated. And Pénicher observed that "if one wished to record and put into a book all the excellent, curious and erudite preparations to be derived from the precious and rare Mummy . . . there would be no end to it."[69]

However, such great advances were not to carry over into the following century. In spite of some successful treatments recorded by the occasional provincial doctor,[70] the use of mummy went into a decline, and after 1749 it was almost never prescribed in Paris. Nor did its detractors have any trouble changing the public's opinion, who now found it "disgusting."[71]

CONCERN AMONG THE SCENT EXPERTS

Criticism of the use of any kind of perfume or odor in the treatment of plague became even more widespread in the nineteenth century, and its use in this regard was all but abandoned. However, the purported purifying and vital powers with which odors had been endowed for centuries ensured that their application continued to play a part in the cure of other diseases.

Sanitary regulations dating from 1835 state that the physicians of the day are to wear clogs and dress in baize (coarse fabric) when they enter any sickroom. Perfumes are to be burned before they enter. Such precautions, however, were vestiges of the past. Article 616 specifies that perfumes can, at the most, "attenuate" the unhealthy effects of pestilential emanations.[72] The medical examination was still performed from a distance of at least twelve meters and from behind an iron partition. Long-handled instruments were to be used to touch the plague victim, and should a surgeon's "manual intervention" become absolutely necessary "one should select a surgery student, who can then be shut up with the patient; however, such a procedure should only be used as a very last resort."[73] Indeed, the lancing of a bubo was seen as such a threat that every possible step was to be taken to persuade the patient to operate on himself before losing consciousness.

The use of odors was not only being questioned to a greater degree but was also beginning to be sharply criticized. In 1839, Grassi, an expert in contagion and a senior physician at the quarantine station in Alexandria, maintained that scents were responsible for all his family's misfortunes. At the same period, Clot-Bey, leader of the anticontagion faction, held that the use of scents was "more the result of old practice than of any scientific logic."[74] Modern chemistry offered more rational and more effective methods of neutralizing miasmas. However, there still seemed to be a gap between the hopes to which chemistry was giving rise and the real help it could actually offer, for Clot-Bey admitted that he had no specific proposals to make . . . other than thorough cleansing, ventilation, and the use of chlorine. In 1843, Aubert-Roche, who had been practicing medicine in Alexandria for years, sneered at all sanitary practices that failed to attack the true causes of the problem: lack of hygiene and unhealthy living conditions. He asserted that the link between perfume and quarantine, which was still made throughout the Middle East, was a system of protection based on a total misapprehension.

When the plague broke out in Egypt, Syria, and what is

now Turkey, Europeans and wealthy indigenous Christians observed quarantines. They began by setting up two wooden grills in front of their houses. In front of the first they placed a tub of water, and between the two they set a receptacle in which they burned an incense made up principally of styrax, along with iron tongs for holding objects. Anyone entering the house had first to undergo purification by water and perfume. Some of the more enlightened used chlorine (even though chlorine, as Aubert-Roche observed, had been totally ineffective in the treatment of yellow fever, cholera, and typhus).[75] When perfume or chlorine was unavailable, they burned chopped and dampened straw. "Thus perfume, water and the grills are purported to be the only protections against the plague. It matters little if you are poor and dirty, that your dwellings are of faulty construction, with low ceilings and poor ventilation. If you happen to contract plague in such places, it is because you have no barrier, no water, no perfume—in short, it is because you did not observe the quarantine."[76] Without openly questioning quarantine measures per se, the French Académie Royale de Médecine in 1846 nevertheless pronounced against the use of perfumes in leper houses. Aromatic fumigations of sulphur and arsenic salts were deemed ineffective and dangerous. Pending a more radical process for destroying pestilential emanations, the Académie favored chlorine, a more modern prophylactic.

The nineteenth century was one of great enthusiasm for camphor and aloes, especially in rural areas. Regarded as powerful and effective panaceas that eliminated the need for a doctor, they were used in different forms to treat such varied diseases as angina, anemia, catarrh, corns, head colds, hemorrhages, indigestion, insomnia, and seasickness. Pharmacies sold vast quantities of them; every family had its bags of camphor and aloes and they could be found everywhere—inserted between the floorboards, stuffed into mattresses, hung in wardrobes to kill moths, and even added to the paste used to hang wallpaper.

"As a result, the smell of camphor is the first thing that strikes you when entering most houses. On Sundays its smell permeates the church."[77] Camphor, as the biologist François-Vincent Raspail stated in 1843, was considered far superior to every other essential oil. Lending itself to a multitude of uses and easy to handle (it did not get sticky or stain clothing), the remedy also had all the qualities required to make it a real "pocket pharmacy." Carried in "hygienic boxes" so that the product would lose none of its effectiveness, camphor was used to treat numerous infections. Taken three times a day in the form of salts, it would have cured a paraplegic girl—had the unhappy creature not been carried off by drinking too much absinthe. A two-year-old child with a tendency to rickets was returned to health by smoking a camphor "cigarette" every day after lunch. These "cigarettes," which were made of bone, ivory, West Indian hardwood, feather shafts, or straws, had to be refilled constantly so that the inhaled air would be kept impregnated with the vapors. In cold weather it was advisable to keep the "cigarette" warm in the hands or a pocket to make breathing the camphor easier. And it was economical: "An ordinary cigarette, if not chewed on, can last at least a week."[78]

Camphorated alcohol fortified the health and muscles. Sedentary men were urged to take an "air bath," morning and evening, in the following manner: "In a 60- to 65-degree room, sponge the naked body with camphorated alcohol while performing such gymnastic exercises as can be done readily: bending at the knees, rubbing the body with the hands and shadow-boxing, running in place, etc . . ."[79] Introduced into the rectum or vagina, camphorated suppositories were used to treat hemorrhoids, vaginitis, diseases of the womb, and fistulas.

There was no limit to the substance's benefits. It could protect hospitals, military barracks, and prisons against the entry of epidemic fevers just as it protected bodily orifices from the invasion of germs. "Anal itching is arrested when it is placed in the bottom, erotic spasms subside when it is sprinkled on the genitals . . . camphor restores calm to the body and modesty to the mind."[80] Its use was indispensible when performing surgery on the male urinary tract, for it provided the surgeon with a powerful means of counteracting "stubborn erections that can compromise or suspend even the most urgent operations."[81] As such, it was strongly recommended for use in boarding schools. Dusted on the bedclothes and in swimming trunks "in the region of the privates,"[82] camphorated powder was the handmaiden of hard work and morality.

Camphor was not the only strong-smelling substance whose virtues were being extolled. The following ardent plea was issued by a man profoundly alert to the powers of smells. In the firm belief that the milk of a wet nurse who had eaten garlic was a powerful vermifuge, he urged wealthy town dwellers to abandon "adulterated" nursing: "I invite our well-to-do ladies who want to nurture their children to feed themselves as if they were in the country and to aromatize all their food; in so doing they will also be practicing preventive medicine on their children."[83] Nor did his interest in odors stop at describing their beneficial or deleterious effects on "animal economy;"[84] as a good scent expert, he also reminded his readers of the important role odors played in medical semiology.

From the late eighteenth century into the nineteenth century, physicians Bordeu and Brieude also believed that certain emitted odors were evidence of certain diseases and illnesses, a notion that dated back to the time of Hippocrates.[85] Revealing as they do important chemical alterations, and varying widely according to the nature and degree of organic change, odors—

especially that of sweat—were even sometimes symptomatic of
certain mental illnesses, circa the 1880s. Nauseating and penetrating, the smell of madness, it was believed, was evocative of
clenched hands, the wild beast, the mouse. . . . So characteristic
was it that some psychiatrists would not hesitate to diagnose a
person emitting it as insane or, conversely, to conclude that a
person who did not produce such an odor was faking. The
physician and surgeon would therefore have to develop their
sensory keenness and strive to be a *"vir bene munctae naris"*:[86]

> Smell is the subtle soul of clinical instruction: its lan-
> guage, mysteriously formed in the practitioner's mind,
> shapes the earliest diagnostic notions and whets, as it
> were, the interest of the careful and close observer.
> With practice, medical nostrils learn to sniff the air
> constantly, attempting to take note of the mysterious
> similarities and secret affinities of olfactory symptoms,
> recognizing them in all the variety of their infinite nu-
> ances.[87]

However, such a lyrical outburst cannot conceal a keenly
felt concern: the long tradition of olfactory diagnosis was already
in its decline. The nose, an organ of wisdom, the body's "ad-
vance guard" and the precious handmaiden of intellectual acuity, had through lack of exercise become—alas!—"like a slothful
king enthroned in the physiognomy whose idleness cannot be
sufficiently deplored."[88] By 1885, Monin, a physician, expressed
indignation that modern man and the contemporary physician
had, most regrettably, lost all nasal finesse. In this cry of alarm
can be heard all the dismay of a practitioner of antiquity being
forcibly dragged into the age of Pasteur.

PART THREE

BLOOD AND INCENSE:
A SEARCH
FOR THE SOURCE OF
PERFUME'S POWER

Both perfumes and bloodletting, whose roots are firmly planted in myth and legend,★ were eventually to meet with a common therapeutic fate. They were used conjointly over the centuries, and their simultaneous rise and fall serve to underscore the close relationship in which medicine has always viewed two substances that are to all appearances quite different: blood and perfume.

We find the same connection being made in the writings of the alchemists, writings that are on the borderline between medicine and magic. Cornelius Agrippa's "occult philosophy," for example, was still handing down the recipes of medieval alchemy in the sixteenth century. Part of a vast network of strong "sympathies" or repellent "antipathies," the perfume

---

★According to a legend recorded by Pliny, the hippopotamus inspired man with the notion of bleeding by practicing it on itself. Another tradition relates that "On his way home from the Trojan War the illustrious brother of Machaon was caught in a violent storm and washed ashore on the coast of Caria. He was found by a shepherd who, learning who the castaway was, advised him to go to the King of the province, Damaethus, whose daughter had just fallen from the ramparts of the palace. Podalirus bled the princess in both arms and managed to save her life—at least, that is what the King her father believed, for he gave Podalirus his daughter's hand in marriage and the region of Chersonesus as dowry."[1]

prescriptions he recommended for helping a person take advantage of some favorable planetary conjunction were lifted more or less directly from the *Secrets* of Albertus Parvus.[2] The moon's perfume was made of a frog's head, the eye of a bull, the seed of the white poppy, camphor, incense, and blood derived either from menses or from a goose. Saturn's perfume included black poppy, henbane, mandrake root, and both cat's and bat's blood. Jupiter's was a compound of ash sap, aloe wood, storax, benjamin, stag's brain, and the blood of either a stork or a swallow. Venus's favor could be won with musk, amber, red roses, finch and pigeon blood; Mercury's with resin, cloves, the brain of a fox or weasel, and magpie blood. Some commentators have maintained that these recipes contain a hidden, encoded meaning. Thus, "frog's head" really refers to a plant of the ranunculus family (buttercups, marigolds, bachelor's buttons); "bull's eye" is really the red carnation; "brain" is the sap of the cherry tree. The "blood" of "dragon's blood" is really the sap of the dracaena, or dragon tree.[3] However, when he marshals evidence to demonstrate the effectiveness of certain balms and salves "to promote love," Agrippa's explication appears to imply the actual use of real blood. Since man's "spirit" is composed of his blood's vapor, "it is fitting that such poultices be made up of unguents derived from like vapors, having thereby a more substantial relationship with our spirit and thus attracting it more strongly through resemblance and transforming it."[4] Whether we read these "perfumes" designed to gain the favor of the planets or of someone we desire as literal recipes or encoded messages, it is obvious that fragrant substances and blood—symbolically or in fact—both play a part in their intermediary function.

We find further illustrations of this in many very different civilizations where similar rituals—particularly those in which there is a question of consulting the gods or of making pacts—are performed employing one substance or the other, and sometimes both. The prophetess of Apollo ate the sacred laurel and was fumigated with it before she prophesied,[5] while in Argos the Pythoness prophesied after having drunk the blood of a lamb. In ancient Egypt Arabs preceded the Pact of the Perfumed Ones by plunging their hands in blood.[6] Both substances are so often involved in the practice of so many rites that we are inevitably led to ask an obvious question: Is there a deeper relationship between blood and perfume than the one based on simple function, a relationship that may explain the importance of the great powers with which scent has been imbued?

BLOOD, INCENSE, AND THE SACRED

▼

Perfumes, sacrifice and unctions
exist and spread their odors everywhere,
they open the portals of the elements and
the heavens whereby man can glimpse through them
the secrets of the Creator.

H. C. Agrippa, *La Philosophie occulte*, 1531

RITUAL PRACTICES

From mankind's dimmest past, cults have made dual use of blood
and perfume. Sacred trees, poles, and stones were often decorated, incensed, and anointed with sweet-smelling oils and with
the blood of sacrificial victims. In Greece, and especially in
Crete, particular stones and trees were anointed with blood and
perfumed libations. In India, animal or human victims were
hanged from the branches of a sacred tree whose trunk had been
smeared with aromatic substances. Linguistic studies hint at the
existence of analogous practices in Palestine: An important
megalithic site in the Land of Moab, in Judea, bears the name El
Mareighat, "The Anointed Stones," and in Galilee there is an

ancient dolmen called the Hajr Ed-Damn, "The Stone of Blood."[1] However, the link between blood and perfumes is hardly confined to primitive religions. It can also be found in the religions, both monotheist and polytheist, of highly developed societies. We shall examine examples from Egypt, the Jewish faith, and Aztec civilization, all of which attest to the connection between blood and incense, both in rites of sacrifice and in those solemn ceremonies in which priests and kings were anointed with the stamp of divinity.

The Mummy and Beef, Egyptian Style

Carved in hieroglyphics on the walls of the temple at Idfu is a recipe for the preparation of the "twice-good" perfume known as kyphi. Its principal ingredients are honey, wine, cyprus, grapes, myrrh, broom, stoenanthe, saxifrage, saffron, juniper, cardamom, patience (a species of dock), and calamus. These are to be ground together to a smooth consistency and put through a fine sieve, after which the most odorous part is to placed in a mortar and made into a paste with the addition of oasis wine. Plutarch himself mentions this rare and refined compound, which was later adopted by the Greeks and the Romans.[2]

Consider this scene: The walls of the Temple at Deir al-Bahri are covered with a frieze depicting an expedition sent by Queen Hatshepsut to the Land of Punt, the archaic term for Arabia. Five ships, each with thirty oarsmen and a huge sail, are shown arriving in the land of the Great God, where the royal emissaries are welcomed by Parohu, the "Lord of Punt," accompanied by his wife, his children, and his servants. The Egyptian ships are then shown returning laden with a precious cargo of ivory, gold, monkeys, leopards, slaves, incense, and myrrh. When they reach Egypt again the gifts are presented to the queen, and in the depiction of that ceremony we see that the greatest admiration is aroused by the gift of thirty-one shoots of the incense tree.[3]

In both papyrus and bas-relief, emphasis is placed on the sacred function of perfumes and aromatic plants as offerings to the gods, to the sovereign, and to the dead. Even the making of perfumes is closely linked to religion. The formula for *kyphi* is carved on the walls at Idfu because such temples always included space for the laboratories in which the priest-perfumers performed their sacred duties. These functionaries daily offered three kinds of perfume to the gods: in the morning, resin; at noon, myrrh; in the evening, *kyphi.* Great religious feast days called for a huge consumption of odoriferous substances, which were carried in solemn processions, as described in the annals of Thothmes III, Ramses III, and Senusret.[4] "On such occasions one might see 120 children bearing golden vases containing incense, myrrh and saffron, cinnamon, cinnamomum, orris and other precious aromatics."[5] On feast days the effigies of the gods were given as many as nine anointings with perfumed oils instead of the one, the *mezet,* they received on ordinary days. The same oils were also used as a royal unction to underscore the king's relationship to the gods.

Widespread and sophisticated, aromatic substances were used in conjunction with blood sacrifices in religious rites. Hieroglyphics at Panhy-Mery-Amen show the pharoah offering a dawn sacrifice of cattle and sweet-smelling gums to the god Amon Ra and then purifying himself with incense. Greek historian Herodotus gives many details of how sacrificial carcasses were prepared. Before being covered with oil and consigned to the flames, they were "stuffed" with "loaves of bread, honey, figs, frankincense, myrrh and other aromatic substances."[6] In the epic Pen-Fa-Ur, carved on the walls of the temple at Karnak, Ramses II, before going into battle, reminds Amon Ra of the offerings hc has made to him: "Have I not honored you in countless dazzling feasts? Have I not sacrificed to you thirty thousand cattle with every sweet-smelling herb and the finest perfumes?"[7]

The funerary rites of the ancient Egyptians also attest to the great importance of perfumes, which were believed to be an intimate expression of divinity and whose use was important on two levels. Perfumed substances retarded the putrefaction of the deceased (a necessary condition for his survival after death), and by giving his body a pleasing smell, they turned him into a god, a "Perfumed One." The dual role of aromatic products is also reflected in the two parts of the ritual embalming process, which included technical instructions for the performing priests as well as accompanying liturgical formulas.

After a lengthy period of treatment, which could last from forty to seventy days during which various specialists performed a number of operations (removal of the hair, brain, and other internal body parts, ablutions with palm wine mixed with spices and aromatic herbs, packing the body with packets of natron or saltpeter and gum resins to absorb its humors, pickling it and then restuffing it with various substances so it would retain its shape), the cadaver was then subjected to a further series of anointings with consecrated oils.[8]

The first anointing dealt with the head. Using a high-quality oil of frankincense, the officiants anointed the head while reciting magical formulas to enable the incense (which was both a divine emanation and "that which maketh divine"[9]) to work its subtle transformation: "O Osiris ———— (enter the name of the defunct being treated)! To thee we offer frankincense from the Land of Opono to give thee better odor and endow thee with the odor of a god. For thee we give the humor of Ra to improve thine odor. . . . The scent of the great god is thy incense; the perfect scent, that will not evaporate from thine mummy."[10]

Next came the perfuming of the body from shoulder to the soles of the feet with ten unguents, intended to regenerate the deceased and provide him with the indispensable viaticum for his journey into the kingdom of the dead.

> Receive the festive perfume that embellishes thy body! For thee, oil of ladanum to enliven thy body and stimulate thy heart with what is given through Ra's grace, thereby enabling thee to reach the great Douat* in peace, and to smell of ladanum within its nomes [provinces]! May the sweat of the gods enter into thee and the protections of Ra extend to all thy body, that thou mayst enter into the holy lands and walk upon the holy ground within the nomes, and that thou mayst do thy will in the Two Lands thanks to the divine sweat from the Land of Opono![12]

Then the priests sealed the entrails of the deceased in jars filled with unguents and kneaded the body with perfumed oils and wrapped it in bandages while constantly invoking the organic, carnal, and humoral connections between the perfumes and the gods, the source of their wondrous virtues. After having massaged the corpse's back with a sweet-smelling oil to make it supple, the embalmers then addressed the deceased as follows: "Receive this oil, receive this unguent! Receive the unction of life. Receive the sweat of the gods, the humor of Ra, the spittle

---

*The *Book of the Dead* describes the world of the dead as if it were Egypt. It is divided by a long river. The Douat consists of twelve regions, corresponding to the twelve hours of the night. The dead crossed over in the solar boat to shine in splendor alongside Ra at the first hours of daylight.[11]

of Chu, the sweat of Geb, the divine bodily issue of Osiris, the oils of regeneration!"

Rites entailing breathing into the mouth and keeping the respiratory passages clear, which were designed to give life to royal and divine statues, emphasized the reconstitutive, purifying, protecting, and mediumistic powers of odorous substances. Prior to filling the body with the breath of life, the chief officiant, the Priest Sem, would purify the mummified body or statue by laying six pellets of incense on its mouth, its eyes, and its arms. Words were then spoken to augment the purification. Next, the priest fumigated the body with very pure varieties of incense to "wash" and "embellish" the corpse and to envelop it completely, imbuing it with the divine substance that would in turn deify it, while reciting the following formula: "Hail, Incense! Hail, Incense! Hail to thee, creation of Horus . . . Through incense thy purity is great, ———, that thou mayst be called 'Purified by Incense,' that thou mayst be called 'Perfumed One.' " Having now become a precious scent, the deceased could join the gods, could rise up through the air to their kingdom and mingle with their sublime effluvia:

> *Behold, ———, thy perfume cometh in the form of incense,*
> *Behold, O Gods, thy perfume cometh unto ———!*
> *Behold, the perfume of ——— riseth unto you, O Gods!*
> *May ——— be with you, Gods, and may you be with ———!*
> *May ——— live with you, Gods, and may you live*
> *with ———!*
> *May you love ———, O Gods. O Gods, shed your love*
> *upon him.*[13]

"Perpetual Incense" and the "Blood of the Covenant"

The covenant between the God of the Hebrews and His people was also founded on blood and perfume. This privileged relationship was first consecrated in the "blood of the covenant" and "perpetual incense." In the Jewish faith these intermediary substances, which are both governed by strict taboos and laws, are frequently linked together.

The "perpetual" incense that the priests offer up to the Lord is different from profane perfume. Its formula was given directly to Moses: "Take unto thee sweet spices, stacte, and onycha, and galbanum; these sweet spices with pure frankincense: of each shall there be a like weight. And thou shalt make it a perfume, a confection after the art of the apothecary, tempered together, pure and holy."[14] It is to be burned upon an altar, also to be constructed according to Divine plans:

> And thou shalt make an altar to burn incense upon: of shittimwood shalt thou make it. A cubit shall be the length thereof, and a cubit the breadth thereof; foursquare shall it be; and two cubits shall be the height thereof: the horns thereof shall be of the same. And thou shalt overlay it with pure gold, the top thereof, and the sides thereof round about, and the horns thereof: and thou shalt make unto it a crown of gold round about. And two golden rings shalt thou make to it under the crown of it, by the two corners thereof, upon the two sides of it shalt thou make it; and they shall be for the staves to bear it withal. And thou shalt make the staves of shittimwood, and overlay them with gold.[15]

The oil of holy ointment—used to anoint the tabernacle of the congregation, the Ark of the Covenant, the tables, and all the vessels and candlesticks, as well as Aaron and his sons, making them priests throughout the generations—was also to be a "compound after the art of the apothecary."[16] Rigorous rules were laid down for its preparation that emphasize the importance of the use of aromatic compounds in Jewish religious practice. Prepared by priests, the ointment was to be holy for the Lord and not to be employed for any other purpose or offered up by anyone other than priests descended from Aaron, on pain of death. Witness the fate of Korah and his company, who flouted Moses's solemn warning and presumed to use the incense, whereupon "the ground clave asunder that was under them: And the earth opened her mouth, and swallowed them up, and their houses . . . and all their goods. They, and all that appertained to them, went down alive into the pit, and the earth closed upon them: and they perished from among the congregation."[17]

The Lord instructs Moses to anoint Aaron and his sons with the oil of holy ointment and with the blood of the sacrifice:

> And thou shalt take the other ram; and Aaron and his sons shall put their hands upon the head of the ram. Then shalt thou kill the ram, and take of his blood, and put it upon the tip of the right ear of Aaron, and upon the tip of the right ear of his sons, and upon the thumb of their right hand. . . . And thou shalt take of the blood that is upon the altar, and of the anointing oil, and sprinkle it upon Aaron, and upon his garments, and upon his sons, and upon the garments of his sons with him: and he shall be hallowed, and his garments, and his sons, and his son's garments with him.[18]

A similar procedure occurs in the sacrifice prescribed to expiate the sinning of a soul through ignorance of any of the commandments of the Lord "concerning things which ought not to be done."[19] It is also worth noting that the preparation of the altar to be used for blood sacrifices included the use of sweet-smelling oil of holy ointment, whereas the annual purification of the altar on which incense was burned, and on which it was forbidden to make blood sacrifices, was consecrated by being anointed with blood.[20]

The Covenant of Blood between God and His people, which is described in the Old Testament and repeated in the New,[21] was renewed and perpetuated in the rite of circumcision: "And he that is eight days old shall be circumcised among you, every man-child in your generations, he that is born in the house, or bought with money of any stranger, which is not of thy seed . . . my covenant shall be in your flesh for an everlasting covenant."[22] The biblical story of Abraham's attempted sacrifice of his son Isaac (in the Land of Moria—*mor* meaning perfume in classical Hebrew) links the symbol of an eternal covenant (circumcision) to a blood sacrifice.

During sacrifices animal blood was employed according to rites that are set forth in great detail in the Old Testament. First sprinkled on the altar, and on the bodies of the offerings, the blood was then sprinkled on the faithful and on the priests. Blood offerings fulfill two functions, one conditioned by the other: They purify and atone, and thereby prepare for those who offer them open communication with God. "For the life of the flesh is in the blood: and I have given it to you upon the altar to make an atonement for your souls: for it is the blood that maketh an atonement for the soul."[23]

"Precious Liquid" and Copal

The religion of the Aztecs carried offerings of human blood to extremes. Aztec blood offering was rooted in a belief that blood libations were necessary to the workings of the universe. In the beginning, all had been shadow and darkness. To bring light to the world, the gods came together and two of them cast themselves into a pit of live coals, thereby giving birth to the sun and the moon. However, once they had risen above the horizon, the two heavenly bodies stood immobile in the sky. In consternation the gods dispatched a messenger to ask the sun why he did not move. His reply was that in order to live and pursue his course across the sky he required the blood of other gods. Whereupon all the gods sacrificed themselves to nourish the sun and moon with their blood.

The practice of human sacrifice commemorated this primal divine holocaust. Aztec iconography and statuary often depict the sun as an eagle clutching a bleeding heart in its talons. The voracious appetite of this bloodthirsty predator must be constantly appeased to prevent the original darkness from again engulfing the earth.

The ideal form of sacrifice was to tear out the living human heart, the method that produced the greatest amount of blood.[24] The victim climbed the steep steps to the summit of the temple, where he was seized by the priests and stretched out on the sacrificial stone, the surface of which was slightly convex so that his chest would be thrust up. While four priests gripped the victim's head and limbs to keep him from moving, the sacrificing priest slashed open his chest with a flint knife and plunged his hand into the cavity to rip out the still-beating heart. This he offered up to the sun, after which it was placed in a ceremonial basin. Meanwhile, using a hollow reed inserted into the victim's open wound, another officiant siphoned off the remaining blood and sprinkled it lavishly over the victim's body. Finally, while the body was still warm, it was thrown from the top of the pyramid and allowed to roll to the bottom of the steps.[25]

Blood also played a part in the daily rituals of Aztec priests. According to Fray Bernardino de Sahagun's sixteenth-century account, they would be roused from their sleep by the blowing of a horn to make gashes in their ears with little obsidian knives. They would then dip thorns of the maguey plant in the wounds.

The amount of blood shed reflected the degree of the priest's devotion.

The rituals were also heavily dependent on perfume. Copal, a white resin, was the aromatic gum of preference. Day and night, the priests offered it up in the temple in long-handled terra-cotta pots that were decorated with bas-reliefs and hung with tiny bells. Each morning and evening the people incensed the many idols placed in their houses and courtyards with copal as well. Incensing was also practiced by the Aztecs in rites other than religious ones; for example, judges burned copal before presiding over trials in order to honor the gods and beseech their protection.

Perfume and blood were integral parts of religious ceremonies and solemn occasions. War that was waged to ensure the essential supply of sacrificial victims was called *Xochiyaoyotl,* "War of Flowers." During his or her presacrificial vigil, the victim would inhale aromatic herbs with intoxicating aromas and, prior to death, the victim to be sacrificed to Xilonen, Goddess of the Corn, would burn offerings of incense at four sites symbolic to the Aztec calendar. "As the satraps passed before the Goddess Xilonen they strewed incense behind them in their paths . . . The female victim climbed to the top of the temple. Offering his own back, one of the satraps held her supine while the other cut off her head. Immediately afterwards, he opened her chest and tore out the heart, which was tossed into a basin . . ."[26] The girl sacrificed to Uixtociuatl, Goddess of Salt, marched to her death garlanded with flowers and wearing "coronets of a sweet-smelling herb known as *iztuahyatl,* which resembles the incense of Castille."[27] The priests charged with throwing the victims into the burning coals first perfumed their victims, "powdering their faces with incense, which they carried in small bags and threw at them by the handful."[28]

The combination was also evident in the ceremonies surrounding the election of the king. The chosen one held in his left hand a bag filled with incense and, in his right, a censer decorated with skulls. Watched intently by the assembled crowd, he mounted the steps of the temple at Uitzilopochtli and incensed the god's statue. Next, his councillors performed the same ritual. The king and his ministers then entered the building to perform acts of penance and to make two offerings of blood and incense to the god at noon and at midnight.

When the ruins of the great temple at Tenochtitlán were rediscovered, many pointed stone knives were found that had copal balls at the end of the hilt. The weapon had been devised so that it would create the spurt of "precious liquid" while also releasing a penetrating perfume. Blood and incense seem fated by nature to fulfill an identical function—to establish communication with the divine.

THE ODOR OF SANCTITY

"To be in an odor of holiness," "to die in an odor of sanctity," are not mere abstract expressions. The lives of the saints make them very real. Some saints or mystics—either during their lives or after their deaths—are said to have emitted delicious aromas, often regarded as a tangible manifestation of their supernatural virtues. "That the human body may by nature not have an overtly unpleasant odor," wrote Pope Benedict XIV, "is possible, but that it should actually have a pleasing smell—that is beyond nature . . . " If such an agreeable odor exists, he went on, "whether there does or does not exist a natural cause capable of producing it, it must be owing to some higher cause and thus deemed to be miraculous."[29] A pleasant odor emanating from a corpse was an indication of sanctity even clearer than the incorruptibility of the flesh. Collin de Plancy's *Critical Dictionary of Relics and Images* tells us that in the thirteenth century the remains of some of Saint Ursula's eleven thousand virgins were moved to a Cistercian monastery. Laid out in the choir, the sacred bones began to give off an unbearable stench. Suspecting some Satanic hanky-panky, the abbot summoned the abominable spirit to show itself. "Of a sudden the huge jawbone of a horse was glimpsed beneath the heap of relics; it was cast out forthwith, and the horrible stench that had filled the place gave way to the sweetest of smells: whereupon the monks praised God."[30] The corpse of a saint cannot emit an unpleasant smell unless the Devil himself interferes, and Collin de Plancy adds, with iconoclastic irony: "Only the impious would question this article of faith."

Smells from the Beyond

We are hardly surprised that a pleasant smell should be associated with holiness. After all, the saint has a special contact with the beyond, and even during his or her lifetime the true saint resides, as it were, in the anterooms of Paradise. Paradise itself was a region traditionally described as filled with exquisite odors, a notion derived directly from pagan antiquity. According to Plutarch, the river Lethe emitted "a delicate and suave exhalation of strangely voluptuous odors, causing an intoxication like that achieved by becoming drunk on wine. Souls were imbibing these delicious scents aglow with pleasure and engaging in concourse each with the other."[31] Lucian evokes the scented Isles of the Blest, where there was a golden city beside a river of myrrh.[32] There is little difference here between pagan Elysium and Christian Paradise. Gregory of Tours, the Frankish prelate, described the latter as "a broad prairie from which rises at all times an extraordinary perfume." Saint Maximus breathed in "an inimitable ambrosial odor that emanated from the loveliest of lovely springtime flowers." The fragrances of Paradise were food and drink to Saint Sauve. When the Lord ordered him to return to earth, he cried out, weeping: "The scent has abandoned me."[33]

As a natural counterpoise in this olfactory picture, Hell and Purgatory, like the Hades of antiquity, are filled with stench; their air is noxious. The fiery, reeking islands awash in blood and mire imagined by Lucian bear a striking resemblance to the Hell described by the twelfth-century Cistercian writer Henry de Saltrey. His hero, the Knight Oenus, first comes upon Purgatory, which is traversed by a fetid and frozen river and surrounded by a flaming pit; he then reaches Hell, which is even more nauseating and filled with sulphurous vapors. "Pestilent smell" and "horrible stench" are also characteristics of the hellish visions vouchsafed to and reported by Saint Teresa and Saint Veronica.[34]

The Perfume of the Mystics

"For we are unto God a sweet savour of Christ," writes Paul in the second epistle to the Corinthians (2:15). In the case of many saints and mystics, the apostle's metaphor can be taken literally. Narratives and eyewitness accounts often attribute to them the ability to emit odors. A search through hagiographic literature reveals that there is not *an* odor of sanctity but, rather, a whole gamut of sacred odors of various sorts. According to Hubert Larcher, Saint Lyddwyne de Schiedam's odor of sanctity had seven components: cinnamon, cut flowers, ginger, clove, lily, rose, and violet. Our contemporary Padre Pio could boast of six, whereas Saint Teresa of Ávila had four, Saint Trévère three, and Saint Basilissa made do with only two. These components combined to form boquets similar to more mundane perfumes. Nor does the analogy stop there: Like "secular" perfumes, holy odors change and ripen over time and according to circumstances. Borrowing the language of perfume makers, we could say that the head notes give way to the heart notes and, finally, to the bodily notes. The odor of sanctity of Saint Teresa of Ávila, for example, changed after her death—the odors of lily and orris expanded to include violet and jasmine.

Thus, the pleasant odor of the saint or the mystic is perceived as evidence of his or her privileged relationship with the Divinity. It also serves as both a means and an end. Spiritual awareness and asceticism tend to separate a human being from man's baser, animal nature and therefore from the odors linked with corruption and decay. At the same time, the sublimation of organic needs and the elevation of a soul focused totally on the other world enable the saint to partake of the perfume of the Divinity. Both an offering to God and a gift from Him, the odor of sanctity is, for ordinary mortals, a sign of the singular nature of the creature emitting it. Because an odor of sanctity is the special attribute of a person who has renounced the flesh and its desires, however, it is an offering, as well. By immolating the body the saint draws nearer to God, but rather than making a blood offering, he or she substitutes the odor of a body sanctified through penitence.

Blood and the Odor of Sanctity

Theoretically, the odor of sanctity attests to the healthy and pure condition of a soul that has managed to include its body in its spiritual ascension. Freed from its corporeal limitations, the body becomes "more agile, suppler, firmer, stronger."[35] However, this notion does not please rationalists, who demand other explanations such as a connection between continence and the emission of pleasant bodily scents: For example, when not released through sexual activity, some substances may act as metabolic inhibitors and trigger the production of these "saintly" odors.

Hagiographers too have dealt with this subject by relating the phenomenon of the odors of sanctity to the incorruptibility of the flesh. Odors of sanctity are frequently noted following the death of the saint and sometimes persist for considerable periods of time. Physical incorruptibility is closely linked to the nonputrefaction of the blood. This correlation is very evident in a story concerning Saint Teresa of Ávila. The witness who examined her body in the mid-seventeenth century first dwells on "the sweet odor it released, the freshness and beauty of the seemingly still-living flesh." He continues, now with a more clinical eye:

> I then began to move it and observe it more attentively; in the upper body I noted an area so colored that I pointed it out to the others, saying that the blood was still circulating. I applied to it a cloth, which instantly became tinged with blood; I asked for another, whereupon the same thing occurred. Yet the skin remained intact, with neither wound nor tear. I peered closely at the shoulder of our Holy Mother, meditating on the greatness of this miracle, for she had been dead for twelve years, and yet her blood still circulated like that of a living being.[36]

Hardly surprising, then, that those seeking a rational explanation of odors of sanctity should turn to the study of the blood, especially since stigmata and other wounds were often the origins of such agreeable smells.[37]

The notion of some link between the odor of sanctity and alterations in the composition of the blood has often been advanced. However, such changes have been explained in widely differing ways. For some, the answer is provided by the ascetic's diet. An exclusively vegetarian diet interspersed with fasting may purify the blood of its usual secretions and cause it to give off the vegetable odor of the ingested food. There would be little or no urea in the blood to carry elements other than those introduced into it by the diet, and, like plants grown in different soils, it would have quite another aroma. "Here, the odor is produced not by a great number of secretions, whether liquid or gaseous, but solely by the gasses natural to the blood."[38]

Some physicians believe such changes in blood composition to be the result of mental unbalance. Connections are made between certain cases of hysteria and the emission of pleasant odors. For others, like physician Georges Dumas, such phenomena are the result of a combination of nutritional and nervous problems. The odors of cinnamon, clove, orange, pineapple, rose, violet, benjamin, etc., are produced by the appearance in the blood of aromatic fluids derived from alcohols (aldehydes, acetones) and ethers through incomplete combustion. If blood combustion is normal, such substances are burned, completely oxidized, and turned into water, carbonic acid, and urea. However, should there be a slowdown in providing nutrition to the tissues, such aromatic elements would be voided via the breath or through the skin in perspiration: "Nutritional and emotional problems can apparently account for the phenomenon that has so impressed hagiographers and, since in the last analysis the basic nutritive process depends on the nervous system, which accelerates or alters its various stages, it is probable that the odor of sanctity is almost always to be found in neuropaths"[39]—in other words, the result of a sort of "holy neurosis."

The presence of acetone in the blood, for example, could be responsible for giving the breath and urine of certain sick persons the agreeable odor some hagiographers describe as "sanctified." The mystery surrounding such odors is thus dissipated, and Teresa of Avila's floral exudations can be viewed merely as indications of diabetes, a disease in which fragrant acetone is manufactured by the body in abnormal quantities.

All these hypotheses impute the origin of blood variations that create the "odor of sanctity" to somatic or pathological causes. However, there is another point of view, which we might call the "psychosomatic." Principally advanced by Dr. Hubert Larcher, it represents an attempt to give the system of cause and effect a spiritual underpinning. Larcher attempts to reconcile the rational and idealist viewpoints and concedes the chemical substratum of such odors as well as the metabolic imbalances that create them. However, the variations in blood composition that produce "holy odors" cannot be reduced to somatic or pathological phenomena alone. The mystic's life, with the profound organic modifications it produces, affects the metabolism and the composition of the blood. The ecstatic state may explain certain instances of incomplete combustion and the presence of new aromatic substances in the blood. The alcohols, ethers, and acetones freed by decreased rates of oxidation in ecstatic trances could synthesize with the red-cell pigments in the blood, causing the release of vegetable scents: "Indeed, it is quite conceivable that the mystical life could result in a slowing down, in certain cases, of the metabolism, especially sugar combustion, and result in the formation of odoriferous compounds."[40]

In other words, the mind acting on the body may set off a chain reaction of phenomena that can culminate in the creation of the "holy" perfumes: Ecstatic states may slow down the combustion processes and lead to the formation within the organism of alcohols and other unusual substances "in such a way that ultimately the condition of the soul controls a chemistry capable of removing some of its somatic links and thus of helping it to take wing."[41]

Peak states of spiritual activity can affect the entire organism, all of whose requirements are thereby altered, and blood syntheses may then occur more easily, apart from bodily concerns, more aesthetically, and more fragrantly. Created by the most spirituous (and most spiritual) fermentations of the blood, the odor of sanctity draws from them its highly unusual capabilities: softness, power, tenacity, and exceptional diffusion, in addition to its antiseptic and nondecomposing properties.

Larcher's thesis also enables him to explain certain phenomena ancillary to the odor of sanctity. The alcohols pumped into the blood during the ecstatic state can lead to mystic intoxication. Like certain drugs used to attain artificial nirvanas, such substances can open the doors of perception into the beyond. These olfactory binges tend to enlighten rather than cloud the mind, making visible and sensible worlds usually hidden from the common person. The shared "celestial visions" reported by the nuns who surrounded Saint Teresa of Ávila's deathbed can be related to this process. "Yet we must also bear in mind the possible action of the molecules involved in the odor of sanctity—which was especially strong and almost unbearable—on the nervous system and psychic functioning of those nuns."[42]

Extremely persistent and amazingly powerful, the odor of sanctity is indeed the offering ideally designed to be pleasing to God, composed as it is of the two principal elements of sacrifice: blood and perfume.

2

LIFE PRINCIPLES: BLOOD AND INCENSE
▼

Odors in and of themselves
make myths possible.

Gaston Bachelard, *Fragments d'une poétique du feu*

BLOOD, SYMBOL OF LIFE

Since time immemorial blood has—quite naturally—been regarded as the very stuff of life, a notion probably based on the
observation that any loss of blood leads to a decrease in physical
strength and that excessive loss of blood leads ineluctably to
death. When blood flows out of the body, life flows with it.
"For the life of the flesh is in the blood," proclaims Leviticus.[1]
Logically, we thus deduce that the above "objective" statement
also underpins the notion that the precious fluid contains the
soul, and even the thinking mind. The invocation in *The Book
of the Dead*—"Hail soul in thy blood, the sun"[2]—connects with

Empedocles's statement that "the principal seat of what we call thought" is in the blood that circulates through the heart.[3]

This "spiritualization" of blood explains the countless taboos and codifications connected with it. The taboo on ingesting blood exists both among the Malepas Indians, a Bantu tribe in the northern Transvaal, and among the Jews. The Old Testament condemns its consumption: "Only be sure that thou eat not the blood: for the blood is the life; and thou mayest not eat the life with the flesh."[4]

For certain peoples the soul can escape by the spilling of blood, which can have unpleasant consequences. There are countless taboos designed to prevent not only the consumption but also the loss of blood. The Siamese "bloodlessly" executed royal miscreants either by starving them to death, by smothering them, by piercing their stomachs with a stake of fragrant sandalwood, by drowning them in cauldrons, or by crushing their bodies with wooden hammers. The list of "clean" executions employed by very different populations is endless. To prevent the blood of a certain Captain Christian, executed in 1660 by the government of the Isle of Man, from seeping into the soil, a ground cloth was laid down around the place of execution. Some Australian tribes placed children to be circumcised on a platform created by the bodies of living men so that the blood would not come into contact with the ground. In the Marquesas and Celebes islands, the blood of a woman in childbirth was collected for similar reasons. In the southern Celebes, where the houses are built up on stilts, a slave woman is stationed below the room in which a woman is giving birth holding a bowl on her head to catch the blood in as it drips through the cracks in the bamboo floor. "Among the Latuka of Central Africa the earth on which a drop of blood has fallen at childbirth is carefully scraped up with an iron shovel, put into a pot along with the water used in washing the mother, and buried tolerably deep outside the house on the left-hand side."[5] Men called *ramangas,* or "blue bloods," who were servants to the nobles of the Betsileos of Madagascar, were given the unusual assignment of lapping up and drinking their master's blood when he was wounded so that that substance, which contained his soul, would not fall into the hands of sorcerers.

The notion that the blood contained the soul was also reflected in the vengeance rituals of non-Islamic Arabs. The victim's soul, which escaped with the flow of his blood, was condemned to wander the earth and could not rejoin its body until it had drunk of the blood of its murderer. Transformed into a bird called the Hama, it flew about, lugubriously cawing for revenge. Judges too were forced to reconcile two contradictory demands: The killer's blood had to be spilled, but as little of it as possible so as to avoid his soul's then harassing everyone by calling for revenge for his spilt blood.[6]

THE SIMILARITY BETWEEN SAP AND BLOOD

There is a basic similarity between sap and blood, the former representing in the plant kingdom what the latter does in the animal. Sap irrigates and nourishes the plant in the same way that blood irrigates and nourishes the tissues of the body. It seeps out of an injured plant and its loss can lead to death. Above and beyond the simple parallelism between two different worlds, however, we find that countless connections were made between sap and blood very early in human thinking. The tree was already an important cult object in prehistoric times. As a source of sustenance, nourishment, and protection, the tree was either divine in and of itself or the residence of a divinity. Thus, sap was not only a vegetable emission but actually akin to blood—and probably, in the beginning, to female blood. The resin of the acacia was believed to be the menstrual blood of its indwelling goddess.[7] This sap-blood also contained a generative power, since prior to its being regarded as impure, the menses had represented quite the opposite and had been considered the purest form of blood, replete with all the mysterious energies of life.[8] As the bearers of occult powers of re-creation, both sap and blood were believed to be generative life forces.

The close links between the two substances are embodied in the beliefs and customs of many widely separated primitive cultures. When he was felling a tree the Basoga woodsman of central Africa would make his first axe stroke and then put his mouth to the gash and suck out the sap. The custom established a relationship with the tree so that it would not feel any ill will toward the brother that was felling it. Such anthropomorphism was even more pronounced elsewhere. A striking example can be found in the cruel punishment the primitive Germans in-flicted on anyone caught tearing the bark from a tree. The culprit was forced to replace the missing tree bark with his own skin. The skin around his navel was cut out and nailed to the bare spot, and the guilty one was then forced to circle the tree he had injured until his entrails were wrapped around the trunk.[9] As late as 1859 there still existed in Nauders, in the Tyrol, a sacred larch that was reported to bleed if it was cut. It was popularly believed that an axe stroke would penetrate the body of an impious woodsman as deeply as his attack on a sacred tree and that his wound would not heal until the tree trunk had regrown its bark.

There was once a widespread belief that blood was capable of engendering plants, a belief nourished by the metaphor of blood taking the form of a life-giving rain and regenerating an arid land, or flowers or trees springing up where blood had been spilled. Egyptian lore contains many such examples. Seth's nose-bleed was turned into cedars; from the blood of slaughtered rebels against Amon Ra a vine sprang up; in the *Tale of Two Brothers* two perseas grow out of the body of a sacrificial bull.[10] Other civilizations have similar beliefs: Around midsummer tiny red wildflowers appear in the fields, the plant *Adonis aestivalis,* sometimes called "Adonis' droplets." They recall one of the elements of the familiar Greek myth according to which Adonis, having been mortally wounded by a boar, shed drops of blood that fell to earth and turned into the red anemone.

In ancient beliefs there is a widespread relationship between sap and blood in the other direction. Examples can be found in such widely differing cultures as those of the Ural-Altaic peoples and the Samoan islanders. According to a Yurak tradition, the flood was caused by the felling of a sacred birch that bled as it died.[11] Samoan legends tell of bleeding trees. There is a grove no man dares cut down: "One day, some strangers tried to fell it, but blood sprang from the trees and the desecrators fell sick and died."[12] Similarly, when woodsmen in the *Quest for the Holy Grail* cut into the Tree of Life they are awestricken to see well up "drops of blood vermillion as roses."[13]

However, were we restricted to a single illustration of the dichotomy of sap and blood we would need go no farther than an extraordinary Mayan myth from the *Popul-Vuh,* which was written in Quechuan in the middle of the sixteenth century.[14] Challenged to an athletic game by the gods of Xibalba, "the Realm of Disappearance and Vanishment," the "Master Magicians" descend into the netherworld, where they are put to death for their treachery and arrogance. The head of the "Supreme Master Magician" is hung in a hitherto sterile tree, which at once bears fruit and is made subject to all sorts of taboos: It is forbidden to pick its fruit or even to come near it. "Since then, the head of the Supreme Master Magician has no more been seen, but has become but another of the fruits of the tree known as the calabash or baobab."

A virgin princess actually named "Blood," the daughter of a Xibalba chieftain known as "Assemble-Blood," decides to break the taboos. Like a Mayan Eve, she approaches the foot of the tree, asking, "Are these the fruits of the tree, and will I perish if I pick them?" Suddenly, the head of the Supreme Master Magician speaks: "What do you seek here? The round fruits in the branches of the tree are naught but skulls. Do you still want them?" Princess Blood insists. "Very well, then, reach out your hand." She does so. "Whereupon the skull spat its saliva onto the young girl's hand; the girl peered at her palm, but the skull's saliva was no longer there. "In that saliva, in my spittle, I have given you my seed," says the voice from the tree. Some months later Princess Blood, now pregnant, is accused of fornication. Commanded to reveal her lover's name, she replies that she has known no man. After having taken counsel together the Xibalba chieftains "Supreme Death," "Principal Death," and her father, "Assemble-Blood," decide that she must be sacrificed. They order her heart torn from her body and brought back to them in a goblet. On the way to her place of execution, however, Princess Blood manages to convince her executioners of her innocence. Determined to spare her, they wonder: "What can we use in place of her heart?" Princess Blood then tells them to cut into the bark of a tree, the dragon tree, and to collect the sap in a goblet. "Whereupon the blood, the sap of the red tree, formed a ball; resembling blood, it was glossy, reddish, formed in a ball in the goblet." While Princess Blood flees to the earth's surface, the sacrificers report back to the Xibalba chieftains. "Is it finished?" asks Supreme Death. "It is finished, O Chiefs. Here is the goblet containing her heart." "Very well," says Supreme Death, "show it to me." And he raises it up. The ruddy sap pours out like real blood. "Stir up the fire and cast it onto it," says Supreme Death. Putting it on the fire, the Xibalba begin to smell its odor; they all become intoxicated, for the perfume they smell in the blood's smoke is indeed truly pleasing to their senses."

The respective roles played in this myth by the calabash and devil trees express in different but convergent ways the path from sap to blood. The symbolism of the princess's magic impregnation by the saliva spat into her palm is obvious: The saliva represents semen. However, coming as it does from the calabash, from the skull-fruit, it is vegetal sap as well. The path of blood, albeit more indirect, is equally effective. From the fecundating juice the girl will bear two children, two blood creatures who will later punish the injustice of the Xibalba chieftains. Unlike that of the calabash tree, the sap of the dragon tree undergoes a direct mutation. "Like blood, the sap did flow," and the substance that flows from the slashed tree trunk into the sacrificial goblet will save the princess's life. The final transformation: Cast onto the fire, the heart produced by the dragon tree burns, emitting a strong-scented smoke. And here, emerging from the cycle of blood and sap, we come to the supplementary element: scent.

THE BLOOD/SCENT CYCLE

Above and beyond the blood/sap linkage, the final episode in the tale of Princess Blood illustrates an even closer relationship between blood and certain saps and gums with aromatic properties. Myths often link the origins of the gods with odorous plants, their gum, their wood, or their flowers.

Thus, Adonis emerges from a myrrh tree; Amon Ra, like Brahma, is born from a lotus; conversely, a lotus springs from Vishnu's breast, a rose from the breast of the goddess Gaia Terra, and for the Egyptians, incense is the "Sweat of the God." A special relationship exists between divinity and pleasing scents, especially ointments. Since sap represents the life principle, saps that exude a pleasant odor have an additional quality that endows them with a divine nature. One aspect of this link with divinity has been discussed by William Robertson Smith, who maintains that the use of incense for sacred purposes derives from the notion that it is the sap/blood of an animate and divine tree.[15] The order of things can also logically be reversed. It is likely that the smell of its incense led to people's regarding as holy the tree producing it. Likewise, plants that produced scents or perfumes, obtained by the crushing of petals or fibers, were inevitably seen as supernatural.

Incense, like other saps, is a vital principle, but its odorous properties make it (with blood) a more evolved and sophisticated symbol. This helps to explain the essential role it plays in religious rites and its constant presence in all communions between mankind and their gods and in other solemn human ceremonies. It was associated with (and sometimes substituted for) blood in sacrifices and oaths in the most distant past because it represented (as did blood) man's most precious possession, one given him by the gods themselves: namely, life.

PART FOUR

THE
PHILOSOPHICAL NOSE

▼

The Greek profile, far from being an outer
and accidental form, is the incarnation of the very
idea of beauty itself. . . . Thanks to it we have
an embodiment of a facial conformation in which the
expression of the spiritual takes pride of place.

Hegel, *Aesthetics*

Annaïk Labornez was a large, pink and plump baby.
She had tiny little eyes and a little tiny mouth,
and her nose was so small you could scarcely see it.
All of which made her parents very unhappy, and every day they
would measure her tiny little nose: "It just doesn't grow,"
they would wail. "Oh, unhappy us! We shall be
the laughingstock of the whole country!" And, indeed, in
Clocher-les-Bécasses it was generally believed that
a person's intelligence was directly proportionate to the
length of that person's nose. This bizarre
dogma had probably arisen from the fact that
during the summer holidays a famous scientist endowed
with a truly formidable nasal appendage always
came to vacation in the village.

Caumery, *L'Enfance de Bécassine*

This comparative investigation into the way the sense of smell and odors were perceived in the past and the different manner in which they are perceived today must of necessity include some reference to philosophers, since in past centuries philosophers were also scientists and deeply involved in contemporary scientific inquiries. Without pretending to an exhaustive examination of all of Western and non-Western philosophy, let us now consider a few typical texts and figures.

1

THE AMBIVALENT STATUS OF THE SENSE OF SMELL AND ODORS IN GRECO-LATIN PHILOSOPHY

▼

Considered by Aristotle to be the most undistinguished of all the senses, our human "nose" is indeed far inferior to most other animals' sharp powers of smell.[1] Theophrastus shared Aristotle's opinion: Every animal, every plant, and even some inanimate things all give off a specific odor, one that we humans do not always perceive, but to which most animals are acutely sensitive: For instance, he tells us, "beasts of burden can smell the barley of Kedropolis [a city in Thrace] and refuse to eat of it because of its evil odour."[2]

Our olfactory shortcomings rest on three factors: the imperfection of our olfactory equipment, the naturally evanescent nature of odors, and the sense of smell's subordination to the emotions.

Our olfactory channels are simply not large enough. Plato stated that the "veins" were too narrow to perceive "particles" of earth and water and too wide to entertain those of fire and air.[3] Aristotle blamed the width of the "channels" for the lack of olfactory finesse and for the frequency with which we must sneeze.[4]

To the handicap created by a sadly inadequate perceptual tool we must add the incompleteness and transiency of pleasant fragrances. According to Plato, odor emanates from a body that is undergoing change and that is therefore unstable. Created by an "intermediary state," by a change, odor "is a half-formed nature,"[5] which makes its perception difficult. For Aristotle, the sensations to which odor gives rise are exceedingly difficult to analyze.[6] At the pivotal point between the "outer" senses of sight and hearing, which rely on some outside stimulation, and the "inner" senses (taste and touch), which react in conjunction with the body, the sense of smell is ambivalent, neither one nor quite the other. It occupies a dual sensory register, hence its ambiguity.[7] Although Aristotle is not really clear on the point, he claims that this dual nature may explain the imprecision of the sense of smell and the evanescence of odors.

Lucretius believed that the fleeting qualities of scents were responsible for the mediocre ability of the human sense of smell. Sensory deficiency was not totally disregarded (after all, even the dog, an animal supposed to possess a highly developed sense of smell, has occasional lapses), but the problem, he believed, probably lay with odor itself. He reasoned that its composition and the manner in which it is produced and propagated must be responsible for its lack of impact. The scent particles cannot surmount the obstacles they encounter:

> It is obvious that odors are made up of elements larger
> than those of sounds, since they are arrested by walls that

allow the voice and sound to pass through without difficulty. Indeed, this is why we often have difficulty in locating the source of an odor. In fact, the odorous emanations cool as they travel through the air and do not arrive swiftly and still warm to affect the sense of smell. This is why dogs often err and have to search out the scent.[8]

In addition, odor forms and spreads with difficulty: "It travels slowly and vagrantly, it gradually fades *en route,* dissipating into the absorbent ambient air; it has difficulty in emerging from the depths of the body in which it is formed." Unlike color, which is superficially fixed and easy to perceive, odor springs from the very heart of substances. Lucretius draws his example from the strong smells produced by crushed or burning materials, in which "odor corpuscles" are instantly produced and released into the air.

He goes on to draw analogies between smell and the soul. Both are buried and hidden within the body, and both consist of tiny atoms whose loss does not result in any change in a body's weight or shape. The soul's departure from its fleshy envelope is like the process of exhalation: It mounts from the depths following the meanderings of the body's interior channels until it reaches the surface pores. Once outside, it then floats in the atmosphere like a vapor. Once in the outer air, however, the life span of both soul and odor is distressingly brief: The soul cannot live outside its protective shelter; odors fade rapidly away.

Aristotle saddles the sensory apparatus and odors with a third element of imperfection—namely, the close links that exist between the act of smelling and human emotions. The fact that the perception of any odor is necessarily accompanied by some feeling of pain or pleasure actually reveals a sense organ incapable of transcending its physical matrix.[9] Indeed, the emotional relationship is generally deemed responsible for our lack of a suitable olfactive vocabulary. The different varieties of smell, Plato says, "have no name, and they have not many or definite and simple kinds, but they are distinguished only as painful and pleasant."[10] Thus they can only be defined relatively, not in and of themselves. For Aristotle, odors—divided, subjective—have no true individual identity. They are related to taste, and they share some of the qualifiers of taste: "Odors, too, are bitter and sweet, tart, astringent and succulent, and fetid odors can be deemed to be analogous to bitter tastes."[11] However, the vocabulary of taste is insufficient when it comes to naming all odors and, as Theophrastus notes, we are inevitably forced to turn to emotional classifications.

Plato recognizes as pleasures only those sensations that are independent of any need, of any desire—pleasures whose verity and purity make them akin to wisdom and the intellect. Thus, the sense of smell can be the instrument of noble pleasures not to be derived from either taste or touch. Plato makes the distinction between those senses capable of providing pleasures that elevate the soul and those that are the source of purely carnal indulgence, which distracts from knowledge and contemplation. However, scents and flowers can, indeed, inflame the appetites of the unstable man and contribute to his ruin, as described in *The Republic:* "And when the other appetites, buzzing about it, replete with incense and myrrh and chaplets and wine, and the pleasures that are released in such revelries . . . awaken in the drone the sting of unsatisfied yearnings, why then this protector of the soul has madness for his bodyguard and runs amuck. . . ."[12] The status of the sense of smell and odors thus varies according to the pleasures they procure; it is positive when such pleasures are aesthetic and negative when they encourage concupiscence.

The same ambiguity occurs in Aristotle, who set up an

ontological distinction between specifically "human" odors and those "common" to both men and beasts. The first, which play no role in survival, have an absolute value. Their pleasant or unpleasant character is not established by a bodily need. They can thus serve as the source for aesthetic pleasures proper to human nature "because, of all the animals, man has perception and takes pleasure in flowers and other analogous substances."[13] Their drying and warming action on the brain also makes them physiologically useful: "It is in man's interest and to preserve his health that this kind of odor has been produced, for it has no other function than that."[14] The second kind of emanation is good or bad incidentally, "by accident"; for example, it is agreeable when one is hungry and unpleasant if one is not. Its value, dependent as it is on individual subjectivity, is relative. Ontologically downgraded, the latter odors also inspire a certain disapproval. They can abet lust and gluttony: "We do not qualify those who derive pleasure from the odors of apples or roses as unbalanced, but we do describe as unbalanced those who relish the odors of unguents or culinary preparations, for unbalanced persons derive pleasure from the fact that such odors remind them of the objects of their concupiscence."[15] Here, Aristotle is in agreement with Platonic thinking. The pleasures aroused by scent should be aesthetic, not carnal. However, notwithstanding its "libertine" aspects, the sense of smell is one of the noble senses that pose no threat to temperance and freedom.

Aristotle's ontological distinction was adopted by Theophrastus, who went on to attempt an objective definition of the pleasant and the nauseating. A good odor relates to the cooked, to that which cannot become putrid; unpleasant odors to the earth and decay. Animal odors can alter with age, constitution, state of health, or organic discharges. In the young and vigorous they are pleasing; they become disagreeable when the creature grows old, is ill, or in heat.

Lucretius's notions differ sharply from earlier ontological or ethical concepts. Disgusting or agreeable sensations are created by the shape of the atoms that affect the organs of the sense of smell. When smooth, they gently penetrate into the nostrils; when rough or sharp, they abrade the olfactory tissue. However, Lucretius goes on to note the existence of elective affinities: "One odor will suit one creature better and another, another creature, according to the different species. Thus, the bee is attracted over great distances by the odor of honey, the vulture by that of a cadaver; hunting dogs will lead you to where the wild beast has left his spoor, and it was from a great distance that the bird that saved the city of the sons of Romulus, the white-plumed goose, caught in the air the odor of its populace."[16]

Lucretius also draws on Epicurus's atomist theory, in which the "order of the atoms" of the receptor plays a part in scent perception.[17] This notion attempted to explain the specific and individual differences in olfactory sensitivity. It also explained how an individual can appreciate the same smell in different ways according to organic variations: If a smell he once found agreeable now seems unpleasant to him, it is because an alteration in his body's atomic order has made him sensitive to different elements.

Lastly, by recognizing the total equivalence of all the senses and their preeminence over the mind, Lucretius rehabilitated the sense of smell. Like the other senses, it is a guide indispensable to life. Its role in nutrition and survival (contrary to what we find in Plato and Aristotle) inspires no pejorative connotations.

The materialism of Lucretius allots the sense of smell an important role in the field of knowledge. Platonic idealism and the school to which it gave rise denied it the scientific value of the sense of sight, while Aristotle, without being an "idealist," adopted a notion very close to that of Plato, with the latter's hierarchy of the senses. In both schools the sense of smell is the unstable point at which the pure and impure senses meet, stabilized only when it causes a certain type of sensation. Without making a totally negative judgment with regard to the sense of smell and odors, such reservations nevertheless contain the seed of future censure.

2

THE INFLUENCE OF CHRISTIANITY IN THE DEVALUATION OF THE SENSE OF SMELL AND ODORS

▼

By accentuating the opposition between body and mind already established in Greek idealist philosophy, Christianity was to promulgate an increased condemnation of olfactory pleasures with an antagonism not found in the Old Testament.

The Old Testament evidences little contempt for the body or its adornment. In hymning the beauty of the "very object of desire," the Song of Songs uses metaphors of the greatest sensuality and refinement.[1] It compares the bodies of lovers to precious stones, to rich fabrics and metals, to rare perfumes, to fragrant flowers, to gardens redolent with exquisite scents. "Thy name is an ointment poured forth," says the fiancée to her beloved; he is a "bundle of myrrh," a "cluster of camphire [camphor]." The beloved's cheeks "are as a bed of spices," his "lips like lilies, dripping sweet smelling myrrh." His members, his belly, his hands are of gold, of alabaster, of ivory, covered with sapphires and topaz. The fiancée is a lily of the field, a garden enclosed, an orchard with pleasant fruits, with camphor, with spikenard and saffron, calamus and cinnamon, with all trees of frankincense, myrrh, and aloes, with all the chief spices. There is no hint of disapproval, no shame at concentrating on the physical body and its desirability. We remember that the wanderings of the Jewish people often brought them into contact with Eastern civilizations in which jewelry, perfumes, and unguents were especially prized.

In the New Testament, however, we continually sense a veiled criticism of the profane use of scent. When Mary Magdalene anoints the feet of Christ "with a pound of ointment of spikenard, very costly," Judas Iscariot asks, "Why was not this ointment sold for three hundred pence, and given to the poor?" "Let her alone," Jesus replies, "against the day of my burying hath she kept this."[2] To counter the indignant reaction of the apostles' treasurer at such futile waste, Christ legitimizes Mary's action (for which she was to become the patron saint of perfume makers) by giving it a sacred significance: The costly spikenard was poured out for a religious purpose, as a funeral rite.

Suspicions with regard to perfumes found strong support in the epistles of Apostle Paul. Anything that is physically pleasant or pleasing raises an obstacle between man and God: "This I say then, Walk in the Spirit, and ye shall not fulfil the lust of the flesh. For the flesh lusteth against the Spirit, and the Spirit against the flesh: and these are contrary the one to the other."[3] Rejection of the carnal body entails a rejection of its adornment: "Whose adorning let it not be that outward adorning of plaiting the hair, and of wearing of gold, or of putting on of apparel; but let it be the hidden man of the heart, in that which is not corruptible, even the ornament of a meek and quiet spirit."[4]

A further step in this condemnation of the sensual is taken by certain Fathers of the Church, who preached mortification of the flesh and anathematized all the artifices designed to create beauty, which they linked to prostitution and debauchery. "There is nothing of good in the flesh,"[5] declared Saint Clement. The man of God must "mortify the works of the flesh . . . master his body, reduce it to servitude and punish it."[6] Tertullian, one of the Church fathers, exhorted Christians not to create vain embellishments to stoke the flames of covetousness in their hearts. He even urged them to make themselves unattractive so as to curb impure desires: "Therefore, since an eagerness for dangerous attractions places at risk both our own fate and that of others, you are henceforth directed not only to eschew calculated artifices to enhance beauty but also to see to it that, through concealment or neglect, your natural charms (which are equally prejudicial to the spectator) pass unperceived."[7] He expressed a blanket disapproval of any ornament used to embellish or flatter the body, which neither strengthened chastity nor helped to withstand the persecutions then being directed against the Christians: "Indeed, I wonder whether the hand accustomed to slide itself through a bracelet can withstand being swollen by fetters, I wonder if the leg habitually graced by an anklet can withstand being bound in irons. I fear that a neck encircled by a rope of pearls and emeralds will not withstand the sword."[8]

In the waning years of antiquity the struggle waged by the Church's bishops against earthly desire was aimed at promoting an ideal chastity that was conceived as the royal road to God. Christian morality was blatantly castrative: "We are the ones the Lord has made to sacrifice and—dare I say—castrate the world. We are the perfect circumcised, circumcised both in the spirit and in the flesh, for we practice circumcision at once spiritually and carnally upon the things of the world."[9] Viewed in this light, anything that pleases the body and favors concupiscence is forbidden. Whereas the salves and perfumes of the Greek courtesan served to accentuate her marginal position outside the legitimate bonds of the institution of matrimony, the Christian woman who did not renounce jewelry was actually committing sin—in addition to emulating the pagans—because she was arousing desire ("Paint your faces that others may be lost,"[10] fulminated Tertullian). To persuade the "handmaids of the Lord" to distinguish themselves from those of the Devil, the Carthaginian theologian even went so far as to threaten bugbears that may have been even more frightening than eternal damnation: baldness and insanity. "Women with flame-colored tresses face a dangerous fate! They think to embellish that which they destroy: for it is a fact that the corrosive power of drugs destroys the hair and, further, that the repeated application of any liquid, be it ever so pure, will lead to the sure deterioration of the brain."[11] The Church railed against Christian women who not only diverted aromatic substances from the pious use for which it was intended, but also turned their heads into altars onto which they poured perfumes to honor a foul spirit. Did all these flighty creatures, asked the Church Fathers, truly believe that on Judgment Day they would rise again in their paint, their rouge, their perfumes, and their elaborate coiffures? The only acceptable odors were those offered up by fervent souls to God.

Saint John Chrysostom contrasted the pleasing perfume of repentance and prayer with "the black and stinking smoke" that emanated from sinners.[12] While the pure in heart gave off delicate odors that obtained for them pardon and protection, the sinners, sick of an "invisible plague," emitted a smell that brought down Divine wrath:

> If in this city one were to come upon a man bearing
> through the streets a stinking corpse, who would not

flee him and hold him in disgust? You yourselves are
that man, bearing as you do wherever you shall go a
dead soul eaten up by worms and filled with rottenness.
How do you dare, filled as you are with offal and filth,
to enter into the church of God and show yourselves in
His Holy Temple? What will befall you, who unblush-
ing come to infect this sacred temple of Jesus Christ
with your unbearable stink? Do you think to imitate
that sainted sinner who perfumed the Savior's feet with
a precious balm whose odor filled the house? On the
contrary, you come here reeking to heaven, and you do
not even smell it.[13]

The struggle against concupiscence, a top priority of Christian ethics, continued for centuries; indeed, it continues today.
The repression of sensual pleasure, a prerequisite for salvation,
was preached constantly. The perfumed, adorned, and desirable
body of the Song of Songs gradually became a mortified mass of
flesh that must under no circumstances arouse the slightest stir-
rings of desire. Only when it had been castrated and all desirability eradicated was it acceptable at all. Ascetics practiced celibacy
to make themselves into sweet-smelling offerings. Chastity, "the
precious balm of incorruptibility,"[14] blessed the living who had
renounced the flesh. The saint's effort entailed more than merely
making the putrefying body produce pleasant odors; a saint had
to "garden" to please the Divine nostrils as well: "How happy
I would be could I cultivate the flower of your youth and offer
its sweet perfume up to God!" wrote Saint Bernard to the
provost of Beverla. The only scents approved for the mystic rite
were the smell of incense, which rose up to God like prayer, the
smell of flesh made incorruptible by chastity, the disembodied
perfume of the elect—those chosen for salvation—and, above
and beyond all the rest, the odor of the sacrificed Christ.

Saint Thomas Aquinas's treatment of the sense of smell and odors reflects his concern to reconcile Aristotelianism and the Christian faith. He bases his consideration on a hierarchy of the senses drawn up according to the "mode of modification" affecting both the sense organ itself and the object of its perception.[15] Sight, which reacts without any physical organic change in the organ, is the most perfect, the most universal, and the most spiritual of all the faculties. Next come hearing and smell, which entail a physical change in the object. Taste and touch, which entail physical change in both organ and object, are the most material of all the senses. Halfway between the noble senses and the base, for Aquinas, the sense of smell has a status very similar to its position in Aristotelian philosophy. However, it can procure even higher pleasures, pleasures that are not merely aesthetic but "immaterial." Such olfactory bliss is accessible only to those who have the acuity needed to perceive the subtlest of smells.

The elect themselves exude a special perfume, a sublimation of the carnal odor at its highest degree of perfection. The odor of glorified bodies is neither gaseous nor corrupt; it has lost its usual sensual substratum. Can such an exhalation be apprehended? Thomas Aquinas attempts to convince the skeptical by employing a curious comparison. There exist, he says, instances where a smell "produces in the atmosphere and in the organ only an immaterial impression, without emanation."[16] Take, for instance, a corpse that can attract vultures from a great distance: It cannot reasonably give off effluvia capable of traveling such distances, yet the birds of prey perceive it.

The quintessential odor, however, is that of the Christ offered as sacrifice to God, the perfume of Wisdom and Knowledge. The rite of incense was highly complex: First, the altar was incensed, a symbol of the grace that suffused Christ like a sweet smell, according to Genesis: "See, the smell of my son is as the smell of a field which the Lord hath blessed."[17] Next came the incensing of the faithful, a reflection of the grace shed upon them by Christ, who, as written in the Epistle to the Corinthians, "maketh manifest the savour of his knowledge by us in every place."[18]

Thomistic philosophy contains no definitive rejection of the body, no categorical disparagement of the sense of smell. For Thomas Aquinas, however, as for Aristotle, the soul is the body's "form"—in other words, its life principle, its organizing force. Thus, the sense of smell and odors has value only when what it perceives has been purged, refined, purified, and made spiritual.

3

MONTAIGNE AND ODORS

▼

From the fourteenth to the sixteenth century, philosophical considerations of the status of the sense of smell and odors are few and far between. Throughout this period, during which the plague, after some six centuries of hibernation, reappeared in the West "with unimaginable brutality,"[1] writings on the apparatus of smell were confined to attempts to link it in some way with the awful epidemic and to understand and deal with the exhalations that accompanied it. With Montaigne, however, we find a writer returning to the themes of the sense of smell and odors in a manner that is not insistently (or at least not primarily) concerned with ethics.

Writing about the poet Joachim du Bellay and other Renaissance men, Lucien Febvre called them "men of the natural world, seeing, but also smelling, sniffing, listening, touching, absorbing nature through all their senses . . . and refusing to discriminate in favor of any of the organs that afforded them security and a sense of community, the senses that, 'Governing their most important parts/Served them the best and with the fittest arts.' "[2]

Among all the men who have lived fully with their bodies as well as with their minds, Montaigne occupies a special place. He made no attempt to keep soul and body separate. Affirming the oneness of the human person, he sought to achieve a balance between sensual pleasure and spiritual delight. Although he felt the senses should be governed by reason, "they are our masters . . . Knowledge begins through them and is resolved into them. After all, we would know no more than a stone, if we did not know that there is sound, smell, light, taste, measure . . . Whoever can force me to contradict the senses has me by the throat; and he could not make me retreat any further. The senses are the beginning and the end of human knowledge."[3] Montaigne's *Essays* reveal his olfactive hypersensitivity and the special attention he paid to smells:

> . . . I like very much to be surrounded with good smells, and I hate bad ones beyond measure, and detect them from further off than anyone else:

> *Namque sagacius unus odoror*
> *Polypus, an gravis hirsutis cubet hircus in alis,*
> *Quam canis acer ubi lateat sus.*

> (My scent will sooner be aware, Polypus,
> Where goat-smells in hairy arm-pits lurk,
> Than keen hounds scent a wild boat's lair.)—Horace[4]

Montaigne's olfactory acuity was augmented by his body's remarkable ability to retain odor. His skin—and especially his thick mustache—"imbibes" it. "It betrays the place I come from. The close kisses of youth, savory, greedy, and sticky, once used to adhere to it and stay there for several hours after."

Montaigne also remarked upon the varied effects odors had on him: "I have often noticed that they make a change in me and work upon my spirits according to their properties." He approved of the notion that the use of incense and perfumes in churches was intended to delight, to arouse and purify the senses, and to make men more fit for contemplation. Indeed, his examination of the whole topic of smells led him to suggest that physicians "might derive more use from odors than they do." His curiosity and interest in scientific progress were that of a sensual man: "I should like, in order to judge of it, to have shared the art of those cooks who know how to add a seasoning of foreign odors to the savor of foods, as was particularly remarked in the service of the king of Tunis." With a greedy nostalgia he writes of the king's expensive peacocks and pheasants, sumptuously "stuffed with aromatic substances," and he writes that "when they were carved, they filled not only the dining hall but all the rooms in his palace, and even the neighboring houses, with sweet fumes which did not vanish for some time."

Yet such a high degree of sensitivity had what is now called its "down" side: Montaigne was more affected than most men by fetidness. The stench from the Venetian swamps and the Paris mire "weakened his fondness" for those cities. He found the smell of the human body unpleasant, and he marveled at the fact that Alexander the Great's sweat had emitted a sweet odor "owing to some rare and extraordinary constitution." He considered any bodily smell disagreeable, and he quoted the Roman playwright Plautus, *"Mulier tum bene olet, ubi nihil olet"* (A woman smells good when she does not smell), before going on to state: "The most perfect smell for a woman is to smell of nothing, as they say that her actions smell best when they are imperceptible and mute." Montaigne's writings have elements that tend to confirm this evidence of misogyny, and indeed, the foregoing passage follows one in which he writes of the "sweetness" of the breath of "very healthy children," about which there is "nothing more excellent . . . than to be without any odor that offends us." Nor should a child's speech offend—even etymologically, a child is without speech (the root word in Latin being *infans*, meaning both young and incapable of speaking). Is Montaigne's recommendation that a woman smell of nothing not tantamount to asking for her silence as well? A woman should smell of nothing, but there is nothing to prevent her from using scents, as did the Sythian women, who, even amid "the densest barbarism," manage to indulge in extraordinary refinements: After having bathed, they "powder and plaster their whole body and face with a certain odoriferous drug that is native to their soil; and having removed this paint to approach the men, they find themselves both sleek and perfumed." On the other hand, he frowns on the use of perfume to camouflage a lack of hygiene, in which case "to smell good is to stink."

It was Montaigne's humanist ambition to "smell as much as one can"[5] so as to explore the human condition, and he regarded the senses, including the sense of smell, as valuable instruments for knowledge and enjoyment. On the other hand, his heightened intolerance of certain smells—a condition rarely mentioned by his contemporaries and something of a paradox in a thinker so accepting of the body and its functions—ought not make us forget his resounding and unconditional "Yes" to life and his love for pleasant smells—the equivalent of which cannot be found among Cartesians, who actually set out to distance themselves from "anything related to life or to its dynamism."[6]

4

THE ALLIANCE OF RATIONALISM AND CHRISTIAN THOUGHT IN DEPRECIATING THE SENSE OF SMELL AND ODORS IN THE SEVENTEENTH CENTURY

▼

Following the practice of antiquity, the Cartesian hierarchy of the senses allots a neutral, middle place to the sense of smell. Less uncouth than the senses of touch and taste, smell falls short of the subtle qualities of both hearing and, especially, sight.[1] This opinion is based on a special anatomical view of the olfactory apparatus, which is regarded as an extension of the brain into the nasal area, above "the two small, dimpled areas anatomists have sometimes compared to the nipples of a woman's breasts."[2] According to Descartes, the two nerves of which the olfactory organ are composed do not differ from those of taste other than that they are narrower, more sensitive, and activated by more tenuous stimuli. When the human "mechanism" breathes, small fragments of earthly "bodies" floating in the air penetrate into the nose and are filtered through the narrow pores of the ethmoid bone, which allows only the most rarefied of them to pass through. The bodies then activate the extremities of the olfactory nerves in different ways, mechanically inspiring "various odorous feelings" in the soul.

Like all the senses, Descartes believed, the olfactory exists only intellectually: colors, smells, tastes are "mere feelings"[3] that have no existence outside the mind. Odors, sounds, colors, tastes—all are caused by physical movements within the "bodies" that contact our nerves. From the viewpoint of Descartes, feeling and thinking are a single phenomenon. The body is not known through feelings (a weighty statement). Notwithstanding all that Platonic thinking has taught us, there is no such thing as physical reality—no sensory object or intelligible reality subject to the intellect or to the understanding.[4]

The olfactory sense, like the other senses, does not enable us to apprehend matter. That can only be accomplished through a "mental operation," which penetrates beneath sensed and changing appearances. Thus, the analysis of a piece of wax:

> What did we recognize in this piece of wax, what made it so distinctive? There must be more to it than what I had discerned via the intermediary of my senses, because all those things that affect taste, smell, sight, touch or even hearing may change, but the piece of wax is the same. Perhaps it was really only what it now seems to be—that is, it was not the sweet smell of honey, not that pleasant, flowery scent, not that whiteness or that shape or that sound, but, rather, a mere object that appeared to me in such wise a while ago and that has now taken on other qualities.

In short, "we are left with a mere object having a consistency, flexible and unstable."[5]

Therefore, smell, like all the sensory qualities John Locke was to qualify as "secondary," has nothing to do with the substance of the wax itself. Like color, softness, and taste, its odor is one of its "vestments." The scientific value of olfactory data and the testimony of the senses in general are rejected. Their only purpose is to protect the body: Our senses teach us nothing about the true nature of things; they only tell us whether things are useful or harmful.[6]

The French philosopher Nicolas Malebranche also set out to exclude sense perceptions from the realm of truth. Perfectly adapted to utilitarian ends, sense data lack all credibility on the theoretical level: "Indeed, it is now very easy to demonstrate that we are prey to an infinite number of errors with regard to light and colors and, in a general way, to all the sensations like cold, hot, smells, tastes, sound, pain, tenderness."[7] The senses are "false witnesses" to the truth.[8] Truth demands ascesis, and the scientific view of the senses entails their silence. As a Christian philosopher, Malebranche extended his criticism to a general moral warning about the senses: They bear the weight of sin. Prior to his act of disobedience, Adam had known from his pleasures, his pains, and his squeamishness what his body required, what was "good" for it. Since he was in total control of the "corporeal movements" of his body, he did not risk enslavement or unhappiness. Once he had committed his "sin," however, his senses, which had previously kept him duly informed, now treated him with less consideration, and revolted. Less closely linked to God since man's first fall, human beings no longer had the strength to preserve their freedom and happiness. Sin had inverted the preeminence of the mind over the body, which now spoke more loudly than God himself—although it never spoke the truth. Troubled by concupiscence, the human creature could no longer master his thoughts and was forced to engage in a continual struggle to emerge from the "shadows" of sentient ignorance and enter into the "light of ideas."

Seventeenth-century spirituality further strengthened the contempt for the senses and hatred of desire by "systematizing austerities."[9] The French prelate Jean-Baptiste Bossuet took up the notion (dear to Malebranche) that the body is joined to the soul to provide the latter with something to sacrifice, and he emphasized the need to fight against sensuality: "Evil is within us, it cleaves strangely to our entrails, and either we give in to sensual pleasure or we must combat it with continual resistance. . . . If we are to avoid the consummate evil of consent, we must continually resist the desire that gives birth to it."[10] Since disorder is created by the flesh, anything that affords sensual pleasure must be energetically condemned. Olfactory pleasures present especially redoubtable pitfalls because they do not seem to be overt threats to chastity. Bossuet inveighs against the woman in Proverbs who perfumes her bed with myrrh, aloes, and cinnamon and cries: "Come, let us take our fill of love until the morning, let us solace ourselves with love." Such words clearly show where "pleasant odors prepared to weaken the soul and attract it to sensual pleasures" can lead, for the soul accepts them with fewer misgivings since "they do not appear to represent a direct offense against modesty, but nonetheless they can cause it to let go and distract its attention from what should be its natural occupation."[11]

The separation of mind and body was made the subject of methodical attempts to suppress the instincts and prevent them from enjoying the satisfactions they seek. Disgust for the body was to be given its most extreme expression in the next century with the famous "salutary maxim" of Saint Alphonse Marie de Liguori: "Suffering is better than pleasure here below."[12] The founder of the order of Redemptorists laid great stress on olfactory mortification:

> As for the sense of smell, do not be so vain as to surround yourselves with amber perfumes and other sweet-smelling compounds or to use toilet water, all of which have little to recommend them, even to the laity. Rather, habituate yourselves to tolerating without disgust the unpleasant smells that so often emanate from the sick, like those saints who labored with joy in the vilest sick wards as if they were in the midst of a garden filled with the most delicious flowers.[13]

5

REHABILITATION OF THE SENSE OF SMELL IN THE AGE OF ENLIGHTENMENT

▼

In reaction to the rigorist and intellectualist philosophies of the previous century, many eighteenth-century thinkers began to reestablish the importance of the senses in the acquisition of knowledge. The philosopher Julien Offray de La Mettrie, for example, stated that all thought was based on the senses, which are alone capable of enlightening the mind in its search for truth. Were man only mind, he could know nothing: "The soul is basically dependent on the body's organs, by which it is shaped, grows and declines."[1] The rehabilitation of smell was nearly total: For this materialist thinker, the senses were his surest guides, his "philosophers." The philosopher Helvétius also reduced all the mental processes to the senses, expressing himself in the lapidary formula: "Juger est sentir—to think is to feel."[2]

The reevaluation of the body as a branch of knowledge was accompanied by changes in the old classical hierarchy of the senses. Sight, hitherto prized as the most intellectual sense, ceded its prestigious place to touch, which was more concrete.

These readjustments served to raise the status of the sense of smell, which now enjoyed a refound favor, and its newfound position was reflected in the famous example of the philosopher Condillac, who sought to demonstrate that all forms of intellectual activity have their beginning in sensation. He proposed endowing a statue with each of the senses, beginning with the one least suited to participate in knowledge: "We thought it fitting to begin with the sense of smell, since of all the senses it is the one that seems to contribute the least to the operations of the human mind."[3] Possessed of only the sense of smell, the marble effigy gradually comes into possession of every faculty:

> Having proved that our statue is capable of focusing its attention, of remembrance, of comparison, of judgment, of discernment and imagination; that it can deal with abstractions and concepts of number and duration; that it can recognize both general and particular truths; that it is capable of desire, of feelings, that it loves, hates and wills; that it can hope, fear and be amazed; and, finally, that it can form habits: we must therefore conclude that with but a single sense the understanding has as many faculties as it would were it in possession of all five senses.[4]

The olfactory sensation thus incorporates all the faculties of the soul, and what is true for the sense of smell can be applied to the other senses as well. However, although the senses are on an equal footing, the sense of touch plays a special role when it comes to the generation of faculties, for it is the only one that enables us to gain knowledge of the exterior world. Without its help, the statue endowed only with the sense of smell and given a rose to smell "smells the odor of the rose" but has no picture of the object being smelled: "Thus, there will be a smell of roses, a smell of carnations, of jasmine, of violets, according to the objects acting upon the organ. In short, as far as the statue is concerned odors represent its own inner modifications or modes of being."[5] The sense of smell must therefore be informed by touch. Its "exploratory mobility"[6] will instruct the statue that odors are not mere variations of itself, but emanate from external objects.

With a similar end in view, Diderot set up a hierarchy of the senses in which sight abdicated its sovereignty in favor of touch, a reversal of values that benefited smell. Sensuality was brought out of the closet, as it were: "I found that of all the senses the eye was the most superficial, the ear the most arrogant, smell the most voluptuous, taste the most superstitious and capricious and touch the most profound, the most philosophical."[7] The rehabilitation of the most underappreciated senses took place within the context of a materialist proclamation of faith, in which the body and emotions played a primary role in knowledge.[8] The most material senses can also be abstract: Sight, smell, and taste are even capable of realizing scientific advances. "As thinking beings we have senses that are all capable of rising to the most sublime arithmetical and algebraic speculations, of plumbing analytical depths, of posing amongst themselves the most complex questions about the nature of equations and of solving them as if each were a Diophantus."[9]

Rousseau held the senses in equally high esteem, for to him their operations determine the development of reason. Sensory education and health are essential components of any successful intellectual training: "In learning to think we must exercise our members, our senses and our organs, all instruments of our intelligence; to derive all possible benefits from these instruments, the body that contains them must be strong and healthy. Thus, man's true mind is not formed independently of his body—far from it: in fact, a good physical constitution facilitates the mental processes and makes them reliable."[10] This sensual rationalism, which sees the senses and emotions as of fundamental importance, affirms the primacy of the sense of smell. Like "our feet, our hands, our eyes," the nose is one of our "earliest teachers of philosophy,"[11] and is a basic component of Rousseau's philosophy, which was inspired by Condillac, but even more importantly, by the naturalist Buffon.

Indeed, when Buffon came to consider the sense of smell, he drew a very clear distinction between animal and human smell. "An admirable sense," the animal sense of smell was capable of replacing all the others:

> A universal organ of feeling, [the nose] is an eye that can see objects, not only where they are, but even where they have been; it is a taste organ by which the animal can savor not only what he can touch and seize upon, but even that which is far away and unattainable; it is the sense by which he is first, most frequently and most certainly given warning, by which he acts, by which he decides and by which he recognizes what is either suited or contrary to his nature, the sense, finally, by which he perceives, feels and chooses what can satisfy his appetite.[12]

In man, who is guided by a higher principle of "judgment and reason,"[13] the sense of smell occupies the lowest position in Buffon's eccentric sensory hierarchy, which begins with touch and is followed by taste, sight, and hearing. This total reversal of the relative importance of smell in the human and animal kingdoms denotes an important difference in the end being sought: "Man must think more than he must crave, and the animal must crave more than he must think."[14]

It is therefore not surprising that Rousseau, who had read and admired Buffon, should have drawn inspiration from his theory when he, in turn, posited two kinds of smell, one primitive and common to both animal and untamed man, and the other more refined, the attribute of a civilized man. Limited to his appetites, the "natural man," like the beast, develops only the faculties he most needs to protect himself. Yet, instinctive and "untutored" as this sense of smell is, it can be improved. As Buffon had stated earlier, "art and habit"[15] both play a part in its development. Used for "attack and defence,"[16] the savage's sense of smell is extremely powerful. It is hardly surprising, then, that "the American Indians can track the Spaniards by smell, like the finest dogs." In Canada, Indians developed a sense of smell so keen that they could hunt without animal assistance and "acted as their own dogs."[17]

However, there were limits to their powers of smell that could not be overcome even by practice. "Forced by nature to rely on instinct alone,"[18] Rousseau's natural man, like the beast, was deprived of the aesthetic enjoyment of odors. Solely for utilitarian purposes, his sense of smell, albeit highly developed, was nonetheless primitive. "Our otiose sensations—the wafted fragrance of a bed of flowers—must be hardly perceptible to men who walk too much to enjoy strolling and who do not work enough to enjoy the delights of repose. People who are always hungry cannot take great pleasure in odors that do not represent something to eat."[19] Only in the civilized life can this sense truly be cultivated.

And, indeed, the transition from a state of nature to civilization is accompanied by a change in the adaptive tool: Instinct guides the natural man in his physical world, but reason guides the civilized man in the social environment. Abandoning his animal existence, civilized man dulls the keenness of his sense of smell. However, by using his imagination he also expands it in a way not open to the savage. This faculty, which is latent in the natural man confined in the present and "devoid of foresight and curiosity,"[20] can only be activated by the civilized man. Although "odors in and of themselves are but weak sensations," they can "move the imagination more than the senses, and their effect is due not so much to what they offer as to the anticipation they create."[21] The evolution is hardly negative: What the sense of smell loses in power it gains in refinement.

Rousseau goes on to posit that, in society, the imagination has such a strong effect on the sense of smell that it tends to become confused with it, although both play a decisive role in lovemaking. Whereas imagination "has nothing to say to savage hearts," "restricted as they are only to the physical aspects of love-making," and subject because of their natural impulses to the "heat of their amorous temperament,"[22] it can act in concert with the sense of smell to arouse and sustain desire in the civilized man:

> The sense of smell is the sense of imagination; giving a stronger tone to the nerves, it greatly disturbs the brain; which explains why it can arouse the amorous temperament momentarily, but eventually exhausts it. Its effects in love-making are well known; the sweet perfume of a dressing-room is not so flimsy a trap as we might think; and I do not know whether to congratulate or to pity the prudent and unfeeling man who has never thrilled to the scent of the flowers on his mistress's bosom.[23]

The sense of smell is intellectualized: It encourages dreaming and fantasizing. However, it is also affected by the pitfalls of the imagination. Indeed, whether in lovemaking or in hunting, the sense of smell is an instrument for capture. But where, in the natural state, it guided the hunter's pursuit of his prey, in the civilized state it now serves to lure man into a sensual "trap."

In Rousseau's mind, the special relationship between the sense of smell and the imagination has led to important qualitative differences in olfactory ability. Women, who are more imaginative than men, are highly sensitive to all kinds of exhalations. On the other hand, infants and young children, whose imaginative faculties, Rousseau felt, are undeveloped, like that of the savage, display an indifference to smells as do some animals, "not because their senses are not as keen as an adult's, and perhaps more so, but because, not linking odor with any other notion, they are not easily aroused by it to any feeling of pleasure or of pain, [and therefore] it does not delight them or offend them as it does us."[24] Not until children reach the age of two or three years does their sense of smell, stimulated by the imagination, awaken from its "hebetude." The olfactory insensitivity of very young children enables Rousseau, following Hobbes,[25] to emphasize the relative nature of "pleasant" and "unpleasant" smells. Although infants are aware very early on of differences in odor intensities, they make no qualitative distinctions: "sensations derive from nature; preference or aversion do not."[26]★

The relationship between taste and the sense of smell also

★Experiments, for example those carried out by the biologist Steiner in 1979, contradict this purely cultural notion of olfactory tastes and distates. When exposed to rotten eggs or fish, which adults usually find unpleasant, babies less than twelve hours old mimic disgust. On the other hand, the smells of banana, vanilla, and chocolate give rise to facial responses of acceptance and pleasure. Although such observations demonstrate an innate sensitivity to pleasant and unpleasant odors, they do not totally exclude the role of acquired taste.

determines distinctions between pleasant and unpleasant odors. Taste, which is conditioned by a person's way of life, affects the odors that precede and predispose it. The savage's sense of smell would not react in the same way as ours and would make very different judgments: "A Tartar must sniff with as much pleasure at a stinking side of dead horsemeat as one of our hunters does at a gamy partridge."[27] And the very close links that exist between the two senses serve to forestall the clumsy tricks sometimes played upon them when we attempt to hide "the disagreeable taste of a medicine" to get a child to swallow it: "The discord between the two senses is too great for it to be fooled . . . to it, a very sweet perfume is just another disgusting smell; and thus our imprudent precautions only add to the sum of unpleasant sensations at the expense of pleasant ones."[28]

Like Rousseau, "who so often depicted nature with an inimitable truth,"[29] the physician Pierre-Jean-Georges Cabanis noted the close links between the senses of smell and taste, lovemaking, and the imagination. "The guide and sentinel of taste," the olfactory sense is also one of sensuality: "The season of flowers is also the season of the pleasures of love: sensual thoughts are linked to thoughts of gardens or fragrant groves, and poets quite rightly endow perfumes with the power to create a sweet intoxication in the soul. Is there a man, even the most sober (unless he be somehow unbalanced), whose thoughts will not be aroused by the scent of a flowering arbor?"[30] Notwithstanding frequent references to Rousseau's *Emile,* Cabanis's break with sensualism is evidenced in his decision not to "deal with odors from the point of view of their peripheral, moral, effects; that is, as reflecting a myriad of impressions not derived directly from their influence, but based solely on a process of association." According to Cabanis's schema, the weakness of odor memory and the sensual emotions odor can nonetheless evoke are purely physiological. Odors in and of themselves have a powerful effect on the entire nervous system and can predispose it to all kinds of sensual pleasures, communicating "that minimal degree of excitation seemingly inherent to them; and odors are able to achieve this because of their special effect on the organs that produce the most acute pleasures available to sentient beings."[31] Thus, although agreeing with Rousseau that the sense of smell and amorous desire go hand in hand, Cabanis pays closer attention to the links between olfactory and sexual activity, and it is quite natural that a physician should be more drawn to the physiological aspect, which Rousseau, more sensitive to the purely mental aspects of love, only evoked.

A true man of the eighteenth century—although his most important work, *Rapports du physique et du moral (The Links between the Physical and the Moral)*, was published in 1802— Cabanis carried on the work begun by Condillac. However, he broke with Condillac's theories when he affirmed the need to link the study of mental data to physiology, singling out instinct as the element connecting the intellectual and the organic. The senses and sensory data, "the sources of all man's moral ideas and habits," must be studied within the context of the entire body, not in isolation. When it smells a rose, Condillac's statue "becomes, vis-à-vis itself, the rose's smell and nothing more, and this way of putting it, which is as precise as it is ingenious, perfectly expresses the simple change that must at that moment occur in the brain." However, the actual olfactory sensation is not confined to the sense of smell alone, nor is it separate from other exterior stimuli; it is far more complex than that, since the sense of smell not only acts in concert with the other senses but also has an "especially sympathetic" relationship with the intestinal tract and the generative organs. The latter connections enable us to understand the effect of certain effluvia that turn the stomach, provoke violent vomiting, and can either excite or calm attacks of hysteria.

In mammals, the principal organ inspiring sympathy or antipathy is smell: "It is quite obvious that each species, and even each individual, emits a particular odor: it gathers around him in a cloud of animal vapors, constantly refreshed by the life he leads: and when that individual moves, he always leaves behind him particles that enable animals of his own species, or of another that has a keen sense of smell, to track him."[32] Thus, we can understand the attractive qualities of the emanations of healthy animals, since they can provide physical pleasures and have salutary effects. Indeed, it is for this very reason that the air in clean and well-tended barns and cowsheds is still recommended in the treatment of certain diseases.

KANT AND HEGEL: AN ANTISOCIAL
AND UNAESTHETIC SENSE

▼

Whether to establish the importance of the mind's reliance on the physical body or to discern the theoretical role of the senses, the philosophes of the Age of Enlightenment clearly evidenced a new interest in the sense of smell. However, their campaign of rehabilitation did not enjoy unanimous support. Immanuel Kant, in particular, stood aloof from the trend.

According to Kant, in a sensory hierarchy based on both empirical and rationalist concepts, the sense of smell occupies a necessarily ambiguous position. It is at once the "most unproductive" and the "most necessary" of senses.[1] "Closely related to taste,"[2] it is also a contact sense. Both smell and taste operate, not mechanically and superficially, as do touch, hearing, and sight, but chemically, within the body. Since they affect the subject directly, without any external mediation (and are thus more "subjective" than "objective"[3]), smell and taste play a greater role in pleasure than in the acquisition of knowledge and tell us little about the true nature of external objects.

Smell, with its minimal participation in acquired knowledge, has little to do with freedom or sociability, and this serves to raise its lowly status. The smell that enters the lungs establishes a contact "even more intimate"[4] than the one between taste and the receptor cavities of mouth and throat. Furthermore, unlike oral absorption, which is a deliberate act, olfactory perception is almost always involuntary. A smell is unavoidable, for it cannot be either voided or avoided through a rejective process like vomiting. "Smell is like an intermediary taste; others are forced, willy-nilly, to share in it. . . ."[5]

Smell's "overly familiar"[6] intrusiveness is aggravated by the fact that "the disgusting subjects it affords (especially in populated areas) far outnumber the pleasant ones."[7] This furtive reference to the revulsion and ostracism created by human effluvia leads Kant to a pessimistic conclusion. In the end, the inconveniences of the sense of smell outweigh its ephemeral appeal, and "it is no use cultivating it or tampering with it to make it more pleasant." Its sole interest lies in its ability to indicate what we might best avoid: "As a negative condition of well-being, when it prevents us from breathing in unhealthy air (emanations from furnaces, the stench of swamps and corpses) or from eating spoiled food, the sense is not wholly without importance."[8]

Rarely in the history of philosophy has such a condescending opinion been expressed with regard to the sense of smell. This severity on the part of a thinker who was hypersensitive to odors and who yet spent several hours a day at table with his friends is somewhat surprising. Perhaps it reflects the attitude of a moralist fond of conviviality but extremely respectful of others, or perhaps it is the parosmic reaction of a man who was reputedly indifferent to perfumes and to flowers.[9] Or maybe it is an example of the celibate Sage of Königsberg's wariness of this most physical and sensual of the senses—attributes that led the eighteenth-century philosopher La Metherie to advise "extreme caution in the use of scents."[10] That recommendation reflects a theme implicit in every philosophical consideration of smell, one that was finally brought into the open by Freud and Marcuse,[11] namely, the banishment of a dangerous sense that can affect and even control sexual attraction.[12] La Metherie noted:

> Civilized man has not yet perfected his enjoyment of the sense of smell to the extent he has perfected his enjoyment of his other senses. The art of tasting flavors has been highly developed. What a variety of foods and beverages there are! Music has created an infinite variety of sounds; the pleasures of sight are enormously varied. And yet nothing has been done to increase the pleasures derived from odors, even though we recognize that such sensations can be highly agreeable. For the continual use of odors leads to sensual pleasure; it is thus unforgivable in a grown man.[13]

Perfumes and flowers, which can be tolerated in small amounts when worn by honest women, are best left to courtesans and roués. On this subject the sensualist physician shares the mistrust expressed by Plato and Kant.

A sense of desire linked to consumption, and in which the mind plays no part,[14] smell is excluded from Hegel's aesthetics even more explicitly than in the case of Kant. The origin of Hegel's rejection is the position of the nose on the face in relation to the other features. A connecting organ, the appendage occupies a strategic site between two antinomic zones of the face: one is "theoretical or spiritual,"[15] i.e., the forehead, eyes, and ears, where the mind resides; the other, "practical," area, consists mainly of the lips and mouth and is especially designed for nutrition. Although he locates the nose in the "practical" or utilitarian zone, Hegel states that it belongs to "both systems." All the ambiguity with which consideration of the sense of smell is fraught is caused by this siting: Straddling the speculative and material zones, the nose is not an automous entity but is, rather, a mere vassal at the service of whichever of its neighbors is momentarily the more powerful.

When a depression clearly marks the separation between the forehead and the nose, the entire organ seems attracted or drawn toward the nutritive apparatus; "the forehead is thus isolated and takes on an expression of firmness and self-centered mental concentration, cut off from the verbal expression of the mouth, which thus becomes a mere organ serving nutrition and which employs the nose as a subsidiary organ that arouses or stimulates a purely physical need by calling attention to odors."[16] In animals, indeed, the predominance of the "practical" zone ensures that the sense of smell will be totally superior, and the prominence of the muzzle, used to satisfy basic needs, gives the animal's physiognomy "the expression of pure and simple utility, devoid of any spiritual ideality."[17]

In contrast, a Greek profile, "the ideal form of human head,"[18] is characterized by an almost unbroken connecting line from nose to forehead. This expresses the triumph of mind over nature, "which is thrust totally into the background."[19] In this instance the nose becomes an extension of the forehead, "the spiritual organ,"[20] and acquires an almost intangible character and expression. The nose, "through its movements, however slight, serves to express appreciations and judgments of a spiritual order."[21] There is no break, no conflict, no flaw in this noble, serene, and confident visage, this embodiment of ideal beauty, whose "lovely harmony is the result of the imperceptible, i.e., continuous, flow of the line between the upper and lower portions of the face."[22]

Thus torn between two conflicting interests and enjoying only a relative autonomy with regard to taste, the sense of smell is in the end relegated to the practical senses, those concerned solely with the material world and incapable of any disinterested aesthetic action. Unlike sight and hearing, which deal only with the form of real objects and do not affect them, smell's action is related to destruction: "The only odors we can perceive are those that have already been consumed."[23] Incompatible with artistic or intellectual interests, a fulcrum between the spiritual and natural senses, smell can hope to acquire a certain dignity only by renouncing its primal and natural activity—smelling—and by suppressing its corporeal connections. In such conditions, the theoretical role Hegel attributes to the sense of smell would be conceivable only when assumed by the stone face of a statue.

TWO PHILOSOPHERS WITH "NOSE": FEUERBACH AND NIETZSCHE

▼

According to Feuerbach, the depreciation of the sense of smell so evident in Kant and Hegel is closely bound up with the idealism that reached its high point in Hegelian philosophy. Feuerbach's critique includes both Hegel's absolute idealism, which held that any true apprehension of the world was impossible owing to the inability to accept the truth of sensory data, and Christianity, which has produced an ideal that is "castrated, bodiless, abstract."[1] Both lead to man's alienation and division. Feuerbach vigorously condemns such impoverished and biased thinking, which distorts both the body and the senses. "I categorically reject such absolute, vague speculation, turned in on itself as it is, speculation that feeds only on itself. A whole world separates me from such philosophers, who would blind themselves the better to think; I need my senses to think."[2]

A pupil of Hegel (although, given his tendency to materialism, hardly an orthodox Hegelian[3]), Feuerbach was to break with his mentor's idealism and come to the conclusion that what his unworldly elder had lacked was a "nose": ". . . the unique, mental organ, the head, universal as it is, is always clearly defined by a nose—pointed or snub, thin or thick, long or short, straight or crooked."[4] He replaces this wan philosophy, "the last great attempt to shore up a weakened and dying Christianity,"[5] with another and wholly carnal philosophy, based "not on philosophy without body, color or name, but on a logic of flesh and blood."[6] His investigation of the sense of smell is a part of a total concept of man, which, affirming as it does his connections with and differences from various materialist tendencies, cannot be given a single name. The "flesh and blood" humanism Feuerbach was to found in 1843 is made up of "eyes and ears, hands and feet."[7] Countering idealism, he boasts of his closeness to the body and frames his ideas in terms of being in harmony with it: "Whereas the old philosophy began with the proposition, 'I am an abstraction, a purely thinking entity, my body is not part of my essential being,' the new philosophy begins with the proposition: 'I am a real being, a feeling being; yes, my body in its totality is my selfhood, my very essence.' "[8]

The belief that the universality and liberty unique to the human being are not the product of reason alone but of the "total being" led Feuerbach to reevaluate the "lower" senses and reclassify them among the highest. Smell and taste were deemed capable, like sight and hearing, of being separated from man's animal nature and of achieving an "autonomous and theoretical significance and dignity." Indeed, a particularly notable characteristic of this process is the fact that it is accompanied by a long pleading in favor of the stomach, usually regarded as the most trivial of organs:

> Even man's stomach, contemptuously as we treat it, is not an animal entity but a human entity, because it is a universal entity, and not restricted to a species-specific diet. It is for this very reason that man is free from that gluttonous rage that causes the wild beast to leap upon its prey. Keep man's mind but give him the stomach of a wolf or a horse: he will surely cease to be a man. . . . Thus, if a man wishes to enjoy a moral and rational relationship with his stomach, he must treat it not as would some bestial creature but as would a human being. To shuck off one's humanity at the threshold to the stomach is tantamount to relegating it to a bestial class, tantamount to authorizing man to eat like an animal.

Like the stomach, the sense of smell cannot be truly "human" if it is subject only to fixed stimuli. The lack of determinacy that has caused it to lose its acuity as humans have evolved and their societies have developed is an absolutely necessary element in its humanization. And what it loses in strength it gains in liberty and universality: If man's sense of smell is inferior to that of a dog, it is because, no longer subject merely to a few particular effluvia, it is now sensitive to odors of every kind. Far from being a sense with strictly destructive relations with objects, smell is capable of "spiritual and scientific actions" that can serve knowledge as well as art.

Nietzsche's reevaluation of the sense of smell was to be far more radical, for he made it an integral part of his critique of idealism and Christianity. Rejecting Feuerbach's fervor, which had been focused on redeeming a sense depreciated by idealistic and Christian thinkers by intellectualizing it, Nietzsche claimed for the sense of smell in particular (and for man in general) an animality that demanded recognition: "We no longer seek man's origin in the 'spirit,' in 'divine nature.' No, we have returned him to his animal rank. We deem him the strongest of animals because he is the cleverest; the mind with which he is endowed is but the consequence of this."[9] The restraints man has placed on his instincts have been his downfall, creating his "bad conscience." And with guilt has come the most serious and frightening of diseases, one from which humans have yet to recover: "Man suffers from man, from himself: the result of a violent break with his animal past, of his leap, his fall, into another state of being, into new conditions of life, of a declaration of war against those former instincts upon which all his strength and pleasure, all that once made him formidable, were based."[10]

Nietzsche violently attacked religion and idealistic philosophy, asserting that they have connived to spread false notions, like the one of a "pure spirit or mind" independent of its fleshy envelope. He also condemned Christianity, "mankind's greatest misfortune,"[11] anti-instinctual, and life hating, with the utmost ferocity. If man has become the least successful animal, the unhealthiest, the one most dangerously cut off from its instincts, the fault lies principally with

a religion that has taught ignorance of the body! . . . which has found "merit" in depriving the body of sufficient nourishment! . . . which regards physical health and well-being as a kind of enemy, the devil, temptation! . . . that is convinced that a "perfect" soul can be housed in a cadaverous body and that has in doing so been forced to create a new notion of "perfection"—a wan, suffering, nebulous and comatose being, a being of so-called "saintliness"—a saintliness that is really nothing but the sum total of the symptoms of an impoverished, enervated and incurably damaged body.[12]

However, Nietzsche also took up arms against the philosophers who viewed the body with contempt. Ignorant of its "great purpose," they set up an illusory morality that was a negation of the body's untapped wisdom: "To be a philosopher, to be a mummy, to exemplify 'monotonotheism' by playing the undertaker! And above all, let him not mention the body—that pitiful sensual obsession!—stained with every sort of logical absurdity, rejected and even impossible, notwithstanding man's impertinence in behaving as if it were real."[13]

Schopenhauer was Nietzsche's principal target. Yet, in maintaining the primacy of the will—i.e., the body[14]—over the intellect, Schopenhauer had distanced himself from a tradition that had tried to depict man as profoundly different from the beast, placing man's essence in his mind or his conscience. Similarly, by making smell the sense of memory ("since it can recall to us more immediately than any other sense the specific impression of an event or a place, however distant in time"[15]) he had cut himself off from the philosophers who denied any intellectual faculty to the sense of smell. However, Schopenhauer had favored the more abstract senses. Sight, the least corporeal of all, was the most intelligent: It is the sense of "understanding."[16] His treatment of hearing was original: Even though hearing is passive and constantly at war with the mind, it encroaches on the prerogatives of sight; it is the sense of the "thinking and conceptual" mind. Above all, however, Schopenhauer had deemed the more carnal senses, smell and taste, to be inferior. "More subjective than objective" (we discern the Kantian heritage in this formula, which repeats the terms used in his *Anthropology*), they are the servants of insatiable desire, a source of suffering from which we can free ourselves only through negation of the life force, of the "will." The notion that pain and suffering are the bases of all life led to a pessimism connoted by the words *asceticism* and *chastity*.

It is this aversion to the physical (shared by Christianity and idealism) that Nietzsche was to inveigh against. "There can be no question that since philosophy has existed (from India to England, to mention only the opposite poles of philosophical endeavor), there has been a veritable annoyance with, a rancor against, sensuality—Schopenhauer is only its most eloquent exponent, and, have we ears to hear, the most captivating, the most fascinating."[17] It was against this somber philosophy, with its "mortuary stench,"[18] that Nietzsche was determined to do battle "from a position diametrically opposed."[19]

Of all the "philosophical species,"[20] Heraclitus is the only one to find favor in Nietzsche's eyes. Such esteem may seem surprising in that the Greek philosopher had also considered the senses to be purveyors of falsehood. However, Heraclitus also had the immense merit of not having raised the usual accusations of undependability and instability. Nietzsche may well have been thinking of the Heraclitan fragment that (apparently) establishes a relationship between smell and knowledge ("Were all things smoke, the nostrils would recognize them,"[21]) when he wrote: "All my genius is in my nostrils."[22]

Indeed, for Nietzsche the nostrils were the most subtle instruments of scientific observation: "The nose, for example, of which no philosopher has ever spoken with veneration and gratitude—the nose is, albeit provisionally, the most delicate instrument at our disposal: it is an instrument capable of recording the most minimal changes of movement, changes that escape even spectroscopic detection."[23] His vindication of smell, however, immediately takes a metaphorical turn; combining it with that of the instincts, his apologia is extended to include all intuitive knowledge. Thus, he answers all the body haters' scorn for the most animal of the senses by emphasizing its role in the thinking processes. The links between smell and wisdom, mental penetration, and sympathy make it the sense of the psychologist, guided by instinct, whose art consists not in reasoning but in "scenting out." Nietzsche, a "born psychologist,"[24] boasts of being exceptionally well equipped for the task he has undertaken: "I am the first to have discovered the truth by virtue of the fact that I am the first to have sensed, to have had the flair to scent out, falsehood as falsehood."[25] A veritable path to psychological and moral knowledge, "flair" enables us to sniff out the cowardice, hypocrisy, and decadence that lurk in those most-secret places into which neither eye nor mind can penetrate. He counters dialectics, the philosophical weapon par excellence ("a rough-and-ready weapon available to desperate men who have no others"[26]) with this formidable ally of truth that can plumb the depths of the hearts and minds of men.

> Dare I mention one last trait of my nature, one that does not make my commerce with other men the easier? I am sensitive—to a disconcerting degree—to cleanliness, to such a degree that I can physically perceive or sense— the proximity—how express it?—the heart, the secret innerness, the "guts," of every soul. . . . This sensitivity has endowed me with psychological antennae that enable me to grasp and even palpate every secret: from almost the very first moment of contact, I am aware of the slimy dross concealed in the depths of more than one nature that is the product of unhealthy blood but covered with the varnish of education. If my observations are exact, such natures, which affront my sense of cleanliness, are also aware of the circumspection with

which my disgust inspires me: which does not make
them any less malodorous. . . .[27]

Thanks again to this subtle olfactory tool, Nietzsche is able
to bare the unhealthy nature of civilized man, castrated by a
morality that has taught him to blush at his basic instincts. No
longer able to give them free reign, man has repressed them and
in so doing, destroyed himself. The process of mutation of this
"human fauna" into a man with a "guilty conscience" emits a
stench, the stench of a creature that is losing its animal nature
and, hence, its "will to power."

> In seeking to become an angel (to avoid using a harsher
> word), man has acquired this spoiled stomach, this
> tainted taste, which have not only given him a disgust
> for animal pleasure and innocence but have also made
> his life insipid—so that often he must hold his nose
> when examining himself and, with Pope Innocent III,
> morosely draw up the catalogue of his natural infirmi-
> ties: "procreating in impurity, given disgusting nourish-
> ment at his mother's breast, secreting bad smells, saliva,
> urine and excrement!"[28]

A veritable bloodhound, Nietzsche can "scent from a distance"[29] the corruption that befouls the most edifying moralities
and the rot inherent in the decadent notions of idealism and
Christianity, which flee reality and cleave to the beyond: "One
need only read any Christian agitator—Saint Augustin, for example—to understand, to get a really good sniff of, the filthy
kind of spokesmen with which one is faced."[30] In many instances the nauseating effluvia of the "shady den in which such
ideals are cooked up," ideals that "stink to high heaven of
falsehood,"[31] oblige him to "hold my nose."[32] His campaign

against morality and false values is waged without "the slightest scent of powder"[33]: Nietzsche proposes to offer "quite different and far more agreeable perfumes" to "sufficiently subtle nostrils."[34]

In the quest for truth the sense of smell—which is also the sense of veracity, drawing as it does upon the sure sources of animal instinct that give the body its great wisdom, providing the tool for a psychologist in search of the fake and the illusory— dethrones the chilly logic that emerges when man struggles against the instinctual.[35] Above and beyond its primary function, smell thus serves as a "sixth sense": the sense of intuitive knowledge.

8

FREUD AND MARCUSE: THE "ORGANIC SUBLIMATION" AND "SURREPRESSION" OF THE SENSE OF SMELL

▼

Freud establishes an even closer relationship between the depreciation of the sense of smell and the development of civilization, one being the necessary condition for the other. Although his argument is not primarily philosophical, per se, it does certainly contain philosophical elements. (In 1896, writing to his friend Wilhelm Fliess, the father of psychoanalysis referred to their shared detour into medicine and confided that "in his very depths" he had always hoped to use medical science as a path toward philosophy: "As a young man I knew no longing other than for philosophical knowledge."[1]) A blotting out of the sense of smell is a part of the overall renunciation of the instincts, but (and much more than in the case of Nietzsche) Freud believed that it also plays a fundamental role in the civilizing process.

In 1930 Freud advanced the hypothesis of a primitive sense of smell superior to that of civilized man, reflecting a similar hypothesis set forth by Darwin in 1871. Noting the preeminence of the sense of smell in animals, Darwin, in line with the principle of evolution, had concluded that the sense must have undergone a transformation with time and that its present inferior status was the result of the fact that it was of little use to man. The modern sense of smell was only a distant vestige of some far-off ancestor in whom it had been a predominant characteristic.[2] Freud too was to establish a connection between weakened olfactory perception and civilization, but he went on to make a series of conjectures. In another letter to Fliess dated 14 November 1897, he wrote: "I have often had a suspicion that something organic plays a part in repression. I was able once before to tell you that it was a question of the abandonment of former sexual zones. . . . In my case the notion was linked to the changed part played by sensations of smell: upright, walking, nose raised from the ground, at the same time a number of formerly interesting sensations attached to the earth becoming repulsive—by a process still unknown to me."[3] This notion of an "organic repression" would be further developed in *Civilization and Its Discontents*. The role of smell had become less important as man began to assume an upright position and distance himself from olfactory stimuli, allowing visual sensations, which favored the sexual process and attachment to one's partner, to become preponderant and to outweigh the exciting power of menstrual odors. No longer based on an intermittent event (menstruation), sexual excitation became constant, which led to the foundation of the family, the first step toward civilization.

Surprisingly, neither of Freud's texts makes any reference to a scientific discovery that tended to corroborate his thesis that the sense of smell had regressed organically—namely, the discovery of the vomeronasal organ. First found in an adult male in the eighteenth century, this secondary olfactory organ was proved to be common to mammals by Ludwig Jacobson, a Danish scientist, in 1809. Some contemporary physiologists like Yveline Leroy believe that the absence of the organ in man (with a few very rare exceptions it disappears in the early months of fetal life) is linked to man's assuming an upright posture and thus to the passage from animality to humanity. The Freudian hypothesis of an organic repression of the sense of smell seems to ignore Jacobson's work. In any event, Freud does link the repression of smell to man's "verticalization" and his break with the animal. Thus, animals walk on all fours, have discontinuous sexuality, and live in isolation; man stands upright, his sexuality is continuous, and he lives in groups.

According to Freud, smell appears to have been a necessary part of the heavy tribute man has paid to the civilizing process. Its weakening, necessary to prevent any return to an anterior phase of human development, entailed an isolation of the female during the menstrual period. The effect of the female's odor on the male now constituted a threat of regression, a risk of the reemergence of some archaic sexual behavior. Progressing out of the animalistic stage therefore required repression and exclusion, and both the sense of smell and the female came to be regarded as complementary pitfalls. This negative female role would persist throughout the ulterior phases of the development of civilization:

> Furthermore, women soon come into opposition to civilization and display their retarding and restraining influence—those very women who, in the beginning, laid the foundations of civilization by the claims of their love. Women represent the interests of the family and of sexual life. The work of civilization has become increasingly the business of men, it confronts them with ever

more difficult tasks and compels them to carry out instinctual sublimations of which women are little capable
. . . Thus, the woman finds herself forced into the
background by the claims of civilization and she adopts
a hostile attitude towards it.[4]

The rise of civilization also requires man to forgo the interests he shares with "olfactory animals," such as canines, a species
attracted to excrement. Repugnance for fecal matter goes hand
in hand with the development of cleanliness, which has much to
do with smell:

The desire for cleanliness emerges from the pressing
need to get rid of excreta that have become disagreeable
to the sense of smell. We know that this is not true in
the case of infants, who are not repelled by them. Education exerts special care to accelerating the passage to
the succeeding stage, at which excreta lose any value
and become the object of disgust and repugnance and
are, therefore, rejected. Such a depreciation would be
impossible if the strong odor of such matter drawn from
the body were not subjected to the same fate as other
olfactory impressions that were also forgone as man
began to walk upright. Thus, anal eroticism is the first
victim of the "organic repression" that occurs along the
road to civilization.[5]

As a necessary part of the civilizing process, the regression
of the sense of smell is nonetheless fraught with danger. The
limitations it places on the libido lessen the individual's capacity
for happiness and can become the bases for psychoses and neuroses. Although both Freud and Nietzsche note the depreciation
of smell in Western civilization, they deal with it in different

ways. Whereas the philosopher is primarily concerned with olfactory regression in relation to knowledge and the limits it
imposes on it, the psychoanalyst approaches it from the point of
view of the restrictions it sets on pleasure. They both, however,
link the regression to instinctual repression and to its harmful
effects on the individual. Freud, nevertheless, assigns it a much
more decisive role, establishing as he does a direct relationship
between the earliest stage of the civilizing process and the organic sublimation of the olfactory sense. Along the same lines,
the French psychoanalyst Jacques Lacan was to state: "Organic
repression of the sense of smell in man has a great deal to do with
his access to the dimension of the Other."[6]

This thesis was to be taken up by the Freudian/Marxist
humanist Herbert Marcuse, with the addition of a further distinction in the analysis of olfactory repression. Smell has been the
victim of a dual repression: the first—primal, fundamental, and
necessary to the legitimate goals of civilization—concerns its
instinctual, coprophilic (i.e., interested in excrement for sexual
excitement) elements; the secondary repression concerns the
olfactory pleasures and serves the interests of social domination.
Smell, and taste too, are repressed more severely than the other
senses because the intense physical pleasures they provide im-
pede the regimentation of individuals and their exploitation:

> Smell and taste give, as it were, unsublimated pleasure
> *per se* (and unrepressed disgust). They relate (and sepa-
> rate) individuals immediately, without the generalized
> and conventionalized forms of consciousness, morality,
> aesthetics. . . . The pleasure of the proximity senses plays
> on the erotogenic zones of the body—and does so only
> for the sake of pleasure. Their unrepressed development
> would counteract the desexualization of the organism

required by its social utilization as an instrument of labor.[7]

A subversive sense, one threatening both to the control and banking of fleeting impulses and to the requirements of a specific social organization, smell provides "a good example of the reciprocal relationship between primal repression and conscious repression." And it is the latter that futilely constrains individuals without usefully contributing to the ends of civilization. Countering the pessimism of Freud, who viewed repression as the very essence of civilization, Marcuse envisages a civilization that will be less coercive thanks to the abolition of conscious repression. Denying this additional sublimation of the sense of smell can thus play a role in man's liberation. Marcuse, however, neglects to indicate how it will work without endangering the primal sublimation of the sense of smell that enabled man to evolve in the first place.

FROM PHILOSOPHY TO POETRY:
FOURIER, BACHELARD,
AND PROUST

▼

Accused by Plato and Aristotle of lacking finesse and language and of procuring pleasures that are less "pure" than those furnished by sight and hearing, viewed as a nuisance by Kant and rated inferior by Schopenhauer, flatly excluded from aesthetic consideration by Hegel and described by Georg Simmel as the most antisocial of all the senses, smell has indeed been much maligned by philosophers—although there are exceptions.

Some philosophers (albeit very few) rebelled when it came to discrediting the sense of smell—the philosophers of the emotions, first, and later such men as Fourier, Feuerbach, and, of course, Nietzsche. However, to mix a metaphor, the latter's advocacy of smell fell on deaf ears, and there have been few attempts to rehabilitate the sense in the twentieth century (aside from a somewhat halfhearted try by Bachelard). Psychoanalysis probably struck the decisive blow. Freud, positing a link between the decline of the sense of smell and the rise of civilization, relegated the sense to the animal kingdom. Classical phenomenology showed little interest in smell. In his *Phénoménologie de la perception,* Merleau-Ponty does not deal with it at all. And in a recent book, the modern French thinker Michel Serres can do no more than note the contempt expressed by numerous philosophers: "Many philosophies make reference to sight; a few to hearing; even fewer to touch or smell. Abstraction cuts up the sensate body, gets rid of taste, smell and touch, and retains for consideration only sight and hearing, intuition and understanding. Abstraction means not so much abandoning the body as it does breaking it down into pieces: analysis."[1]

Schools of thought that esteem the mind and logic tend to denigrate olfaction. Those that exalt the importance of the physical are as a rule more lenient. Although there is a connection between the two schools, there is abundant evidence that their partisans have vastly different opinions on the status of smell. For the first group, the role of smell in knowledge and aesthetics is negligible at best, if not nonexistent, whereas for the second, smell plays an obvious and even primordial role in both areas. According to the psychologist Maurice Pradines, it is a "needful sense" that provides "neither a true knowledge of the world nor a true knowledge of oneself";[2] for the socialist philosopher Jean Jaurès it was an "aesthetic sense" that establishes "a disinterested relationship between ourselves and the real life of this earth from which we come."[3] Whichever, smell has in fact always been assigned a varying and unstable position on the sensory value scale. Quite often, it was merely brushed aside, as if the evanescent nature of its end result undermined any attempt to include it in a system. Hard to grasp through scientific or philosophical concepts, smell has been more amenable to poetic evocations.

Indeed, it has led such different philosophers as Charles Fourier, the "phenomenological dreamer,"[4] and Gaston Bachelard, the "dreamer of words,"[5] down highly poetic paths.

Fourier undertook to concoct a subtle synthesis using the point where science, philosophy, and poetry intersect. The child of shopkeeper parents who sold fabrics and herbs, Fourier was an ardent defender of desire and emotions and dreamed of subjecting "aromas" to true scientific study. His mother's maiden name was Muguet (lily of the valley), and perhaps it was from her that he got his early passion for perfumes and flowers. In any event, he made up his mind to possess every variety of each of the species he set out to cultivate and to attempt to grow them in every possible way. He transformed his bedroom into a hothouse packed with fragrant plants, with "only a narrow path down the middle of the room to get from the door to the window."[6] There, he drew up his "aromal movement or system of distribution of known or unknown aromas that guide men and beasts, that set off winds and epidemics, that regulate the sexual relations of the stars and provide the germs of created species."[7] He had no fear of shocking a century that prided itself on its enlightenment when he accused it of ignoring certain sciences and of having only erroneous insights into others. To contemporary scientists and scholars he suggested themes for research designed to broaden mankind's knowledge of new horizons.[8] Scientific exploration had a "strange blind spot" with regard to the aromal apparatus, which played a superior role in the harmony of the material universe and which had never been the subject of any serious study. "We do not know such aromas as part of any regular system, nor the causes of the influences they dispense, especially when it comes to the stars, which are controlled by aromatic affinities."

Linked to attraction and the emotions, operating both "actively and passively" on all animal, vegetable, and mineral creation, aromas are finally given theoretical dignity thanks to Fourier. Their importance is seen to be fundamental, for all of creation is conceived by the "aromal copulations" of the stars:[9] Prior to the existence of all things, the planets self-created by means of aromatic bursts. In the writings of this philosopher of desire and love, pleasure is so intimately linked with perfume that his vision of souls in heaven takes the form of "aromatic bodies" borne hither and yon within the "aromatic shell" that surrounds each planet like a soap bubble. And should sybarites, gastronomes, and other men fear there will be no place for them in heaven, let them be reassured: The subtle element of which they will then be composed will be far more receptive to odors than is their terrestrial shell of earth and water. Thus, among a myriad of pleasures, they will be able to enjoy "a plethora of scents, both on earth and from the other planets,"[10] whose delights they will also be able to sample. This vision of an afterlife in which odor plays an essential part in pleasure is not unrelated to the lunar world of Cyrano de Bergerac, where the "invisible soul of scented herbs" will rejoice the traveler's nostrils and where one will live on odorous clouds, for "the culinary art will consist in capturing in huge, especially designed vessels the exhalations released by viands as they cook."[11] The philosopher's theory supports the poet's dream.

Far from deploring the lack of any research into the aromal apparatus, Bachelard believed that odors had played all too large a part in scientific investigations. Along with tastes, they were among the "vulgar sensations" that play an important role in "substantialist belief."[12] Such belief emerges when an immediate phenomenon is endowed with substantiality—that is, it is portrayed as being true, not imaginary—and Bachelard denounced these beliefs as characteristic of the kind of prescientific mentality that "stifles questioning."[13] He considered the action of odors to be particularly pernicious in that, owing to their direct and intimate quality, "they appear to be bringing us a certain message from a material reality."[14] The concepts developed by many chemists or physicians in the seventeenth and eighteenth centuries give ample proof of such substantialization. Thus, according to the chemist Pierre Macquer, the virtue of plants rests essentially in their odor.[15] So, "to preserve their odor is to retain their virtue,"[16] and the belief in the effectiveness of a substance is strengthened if it is "accompanied and signalled by a specific odor." In the seventeenth century the physician Charas had inveighed against those who would remove the disagreeable odor from adder's salt, for in so doing they would also be destroying its efficacy.[17] The "guiding spirit" theory propounded by the Dutch physician Hermann Boerhaave holds that each plant and each animal contains a kind of vapor proper to its "spirit" and manifested solely through its savor and, especially, its smell. Highly volatile, the "guiding spirit" quickly dissipates into the air, but since it is indestructible, it preserves its individuality. It is returned via snow, rain, or dew to earth, making the ground fruitful and becoming essence once again:[18] "Exhaled by roses on a spring evening, the odor returns to the rosebush with the morning dew."[19]

Not only have its proponents led so many minds down paths far distant from true scientific knowledge, but odor continues to do more mischief, in Bachelard's view, since "odor can provide substantialism with basic assurances that are later revealed to be actual obstacles to chemical experiment."[20] The discovery of ozone provides a typical example of such a negative role. As early as 1785 the natural philosopher Martin van Marum had demonstrated that an odor (which turned out to be that of ozone) was created when an electric current passed through. He deduced that it was the "odor of the electric matter," a conclusion that was to "imbue experiments with false substantialist liabilities" for some time to come. This deviation was further accentuated by the fact that the smell released in the electricity experiment was the smell of lightning, the same odor present "after heavy summer storms, when the air becomes less heavy, more pleasant to breathe, more balsamic . . . which gives van Marum a cosmic value."[21] Even when the chemist Christian Schönbein began to perceive "the true cause of the electric odor" in 1840 and began looking for some chemical substance, he attempted to reconcile his discovery with the "odorant principle" of substances like chlorine and bromine, and baptized it with the Greek name "ozone," which means "to smell." The overvalue placed on this substance even led some physicians to look for a relationship between its absence or presence and the outbreak or disappearance of certain epidemics, especially cholera. It took nearly a century of groping in the dark and a slow process of "desensualization" to establish the real nature and properties of ozone once and for all.

Although the prescientific mind had regarded odor as an epistemological obstacle, it was to play a positive role in the awakening of man's mind. Bachelard stated: "Had I personally to experience the philosophical myth of Condillac's statue experiencing the primal universe and conscience through smells, rather than say, like it, 'I am the smell of the rose,' I would rather say: 'I am, first, the smell of mint, the smell of water mint.' "[22] The ontological correspondence established between the exhalation of the plant and the breath of life, described as a simple aroma, recalls the myth of the Phoenix, the myth of the fire of aromatic bark and the bird's rebirth at the very brink of death, which is recalled at the beginning of his last, unfinished work.[23] Bachelard, a "philosopher of the iconoclastic" who struggled against "a crafty foe: intuition, sight, form . . . celebrates the sensory qualities of touch . . . connects with the culinary and the odorous."[24] He places great importance on smells—except in the context of science—because of their special links with the imagination and the memory. Dreaming or reverie allows us to recapture the odors in which memories lie encapsulated: "a universe in emanation, an odorous breath objects emit through the intermediary of a dreamer."[25] Indeed, it is this very capacity that explains Nietzsche's aversion to perfumes, a surprising attitude in a philosopher who vigorously reproached his colleagues for their chronic anosmia—their impaired sense of smell. However, according to Bachelard, the "flair" on which Nietzsche so prided himself served only to help him avoid impurities and not to revel in pleasant odors. Only cold and empty air gave him a feeling of youth and liberty: "The Nietzschean imagination abandons odors as it separates itself from the past. Any true sense of the past is redolent with indestructible odors."[26]

Taking up a theme dear to Proust, Bachelard makes odors the guardians of the past, of a past dredged up from the very depths of being, from the farthest limits of memory, nearly timeless. The two writers' methods are strikingly similar. All Combray rises from a cup of tea into which Proust dips a piece of cake one wintry day: The sight of the madeleine had recalled nothing, "but when from a long-distant past nothing subsists, after the people are dead, after the things are broken and scattered, taste and smell alone, more fragile but more enduring, more unsubstantial, more persistent, more faithful, remain poised a long time, like souls, remembering, waiting, hoping, amid the ruins of all the rest; and bear unflinchingly, in the tiny and almost impalpable drop of their essence, the vast structure of recollection."[27] On another occasion, the smell of a wood fire in the chill air of his bedroom, "like an invisible ice-floe detached from some bygone winter," plunges him once again into the "exhilaration of hopes long since abandoned."[28] Even more, the sense of smell makes possible "the commemoration of all that our being has left of itself in minutes long gone by, the intimate essence of ourselves that we emit all unaware but which a perfume once smelled . . . suddenly returns to us."²⁹

Thus, what a once-smelled odor revives for us today is something quite different from some eventful, dated past: It liberates "the permanent and habitually concealed essence of things," and "our true self, which seemed—had perhaps for long years seemed—to be dead but was not altogether dead, is awakened and reanimated as it receives the celestial nourishment that is brought it."³⁰ The same is true for Bachelard: What the memory of a smell awakens in us—living and "poetically useful"³¹—is not part of the world of facts but of the world of dream. For both writers, these singular inner experiences are accompanied by a sensation of happiness. Bachelard was even to borrow an expression of Henri Bosco and write that "a vapor of joy" rose from the memory.³²

Yet the two notions are far from identical. With Proust the intimate values recur involuntarily, thanks to a chance sensation: "And so it is with our own past. It is a labour in vain to attempt to recapture it: all the efforts of our intellect must prove futile. The past is hidden somewhere outside the realm, beyond the reach of intellect, in some material object (in the sensation which that material object gives us), of which we have no inkling. And it depends on chance whether or not we come upon this object before we ourselves must die."³³ Bachelard, on the other hand, sets out to call them up at will by the power of his imagination. He delves into himself, concentrates upon himself, dreams, meditates, and, like "great dreamers who know how thus to breathe in the past,"³⁴ he can then exhale memories and odors: "Odors! The first evidence of our emergence into the world. These memories of by-gone odors can be recaptured by shutting one's eyes. Then, we closed our eyes the better to plumb the depths. We closed our eyes and thus we at once began to dream.

In dreaming well, in dreaming simply in tranquillity, we will find them again."[35] And the "odoral images" will be even more subtle if imagination and memory achieve symbiosis.[36] It is only after a willed process that rejects description and relies solely on dreaming, in a reverie that enables us to "repose" in the past, that we can succeed in evoking the house of our birth, a haven of dreams and odors rather than an actual physical building:

> What good would it do, for example, to give the lay-out of my actual bedroom, to describe the little room at the back of the attic, to say that from its window, across the rooftops, one could see the hills? I alone, in my memories of another century, can open the deep closet that still holds, for me alone, that unique odor, the smell of grapes drying on their wicker tray. The smell of grapes! An odor at the limit, one must imagine hard to smell it."[37]

Analysis and abstract intelligence are powerless to reconstitute beyond the limits of the real past the dreamy regions of intimacy and to home in on their secrets. Visual images are equally inept—too clear—to penetrate that vaguely defined zone of childhood "without proper names and without history."[38] But the imagination that can "teach language to go beyond itself" can also "unseal"[39] vanished worlds and release their perfumes.

Whereas for Proust the sensory impression is necessary to recall the past, a well-chosen word that has retained its odor has the same power for Bachelard: "When we read the poets and find that a whole childhood can be evoked by the memory of an isolated perfume, we understand that smell, in a childhood, in a life, is—if one can use the expression—a vast detail."[40] The precious sublimator of memory, the "nightlight in the bedroom of memory," the "world's root, childhood's truth," odor is primal (even more than in Proust's work, where olfactory sensations—which are the ones most often described—are the only ones privileged to kindle memories). Yet, unlike Fourier, who dreamed of developing a science of aromas, Bachelard, with his scientific rigor and poetic sensitivity, is careful not to confuse the genres, although opinions differ as to whether he actually attempted to establish "the most impermeable of barriers" between them[41] or to combine them in a "kind of polyphony."[42] With great modesty, this "most philosophical of poets and poetic of philosophers"[43] left it to the "great dreamers"—the poets—to evoke the exhalations that can recreate for us "the expanding universes of childhood."[44]

CONCLUSION

▼

Unpleasant smells no longer frighten us. Odors can seduce, but no longer cure. Smells can still be agreeable or disagreeable, but they have lost their powers of life and death. Yet these bald statements should not be taken as representing simplistic views of the history of smells and the sense of smell. The anosmia—the impaired sense of smell—from which our contemporaries suffer is not as recent a phenomenon as we like to think. In his day Aristotle was already complaining that the sense of smell was weakening and that he was unable to exercise his power of smell to the fullest.

As for the repression of smells in our society, this too is a phenomenon with a complex background. For Saint Thomas Aquinas, incense not only had a symbolic function but was also to be used to dispel the unpleasant body odor that filled the churches, "which can provoke disgust."[1] Montaigne felt the same repugnance. As for the drive to deodorize public places, it began in France as early as the sixteenth century, although considerable time went by before the effort was crowned with any success. Nor are disagreeable odors the only ones that have been repressed. The use of pleasant smells for sensual purposes has been condemned by the philosophers of antiquity and by Christian moralists alike. We must set aside the belief that there was once an olfactory past in which the sense of smell reigned triumphant in all things: The environment, highly developed sensory acuity, the importance of intellect, and the powers of smells have all been in decline ever since the dawn of the modern era. The way in which the sense of smell and odors have been perceived by philosophy and medicine reveals important shifts in thinking and contradicts the Manichaean concept that measures our odor-phobic contemporary society against some former odor-philic society in which the sense of smell was given pride of place.

When Antoine-François de Fourcroy, the pioneering French chemist, began to deal with smells toward the end of the eighteenth century, he flatly denounced the errors of antiquity. When it came to smell, the works of the ancient writers contained "nothing but hypotheses, figments of their imagination . . . popular errors, unbelievable data that are impossible to accept." Two authors—Hippocrates and Galen—managed to escape his wrath, which is hardly surprising, for "the best writing on this subject has always been by physicians . . . Observation of nature has been the sole guide of good physicians in this field throughout the centuries, which serves to explain the manifest superiority of their writings on the subject over those of the philosophers of Antiquity."[2] In fact, although philosophers have paid less attention to olfactory questions than have physicians, their analyses have often been more pertinent. However that may be, the important thing is that medicine has always approached the question of smells and their capabilities with a different mind-set.

The centuries-long struggle against the awful threat of the plague is a convincing model. It shows the existence of a real gap between ancient and modern concepts. All of the many therapies based on odors reveal the extraordinary prestige they enjoyed. From antiquity to the end of the nineteenth century, any preventive or curative measure was usually based to a large extent on a use of and improvement in odorous processes and products. Beginning with simple aromatics and ending with strong chemical fumigations, and making use of the most complex, outrageous, and refined concoctions, alternating or mingling pleasant and unpleasant odors and fetid, strong, or pleasant exhalations, the antiplague arsenal was principally made up of smells.

As François Dagognet has shown, ancient medicines, far from being negligible curiosities, are really "true infrastructures that shed light on social groups."[3] They are "logical substances." If this constancy in employing such totally inept (and to us obviously ridiculous) techniques is surprising to a contemporary observer, it was nevertheless faithful to the logic contained in the medical textbooks. As a result, the etiology of the plague was viewed in an olfactory context—hardly surprising, given the fact that for years and years antique or medieval medicine had been forging links between certain odorous emanations and the onset of many diseases. However, upon closer examination we have also seen that the plague itself was thought to be an odor, an essential point that guided opinions on how the disease arose and spread and made logical the choice of aromatherapy (and its offshoots) as the prime and omnipresent method of treatment. That physicians continued to believe in the effectiveness of aromatherapy until the nineteenth century and, in spite of all the obvious failures they experienced, still persisted in attributing the recession or end of each epidemic to it, can only be explained by this concept, which was so deeply rooted in the medical past: The plague *was* smell. The study of the treatment of the disease affords the most detailed illustration of a more general intellectual and practical process: Vital perfumes should be used against deadly exhalations; the extraordinary curative powers that certain effluvia contain are the natural counterparts of the deadly effluvia they combat.

However, although physicians' writings enable us to follow this evolution in therapeutic notions, how can we know that the suggested practices and remedies were actually put to use and became a part of the social image repertoire? One example of the problems created by this question is provided by the contested

history of the "plague costume," whose more-or-less distorted
picture in many plague narratives was described by Antonin
Artaud: "Over the rivulets of thick, noxious blood, the color of
anxiety and of opium, that flow from the cadavers there loom
strange creatures dressed in waxen robes, with glazed eyes and
noses like long pointed beaks, standing on what seem to be
raised Japanese shoes . . . and who move to and fro chanting
ridiculous litanies."[4] Artaud mixes disparate elements: for example, the waxed fabric recommended by Lampérière and the
beaked mask invented by the physician Charles Delorme. In
fact, the mask was only a part of an ensemble of protective
garments made out of Moroccan leather. Was this costume,
created by Delorme in 1619, and in particular the famous protective mask, its sinister beak filled with aromatic herbs, really
worn by plague fighters, especially during the plagues in Rome
in 1656 and the one in Marseilles in 1720? Many texts and
engravings throughout Europe give credence to this. The physicians Bertrand and Fournier, who were present in Marseilles,
were vehement in contradicting such "grotesque" assertions,
which dishonored the medical profession.

On the other hand, cross-checking information often enables us to conclude that the measures prescribed were indeed
carried out. Such was the case with certain methods of disinfection whose violence might make us wonder whether they were
ever actually employed. The "perfuming" of adults with caustic
fumigations is confirmed in the testimony of physicians who
diagnose the death by suffocation of many of their patients and
go on to state that they themselves risked death by submitting to
the same treatment. Similarly, the actuality of the cleansing of
public streets by firing small cannons can be deduced from the
lists of damages caused to dwellings (broken windows, cracked
walls, collapsed buildings) and from the protests to which the
practice gave rise.

In any event, whether the methods it conceived were actually employed or not, medical practice, unlike philosophical reflection, accorded what may appear to us to be an unwarranted importance to olfactory considerations. Olfaction is omnipresent in both theory and practice, the latter of particular importance owing to its repercussions on day-to-day living. From this viewpoint, the powers of smell are not the concern of physicians alone, but of the sick and of the entire population. This is made clear in countless extramedical sources, from Ovid's *Metamorphoses* to Daniel Defoe's *The Journal of the Plague Year,* not to mention Boccaccio's *Decameron,* all of which attest to the fact that popular beliefs were symbiotically linked to medical practice.

How are we to explain the difference in attitude between physicians and philosophers? The first explanation lies in their divergent approaches to the problem. Even if many philosophers, like Aristotle, were interested in biology, and even if many of them were physicians, very few were actual practitioners. Philosophers were principally concerned with evaluating the ontological, cognitive, aesthetic, and ethical aspects of the sense of smell, whereas physicians took a more concrete view, examining the relationships between smell and the body, health, and disease. There are few philosophers for whom the physiological approach, if taken at all, has not been used basically for ontological and moral ends (as in Plato, Aristotle, Descartes, or Kant). Even rarer are those writers like Montaigne or Cabanis who have examined the hygienic and curative effects of exhalations on the "animal economy." True, Cabanis was both a philosopher and a practitioner, and Montaigne was more concerned with questions of therapy. And although they have been unwilling to hand down value judgments, physicians have always been fascinated by effluvia, partly because of what has been called their "substantialist belief." Analysed by Bachelard, this belief, which he held responsible for many prescientific errors, gave rise especially to the contention that odor expresses the actual essence of things.

Medical practice proceeded on the basis of the "sensualist orientation"[5] of science for many years. This is particularly striking with regard to remedies using those medicinal plants whose virtues are closely linked to smell. Whether they were based on an ancient notion or not, in the seventeenth and—especially—the eighteenth centuries, there were many attempts to come up with scientific explanations. To use Fourcroy's words, "his path illuminated by the flame of experimental physics,"[6] physicist Robert Boyle undertook, in the countless experiments described in his book, *De mira effluviorum subtilitate,* to isolate the molecules of smell. The Dutch chemist and philosopher Hermann Boerhaave attempted to fix them in various fluids, concluding that their odor consisted of a principle he dubbed "the guiding spirit," a term taken from alchemy.

The notion that the body, and particular plants, emitted "a kind of vapor . . . impregnated with the constituent nature of the body in which it resides,"[7] guided the work of a great many physicians and chemists. Watery or viscous, the guiding spirit was always characterized as being enormously rarefied, volatile, and expansible—all qualities that led Pierre-Joseph Macquer to suspect that it might perhaps be some special kind of gas.[8] Although it can vary in quantity and strength, some plants being more abundantly provided with it than others, the spirit is present even in apparently odorless plants, which, if cooked in a double boiler, will impart their latent smells to the water. Tracking this volatile component and making it as stable as possible was to become the prime consideration when distilling essential oils. Any victory was bound to be ephemeral, however, for these substances "derive all their specific characteristics from the volatile odorous element they contain, i.e., the guiding spirit . . . and lose those characteristics as they evaporate."⁹ This belief was so solidly entrenched that as late as 1820 Jean-Jacques Virey, in his *Histoire naturelle des medicamens, des alimens et des poisons (Natural History of Medicines, Foods and Poisons),* was able to state flatly that "aromas are proper to the principal virtue of every substance" and that "there are even medicines whose sole efficacity resides in their odor: orange-flowers, lime blossom, the majority of the Labiatae [plants of the mint family], aromatics, antiscorbutics, musk, in all of which loss of effectiveness accompanies loss of odor."¹⁰

The guiding spirit made a slow exit from the scientific scene, and, indeed, continues to haunt artists and writers. Was it what the photographer Joseph Breitenbach captured on film in his extraordinary series of pictures in which he succeeded in materializing the aura of the scents emanating from flowers? Is it not the spirit the hero of Patrick Süskind's novel *Perfume* is trying to appropriate by murdering beautiful young women to collect the quintessence of their being in order to make up a perfume that will give him mastery over men's hearts?

The theory of substantialization, however, does not fully explain the preponderant position accorded smell by the science of medicine in the pre-Pasteur era. There is another belief as well, created by the relationships between odor and blood. Both are regarded as bearers of vital and deadly elements. When unpleasant, smell is a source of disease, epidemic, and death; when pleasant, it fortifies, disinfects, cures. Good blood, "crimson blood," is a life-giving and health-giving medium, and Ambroise Paré believed that there was nothing better for soothing the heart.¹¹ Yet it is also vulnerable to corruption, and it is that internal putridness that can open the organism to outside attack. This twofold concept was expressed by Philippe Hecquet in the middle of the eighteenth century: "True, the blood is life's treasure, but it is also death's—the substratum of the most cruel diseases."[12]

Links between blood and odor are not confined to their shared, contradictory roles; the constancy with which they have been associated throughout history would point toward more than a simple functional parallelism. A study of the methods used to combat the plague has revealed both the preponderant role played by aromatherapy and the accompanying recourse to phlebotomy. The body, healed and reinvigorated by "perfumings," was simultaneously drained of its superfluous or tainted blood by bleedings—a two-part operation with a compensatory purpose, the healing odors replacing, as it were, the contaminated body fluid. The entire evolution of medical treatments using perfumes was based on the desiccating and anticorrupting powers of aromatics, which had been recognized since antiquity. The "fiery element" is not subject to decay; it can combat the threat of putridness.

Indeed, there is frequent reference to its use in the preparation of Egyptian mummies. The philosopher Girolamo Fracastoro explicitly uses that example to explain the action of odorous substances on contagious "germs." However, the mummy, which provides the most concrete example of the substitution of odor for blood, is not just a theoretical reference: It was also an actual remedy. "True" or "false," African or European, the subject of underworld trafficking and violent polemics, "mummy" was prescribed from the Middle Ages through the eighteenth century for the treatment of a whole spectrum of diseases, from leprosy to plague. Among the recipes Paracelsus recommends to those who cannot procure true "liquor of mummy" is one that includes human blood and goes by the revealing names "Balm of Balms" or "Secret of the Blood." This marriage of blood and scent, of which mummy is an extreme example, can be compared with the notion that the effective element of blood is an aromatic spirit that "guards its arcana by which sicknesses are removed, as spottes from linens by soap."[13] A century earlier, Cornelius Agrippa had already described it as a "vapour of the bloode, subtile, pure, brilliant, aerie and unctuous,"[14] terms oddly reminiscent of those used to describe the guiding spirit of aromatic plants.

Religious rites and the odor of sanctity reveal equally close ties between blood and scent. Their mingled effluvia rise up from altars to the heavens, while here on earth the saint's corpse, emitting its marvelous odor (like the mummified body), "is the giver of life and health."[15] And these concordances drawn from the history of religion can also be found in myths, where sap and blood are often capable of generating each other. Sap changes into blood or gives birth to creatures of flesh and blood; spilled blood turns into flowers or trees. The diversity of the societies that secreted these images enables us to draw obvious conclusions. We are not engaged in a comparative interpretation of myths, but merely in observing that these vital principles, animal and plant, are widely believed to perform interchangeable functions. All of which suggests that mythical discourse, with its linking of blood and incense, expresses a basic identification between the two. We now have a new explanation of the prodigious power accorded perfumes in the past: Incense is blood, charged as it is with the mysterious forces of life. Despite the passage of time, during which the original underlying logic has been forgotten, the powers still attributed to scent in Western societies still bear that faded but indelible imprint.

While smell's relationship to blood helps to explain the important powers given to it in former societies, recent scientific research has also established a link between the powers of smell and the human body. Today, however, this does not concern the blood, but, rather, certain secretions called pheromones.

These odorous substances secreted by the body have been observed in many animal species and act like chemical signals to trigger sexual, parental, or social behavior. The sex pheromones in certain mammals, the pig and the monkey in particular, have also been isolated in man. Recent experiments allow us to theorize that such pheromones can influence human behavior just as they do animal.

These discoveries have opened a whole new field of research for perfume makers, who have always dreamed of creating a truly aphrodisiac product. Seductive perfumes containing pheromones are already on the market in the United States, in Great Britain, and in Japan. Andron eau de colognes, one for women and another for men, are purportedly able to "create an intensive magnetic field between the sexes" and silently to transmit inviting signals to the subconscious. In France, too, there has been a great deal of publicity for a perfumed product that incorporates "a molecular complex for maximal attraction," rumored to be capable of seducing anyone within a radius of at least nine and a half meters. The accompanying brochures also describe the way to counter the sexual attraction should it exceed reasonable bounds.

Although the effectiveness of perfumes using pheromones has yet to be verified, the appearance of such substances on the market has led to a reexamination of ancient perfumes purported to arouse the affections. The province of alchemists, they sometimes included (in addition to musk and civet) strange elements like blood and animal or human urine. Some specialists today believe that the civetone secreted by the para-anal gland of the civet cat is a sex pheromone and that the same is true of the muskone emitted by the preputial gland of the male deer. In addition, however, some mammalian sex pheromones are thought to have a chemical similarity with the odorous steroids also to be found in urine. Even human urine owes part of its inherent odor to a pheromone (delta-2 androsterone-one-17). Such scientific discoveries may provide an a posteriori explanation—and, indeed, justification—for the ancient compounds that could still be found in use as late as the eighteenth century and that have always hitherto been regarded as mere alchemistic oddities.

At the conclusion of this investigation into the realm of the sense of smell and of scents and odors, from antiquity down to the present time, there are still unanswered questions with regard to the true significance of the existing silence that surrounds smell in our societies. Paradoxically, far from evidencing a general indifference to smell, the silence is a betrayal of our hypersensitivity, for never have so-called unpleasant or bad odors been so systematically pursued. The repression is especially evident with regard to bodily odors. The increase in odor phobias in the most industrialized countries is probably the most remarkable expression of this uneasiness about bringing the subject of odor out into the open. Today's ideal is the realization of bodies and spaces which, if not totally without odor, are at least odor neutralized by perfumes that mask their natural smells. In any event, today's sensitivity is basically negative; it is not counterbalanced by a culture rooted in and enjoying a rich and diverse olfactory environment that is conducive to sustaining, developing, and educating the sense.

Recently, however, we have witnessed the tentative emergence of a new interest in the olfactory. In France, for example, some games based on smell have been developed, and in the realm of education various attempts have been made to awaken the sense of smell; a growing number of courses in wine tasting have been made available to the general public, and at the new Cité des Sciences at La Villette, in Paris, an "Odorama" has been set up in which images and smells are combined—all parts of the new movement favoring education of the sense of smell, hitherto the almost exclusive domain of perfume manufacturers and oenologists.

A similar trend has emerged in Japan, especially around the reawakened passion for "Kodo," the incense ceremony. This highly refined form of entertainment consists in recognizing the odors of different aromatic woods and other scented compounds by burning them and associating them with literary themes. An extremely ancient practice (it dates from the sixth century and reached its high point among the seventeenth-century aristocracy), Kodo has reemerged today after a long period of comparative neglect, and is enjoying extraordinary devotion and considerable popularity.

This rediscovery of scent is also evident in the health field. After a long period of neglect, there has recently been a renewed interest in treatments using aromatic plants. A new "instinctotherapy" has emerged that purports to prevent (and even cure) various complaints by encouraging the patient to be guided exclusively by the sense of smell in making dietary choices. Such practices, insofar as they fall outside the control of the medical profession, which views them as regressive and unscientific, have been met with strong opposition and, indeed, hostility. However, the development of a modern aromatherapy is high on the agenda in many countries. We are witnessing the emergence of a "neo-Hippocratism"[16] bent on finding a rational use of the resources provided by nature. Today, the beneficial effects of aromas are being put to many highly progressive uses, particularly in Japan. In an attempt to improve working conditions and improve production, large companies are beginning to install equipment to emit refreshing and relaxing odors into the workplace, varying them according to the time of day.[17]

In addition, a great deal of research is being done to develop new forms of medicines that can be administered nasally. The highly vascular makeup of the nasal mucuous membrane facilitates the entry of medicines directly into the bloodstream, thereby bypassing the liver, which destroys, breaks down, or eliminates an important part of many active substances. Special experiments are being carried out in the fields of contraceptives and antidiuretics and in the treatment of endometriosis, fibrous tumors, and hormonal-dependent cancers.

The renewed interest in smell is also reflected in the work being done in determining whether various serious diseases may be contracted via the olfactory passages and in investigating pathological emanations. Some American scientists have advanced the hypothesis that certain conditions like Parkinson's or Alzheimer's disease may be caused by a substance carried to the brain through the olfactory canals. Richard Doty, director of the Taste and Smell Center at the University of Pennsylvania School of Medicine, has also suggested that the act of smelling can carry to the brain noxious agents such as the polio virus and perhaps even larger molecules.[18]

Various other experiments have justified and lent support to the field of olfactory diagnostics. In addition to the practitioner's sense of smell, however, emphasis has now also been laid on the much more acute senses of certain animals. Kathleen Smith and Jacob Sines have observed that rats are able to distinguish the disagreeable odor emitted by the sweat of schizophrenics from the odor of the sweat of the mentally healthy at a concentration as low as 0.0001, while human subjects are able to distinguish the same samples at concentrations of 0.005.[19] Some psychiatrists have even admitted that this highly unique odor, which is present in acute cases of the disease, is a determining diagnostic factor.[20] Similarly, the work of Hubert Montagner has enabled him to establish that the canine sense of smell makes dogs extremely keen detectors of human emotions and can even be used to sniff out, as it were, certain pathological states, like psychoses. Autistic and psychotic children give off exhalations that are repellent to dogs. Confronted with two dummies, one dressed in underwear impregnated with the odor of a psychotic child and the other in the underwear of a "normal" child, the animal will very obviously avoid the former. Should such results be confirmed, the dog might well become a valuable tool for detecting psychic deficiencies in children as well as problems with metabolic and endocrinal functions, since the endocrine glands that emit odors are dependent on the autonomic nervous system.

Far from being restricted by advances in scientific knowledge, the powers and uses of smell enrich and even inspire new developments. With that in mind we can readily appreciate the alacrity with which some perfume manufacturers have seized upon the discovery of pheromones to develop purportedly aphrodisiac perfumes. The persistence of the olfactory imagination often proves to be firmly rooted in reality, as demonstrated by one highly important recent discovery: It has been found that aromatic molecules are one of the basic components of the interstellar space in which new stars are constantly being formed. This interstellar "atmosphere" or gas is also the almost-direct source of the atoms of which we ourselves, along with the earth and the other planets, are made.[21] The results of the "Arome" experiment carried out by the French National Center for Scientific Research (CNRS), using a stratosphere balloon furnished by the National Center for Space Studies, reflect the nineteenth-century theories of Charles Fourier, who intuitively sensed the importance of aromas in the formation of the universe and envisaged an "aromal movement" by which the germs of created species were produced and the stars controlled. Hardly mere sterile speculation, the insights of the utopian philosopher anticipated the results reported by contemporary astrophysicists by nearly two hundred years, proof positive that account must be taken of the existence and power of the olfactory imagination.

NOTES

▼

PART ONE. FROM PERFUMED PANTHER TO GERMAN
BROMIDROSIS: THE POWERS OF SMELL TO REPEL
AND ATTRACT

Chapter 1. Smell and Capture

1. Cf., Lucian, *Lucius* or *The Ass;* Apuleius, *Metamorphoses.*
2. Lucian, op. cit.
3. Testimony of Father du Pont, in Michel de Certeau, *La Possession de Loudun* (Paris: Gallimard, 1980), p. 50.
4. Cf., François de Rosset, *Les Histoires tragiques de notre temps* (1620) (Lyons, 1685), p. 56.
5. Pierre de Lancre, *L'Incrédulité et Mécréance du sortilège* (Paris, 1622), p. 73.
6. Cf., Henri Boguet, *Discours des sorciers* (Lyons, 1602), pp. 243–244.
7. Cf., I. de Nynauld, *De la lycanthropie* (Paris, 1615), p. 48.
8. Laurent Catelan, *Rare et curieux discours de la Plante appelée Mandragore . . .* (Paris, undated), p. 31.
9. Pierre de Lancre, op. cit., p. 72.
10. François Azouvi, "La Peste, la mélancolie et le diable, ou l'imaginaire réglé," *Diogène,* No. 108 (October–December 1979), pp. 130–131.
11. Jean Bodin, "Jean Bodin au lecteur salut," in *De la démonomanie des sorciers* (Vol. I, 1580).
12. H. C. Agrippa, *La Philosophie occulte* (1531), Vol. I (The Hague, 1727), p. 111.
13. Cf., Georges Mucherey, *Magie astrale des parfums* (Paris: Librairie Leymarie, 1971).

14. Cf., Lucienne A. Roubin, "Perspectives générales de l'exposition hommes parfums et dieux," *Le Courrier du Musée de l'Homme,* No. 6 (November 1980).

15. Cf., Remy Chauvin, *Le Comportement social chez les animaux* (Paris: P.U.F., 1973), p. 63.

16. Cf., Yveline Leroy, *L'Univers odorant de l'animal* (Paris: Boubée, 1987), pp. 48–51.

17. Cf., Ernest Schoffeniels, *Physiologie des régulations* (Paris: Masson, 1986), pp. 74–75.

18. Cf., Remy Chauvin, "Le Langage des odeurs," *Le Figaro* (December 30, 1985).

19. Cf., Yveline Leroy, op. cit., p. 97.

20. Cf., Ernest Schoffeniels, op. cit., p. 75.

21. Cf., Jean D. Vincent, *Biologie des passions* (Paris: Editions Odile Jacob, 1986), p. 267.

22. Cf., P. Langley-Danysz, "La Truffe, un aphrodisiaque," *La Recherche,* No. 136 (September 1982), p. 1059.

23. Ernest Schoffeniels, op. cit., p. 75; Yveline Leroy, op. cit., p. 307; on the vomeronasal organ, cf., infra., pp. 278–279; H. Montagner, quoted by Guy Lazorthes, *L'ouvrage des sens* (Paris: Flammarion, 1986), pp. 74–75; M. Stoddart, "La Chimie de l'amour," *La Recherche,* No. 213 (September 1989), p. 1079.

24. Auguste Galopin, *Le Parfum de la femme et le sens olfactif dans l'amour* (Paris, 1886), p. 157.

25. Wilhelm Fliess, *Les Relations entre le nez et les organes génitaux de la femme* (1897), translated from the German by P. Ach and J. Guir (Paris: Le Seuil, 1977), p. 24.

26. Cf., Collet, *L'Odorat et ses troubles* (Paris, 1904), p. 51; R. Jouet, "Troubles de l'odorat," in *Bulletin d'oto-rhino-laryngologie* (Paris: Ballière, 1912); Sigmund Freud, *Civilization and Its Discontents* (1929), translated by James Strachey (London: W. W. Norton & Company, 1961).

27. Cf., Sigmund Freud, op. cit., p. 53.

28. Cf., J. Le Magnen, *Odeurs et parfums* (Paris: P.U.F., 1961), p. 54.

29. Marcel Proust, *"The Cities of the Plain,"* in *Remembrance of Things Past,* Vol. II, translated by C. K. Scott Mancrieff and Terence Kilmartin (New York: Random House, 1922), p. 733.

30. Petronius, *The Satyricon,* translated by J. P. Sullivan (New York: Penguin Classics, 1965), p. 145.

31. Cf., Marcel Detienne, *Les Jardins d'Adonis, La Mythologie des aromates en Grèce* (Paris: Gallimard, 1972), pp. 172–181; and Georges Dumézil, *Le Crime des Lemniennes* (Paris, 1924), pp. 13, et seq.

32. Cf., H. Wiener, "External Chemical Messengers—II. Natural History of Schizophrenia," *New York State Journal of Medicine* (1967), p. 1154.

33. Cf., F. H. Connolly and N. L. Gittleson, "The Relationship between Delusions of Sexual Change and Olfactory and Gustatory Hallucinations in Schizophrenia," *The British Journal of Psychiatry,* 199 (1971), pp. 443–444.

34. Cf., Sigmund Freud, *Five Psychoanalytic Case Studies;* K. Abraham, *Oeuvres complètes,* Vol. I (Paris: Payot, 1965), pp. 90–98; H. Wiener, "External Chemical Messengers—III. Mind and Body Schizophrenia," *New York State Journal of Medicine* (1967), p. 1288.

35. Hubertus Tellenbach, *Goût et atmosphère* (Paris: P.U.F., 1983), p. 118.

36. Cf., William Pryse-Phillips, "Disturbance in the Sense of Smell in Psychiatric Patients," *Proceedings of the Royal Society of Medicine,* Vol. 68 (1975), pp. 472–473.

37. Hubertus Tellenbach, op. cit., p. 106.

38. I Kings, 10:10–12.

39. E. G. Gobert, "Tunis et les parfums," *La Revue africaine* (1961–1962), p. 61.

40. Esther, 2:12.

41. Judith, 10:3–4.

42. William Shakespeare, *Antony and Cleopatra,* Act II, Scene 2.

43. Solange Petit-Skinner, "Nauru ou la civilisation de l'odorat," *Objets et Mondes,* Vol. 16, No. 3 (1976), unpaginated.

44. Cf., Lucien Lévy-Bruhl, *La Mentalité primitive* (Paris, 1922), p. 352.

45. Cf., Andre Georges Haudricourt, "Note d'ethnozoologie: le rôle des excrétats dans la domestication," *L'Homme*, XVII (2,3) (April–September 1977), p. 125.

46. Cf., Solange Petit-Skinner, op. cit.

47. Cf., B. Jullierat, "Mélanésie," *Le Courier du Musée de l'Homme*, No. 6 (November 1980), unpaginated.

48. Cf., Luc Bouquiaux, "L'Arbre ngbè et les relations amoureuses chez les Ngbaka," *Langage et culture africaine* (Paris: Maspero, 1977), pp. 106–107.

49. Aristotle, *Problems,* Vol. I, Book XIII (London: Heineman, Loeb Classical Library), pp. 307–308.

50. Cf., André J. Festugière, "Le bienheureux Suso et la panthère," in *Revue de l'histoire des religions,* No. 191 (Paris: P.U.F., 1977), p. 82.

51. Theophrastus, *De causis plantarum,* VI.5.2 (Leipzig, 1821), p. 363.

52. Aelian, *On the Characteristics of Animals,* Vol. 40, translated from Greek by A. FF. Scholfield (London: Heineman, Loeb Classical Library, 1958), p. 335.

53. Cf., M. Detienne, op. cit., pp. 164–165.

54. *Physiologus,* edited by F. Sbordone (Milan-Rome, 1936), p. 61.

55. Ibid.

56. Ibid.

57. *The Ashmolean Bestiary* (named after the well-known English collector Elias Ashmole, 1617–1692, and now in the Bodleian Library, Oxford. It dates from the late twelfth or early thirteenth century).

Chapter 2. Smell and Discrimination

1. Cf., Pierre Debrary-Ritzen, *Psychologie de la création, de l'art des parfums à l'art littéraire* (Paris: Albin Michel, 1979), p. 66.

2. Jean-Paul Sartre, *Baudelaire* (Paris: Gallimard, 1963), p. 221.

3. Cf., Jacques Le Magnen, *Odeurs et parfums* (Paris: P.U.F., 1961), p. 116.

4. Cf., H. Montagner, *L'Attachement. Les débuts de la tendresse* (Paris:

Odile Jacob, 1988), p. 122. See also: Andre Holley, "La perception des odeurs," *La Recherche,* No. 58 (July–August 1975), p. 630; Rene Diatkine, "Fécondation in vitro, congélation d'embryons et mère de substitution," in *Actes du colloque génétique, procréation et droit,* Hubert Nyssen, editor (Arles: Actes Sud, 1985), p. 282.

5. Cf., Remy Chauvin, pp. 113–114.

6. Cf., Henri Piéron, "Contribution à l'étude du problème de la reconnaissance chez les fourmis," *Extrait des comptes rendus du 6e Congrès international de zoologie,* Berne Session, 1904, pp. 483–490.

7. Cf., Gale Peter Largey and David Rodney Watson, "The Sociology of Odors," *American Journal of Sociology,* Vol. 77 (1972), p. 1027.

8. Cf., Ruth Winter, *Le Livre des odeurs,* (Paris: Le Seuil, 1978), p. 50.

9. Auguste Galopin, *Le Parfum de la femme et le sens olfactif dans l'amour* (1897), translated from the German by P. Ach and J. Guir (Paris: Le Seuil, 1977), p. 111.

10. Cf., Boleslaw Prus, *Lalka* (Warsaw: Governmental Publishing House, 1969), p. 68.

11. Georg Simmel, *Mélanges de philosophie relativiste* (Paris: F. Alcan, 1912), p. 36.

12. Ernst Bloch, "Le Temps de la peste, mensurations politiques, le Vormärz" (1830–1848), *Change,* Paris, Edition Seghers/Laffont, No. 37 (March 1978), pp. 96–97.

13. Dr. Bérillon, "La Bromidrose fétide des Allemands," in *Bulletin et mémoires de la Société de médecine de Paris* (Paris, 1916), pp. 142–145.

14. Cf., Georges Deschamps, "Dégoûts . . . et des couleurs," *Sporting* (January 31, 1917).

15. Ibid.

16. Ibid.

17. Georg Simmel, op. cit., p. 34.

18. Louis Speleers, *Traduction, index et vocabulaire des textes des pyramides égyptiennes* (Brussels, 1934), p. 89.

19. Job, 19:17–18.

20. Cf., Louis Golding, *The Jewish Problem* (London, 1938), p. 59. See also C. Klineberg, *Race Differences* (New York, 1935), p. 130.

21. Cf., Andre Corbin, *Le Miasme et la Jonquille. L'odorat et l'imaginaire sociale, 18e-19e siècles* (Paris: Aubier-Montaigne, 1982), p. 170.

22. Cf., Guillaume de Nangis, *Chronique latine de 1113 à 1300,* with *La Continuation de cette Chronique de 1300 à 1368* (Paris: H. Géraud, 1843), pp. 31–35.

23. *Traité de la peste avec remèdes certains et approuvés pour s'en préserver et garantir. Nouvellement faict par le collège des maistres chirurgiens de Paris* (Paris, 1606), p. 13.

24. Angelus Sala, *Traité de la peste* (Leyden, 1617), p. 33.

25. Cf., Victor Laval, *Des Grandes épidémies qui one régne à Nîmes* (Nîmes, 1876), p. 117.

26. Cf., Maurice de Toulon, *Le Capucin charitable enseignant la méthode pour remédier aux grandes misères que la peste a coutume de causer permi les peuples* (Paris, 1662), p. 115.

27. Philipe Hecquet, *Traité de la peste òu, en répondant au questions d'un médecin de Province sur les moiens de s'en préserver ou d'en guérir, on fait voir le danger des barraques et des infirmeries forcées, avec un problème sur la peste pour un médecin de la Faculté de Paris* (Paris, 1722), pp. 2145, et. seq.

28. The terms are those used by Garnier. Cf., Jean Garnier, *Une visite à la voirie de Montfaucon* (Paris, 1844), p. I.

29. L. Roux, *De Montfaucon, de l'insalubrité de ses établissements et de la nécessitieé de leur suppression immédiate* (Paris, 1841), pp. 18, et seq.

30. Ibid., pp. 12–13.

31. Ibid., p. 25.

32. Dominique Champault, "Maghreb et Proche-Orient," *Le Courier du Musée de l'Homme,* op. cit., No. 6. (November 1980).

33. John Dollard, *Caste and Class in a Southern Town* (New York: Doubleday, 1957), p. 381.

34. Cf., William Brink and Louis Harris, *The Negro Revolution in America* (New York: Simon and Schuster, 1969), p. 141.

35. Georg Simmel, op. cit., p. 34.

PART TWO. THE STENCH OF PESTILENCE

1. Jean Ruffié and Jean-Claude Sournia, *Les Epidémies dans l'histoire de l'homme* (Paris: Flammarion, 1984), p. 81.
2. Jean-Henri Baudet, *Histoire de la médecine* (Dumerchez-Naoum, 1985), p. 57.
3. See, for example, the preface to the Italian translation of Alain Corbin's book, *Le Miasme et la Jonquille. L'odorat et l'imaginaire social, 18e–19e siècles* (Paris: Aubier-Montaigne, 1982), in which Piero Camporesi mentions some of the links between the plague, corruption, and smell, particularly in seventeenth-century prophylaxis. See also Jamine Bazin, *L'Evolution du costume du médecin de peste en Europe de 1348 à 1720* (Paris: EMU, 1971).

Chapter 1. The Deadly Powers of Smell

1. Cf., Mirko Drazen Grmek, "Les Vicissitudes des notions d'infection, de contagion et de germe dans la médecine antique," in *Textes médicaus latins et antiques* (Saint-Étienne: Centre J. Palerme, 1984), p. 65.
2. Cf., Hippocrates, *On the Nature of Man; On winds.*
3. Cf., Lucretius, *On Nature.*
4. Seneca, *Physical Investigations,* Vol. I, Book II, LIII.
5. Ibid., VI, XXVIII.
6. Cf., Rufus of Ephesus, *Works.*
7. Philo of Alexandria, *De aeternitate mundi.*
8. Claude Galen, *De febrium differentiis.*
9. Consultation on the epidemic among members of the Faculté de Médecine de Paris in 1348, cited in Henri Emile Rébouis, *Étude historique et critique de la peste* (Paris, 1888), p. 77.
10. Cf., Pierre Rainssant, *Advis pour se préserver et pour se guérir de la peste de ceste année 1668* (Rheims, 1668), p. 5.
11. Thomas Sydenham, *Practical Medicine* (1685).
12. Daniel Defoe, *A Journal of the Plague Year* (New York: The Modern Librray, Random House, 1948), p. 568.

13. Ibid., p. 574.

14. Ibid.

15. Ibid., p. 569.

16. Jean Fournier, *Observations sur la nature et le traitement de la fièvre pestilentielle ou la peste avec les moyens d'en prévenir ou en arrêter les progrès* (Dijon, 1777), p. 104.

17. Ibid., p. 94.

18. Cf., Jean–Baptist Bertrand, *Relation historique de la peste de Marseille en 1720, nouvelle édition corrigée de plusieurs fautes* (Amsterdam, 1779), p. 22.

19. Richard Mead, "Traité de la peste" (1720), in John Howard, *Histoire des principaux lazarets de l'Europe, accompagnée de différens mémoires relatifs à la peste, aux moyens de se préserver de ce fléau destructeur et aux différens modes de traitement employés pour en arrêter les ravages* (Paris, Year IX), p. 284.

20. Ibid., p. 249.

21. Ibid., p. 250.

22. Antonio Laurent de Lavoisier, "Mémoire sur la combustion des chandelles dans l'air atmosphérique et dans l'air éminemment respirable" (1777), in *L'Air et l'Eau* (Paris, 1923), p. 63.

23. Jean-Jacques Ménuret de Chambaud, *Essai sur l'action de l'air dans les maladies contagieuses qui a remporté le prix proposé par la Société Royale de Médecine* (Paris, 1781), p. 17.

24. Ibid., p. 47.

25. Jean-Jacques Ménuret de Chambaud, *Essai sur l'histoire médico-topographique de Paris ou Lettres à M. d'Aumont, professeur en médecine à Valence, sur le climat de Paris, sur l'état de la médecine, sur le caractère et le traitement des maladies et particulièrement sur la petite vérole et l'inoculation* (Paris, 1786), p. 31.

26. Danilo Samoilowitz, *Mémoire sur la peste qui, en 1771, ravagea l'Empire de Russie, surtout Moscou, la capitale, et où sont indiqués des remèdes pour la guérir et les moyens de s'en préserver* (Paris, 1783), p. XIX.

27. Jean-Noël Hallé, *Recherches sur la nature et les effets du méphitisme des fosses d'aisances* (Paris, 1785), p. 11.

28. Alain Corbin, *Le Miasme et la Jonquille. L'odorat et l'imaginaire sociale, 18e-19e siècles* (Paris: Aubier Montaigne, 1982), p. 123.

29. "Rapport fait à l'Académie Royale des Sciences le 17 mars 1780 par MM Duhamen, de Montigny, Le Roy, Tenon, Tillet et Lavoisier, rapporteur," in *Mémoires de l'Académie des Sciences,* 1780, Lavoisier, *Oeuvres,* Vol. III, pp. 492, 493.

30. *Rapport des commissaires chargés par l'Académie de l'examen du projet d'un nouvel Hôtel-Dieu,* by MM. de Lassone, Daubenton, Tenon, Lavoisier, Laplace, Coulomb, d'Arcet, Bailly, rapporteur, Ibid., p. 647.

31. Pierre A. Garros, *Défense du gymnase devant la justice et les hommes éclairés,* Year IV, p. 48.

32. Stephen Hales, *Plant Statistics and Analysis of the Air. New Experiments presented before the Royal Society, London,* translated into French by Buffon (Paris, 1735), p. 221.

33. Emile Pingeron, "Lettre sur les agréments de la vie champêtre," translation into French in *Sentimental Magazine* (June, 1773), published in *Recueil de différens projets tendans au bonheur des citoyens* (Paris, 1789), pp. 146–147.

34. Joseph H. Pott, *Des éléments ou essai sur la nature, les propriétés, les effets et l'utilité de l'Air, de l'Eau, du Feu et de la Terre,* Vol. I (Paris, 1782), p. 43. See also A. Corbin, op. cit., p. 93.

35. Jean-Baptiste T. Baumes, *Essai d'un système chimique de la science de l'homme* (Nîmes, 1798), p. 92.

36. "Rapport des mémoires et projets pour éloigner les tueries de l'intérieur de Paris," by MM. Daubenton, Tillet, Lavoisier, Laplace, Coulomb, d'Arcet, Bailly, rapporteur, in *Mémoires de l'Académie des Sciences,* 1787, Lavoisier, *Oeuvres,* Vol. III, p. 585.

37. Cf., Jacques Guillerme, "Le Malsain et l'économie de la nature," *Dix-huitième siècle,* No. 9 (1977), p. 66.

38. Cf., Prus, *Rapport à l'Académie Royale de Médecine sur la peste et les quarantaines fait au nom d'une commission, accompagné de pièces et documents et suivi de la discussions dans le sein de l'Académie* (Paris, 1846), p. 25.

39. Cf., "Discussion dans le sein de l'Académie de Médecine, séance

du 14 juillet 1846, opinion de M. Pariset," in Prus, ibid., pp. 935, et seq.

40. François Laurent, *Copies de mémoires présentés à S.M.I. Napoléon III, empereur des français* (Montmédy, 1858), p. 25.

41. Ibid., p. 16.

42. M. Rouffiandis, "Théories chinoises sur la peste," in *Annales d'hygiène et de médecine coloniales* (Paris, 1903), p. 342.

43. Cf., Marguerite Dupire, "Contagion, contamination, atavisme. Trois concepts Sereer-ndut (Sénégal)," *L'Ethnographie* (Paris, 1985), pp. 123–139.

44. Carmen Bernand, "Idées de contagions dans les représentations et les pratiques andines," *Bulletin d'ethnomédecine,* No. 20 (March 1983), p. 12.

45. Ibid., p. 13.

46. Lucretius, *De Naturam.*

47. Diemerbroeck, quoted by Jean-Jacques Manget, *Traité de la preste recueilli des meilleurs auteurs anciens et modernes et enrichi de remarques et observations théoriques et pratiques* (Geneva, 1721), p. 35.

48. Jean Fournier, op. cit., p. 10.

49. Lucretius, op. cit.

50. Ibid.

51. Michel de Montaigne, "Of Smells," in *The Essays of Montaigne,* translated by Donald M. Frame (Stanford, California: Stanford University Press, 1957), p. 801, et seq.

52. Jean Fournier, op. cit., pp. 15–16.

53. "Mandement de l'évêque de Marseille," in J.-P. Papon, *De la peste ou les époques mémorables de ce fléau et les moyens de s'en préserver,* Vol. I (Paris, 1800), p. 42.

54. Jean Fournier, op. cit., p. 14.

55. Saint John Chrysostome, *Homilies ou sermons* (Paris, 1665), pp. 360–361.

56. Quoted by Alain Corbin, op. cit., p. 276.

Chapter 2. The Curative Powers of Smell

1. Claude Galen, *Ad pisonem de theriaca*, p. 281.

2. Rufus of Ephesus, *Works*, p. 439.

3. Cf., Claude Galen, *De febrium differentiis*, p. 294.

4. Cf., A. Couques, "Mahomet, les parfums et les cosmétiques colorants," *Presse Médicale*, Nos. 25–26 (March 13–15, 1940), pp. 5–6.

5. Jean Michot, "L'Épître d'Avicenne sur le parfum," *Bulletin de philosophie médiévale*, Vol. 20, No. 20 (1978), p. 56, et seq.

6. Consultation on the epidemic among members of the Faculté de Médecine de Paris in 1348, cited in H. E. Rébouis, *Étude historique et critique de la peste* (Paris, 1888), p. 131.

7. Olivier de La Haye, p. 80.

8. Ibid., p. 82.

9. Ibid.

10. Cf., Consultation on the epidemic, op. cit., p. 135.

11. Olivier de La Haye, op. cit., p. 80.

12. Ibid., p. 79.

13. Cf., E. Launert, *Scent and Scent Bottles* (London: Barrie and Jenkins, 1974), p. 39.

14. Consultation on the epidemic, op. cit., p. 137.

15. Olivier de La Haye, op. cit., p. 146.

16. Consultation on the epidemic, op. cit., pp. 137–139.

17. Ambroise Paré, *Traité de la peste, de la petite vérole et rougeole* (Paris, 1568), p. 44.

18. Consultation on the epidemic, op. cit., p. 119.

19. Cf., Marsile Ficin, *Antidote des maladies pestilentes* (Cahors, 1595), pp. 76, et seq.

20. Ibid., p. 74.

21. Ibid., p. 55.

22. Ibid., p. 16. Cf., Georges Vigarello, *Le Propre et le Sale. L'hygiène du corps depuis le Moyen Age* (Paris: Le Seuil, 1985), p. 42.

23. Ibid., p. 80.

24. Ibid., p. 55.

25. For the "cleansing" role of perfumes, cf., Georges Vigarello, op. cit., pp. 97–102.

26. Ogier Ferrier, *Remèdes, préservatifs et curatifs de peste* (Lyons, 1548), p. 52, et seq.

27. Henri de la Cointe, *Rapport des médecins d'Amiens sur les ayriements qui se doivent faire des maisons et meubles infectés en la dite ville* (Amiens, 1634), p. 45.

28. Ibid., pp. 44–45.

29. M. E. Alvarus, *Sommaire des remèdes tant préservatifs que curatifs* (Toulouse, 1628), p. 27. Cf., J.-N. Biraben, *Les Hommes et la Peste en France et dans les pays européens et méditerranéens*, Vol. I (Paris-The Hague: Mouton, 1975–1976), p. 15.

30. Henri de la Cointe, op. cit., pp. 43, et seq.

31. Cf., Angelus Sala, "Traité de la peste" (Leyden, 1617), pp. 21, et seq.

32. Cf., François Ranchin, "Traité de la peste," in *Opuscules ou traités divers et curieux en médecine* (Montpellier, 1640), p. 237.

33. Du François, *Traité de la peste, de ses remèdes et préservatifs* (Paris, 1631), p. 69.

34. Jean de Lampérière, *Le Traité de la peste, de ses moyens et de sa cure* (Rouen, 1620), p. 165.

35. David Jouysse, *Examen du livre de Lampérière sur le sujet de la peste* (Rouen, 1622), p. 267.

36. Ibid., p. 268.

37. Jean de Lampérière, op. cit., p. 412.

38. Ibid., p. 413.

39. David Jouysse, op. cit., p. 289.

40. Arnaud Baric, *Les Rares Secrets ou remèdes incomparables, préservatifs et curatifs, contre la peste des hommes et des animaux, dans l'order admirable intérieur et extérieur du désinfectement des personnes, des animaux et des étables* (Toulouse, 1646), pp. 65, et seq.

41. Ibid., p. 46.

42. François Ranchin, op. cit., pp. 273, et. seq.

43. Ibid., p. 262.

44. Jean-Baptist Bertrand, *Relation historique de la peste de Marseille en*

1720, nouvelle édition corrigée de plusieurs fautes (Amsterdam, 1779), p. 372.

45. Janin de la Combe-Blanche, *L'Antiméphitisme ou Moyens de détruire les exhalaisons pernicieuses et mortelles des fosses d'aisances, l'odeur infecte des égouts, celle des hôpitaux, des prisons, des vaisseaux de guerre, etc.* (Paris, 1782), p. 24.

46. Cf., Louis Reutter de Rosemont, *Histoire de la pharmacie à travers les âges,* Vol. I (Paris, 1931), p. 541.

47. Cf., Louis de Serre, *Les Oeuvres pharmaceutiques de Sr. Jean de Renou, conseiller et médecin du Roy à Paris; augmentés d'un tiers en cette second édition par l'Auteur, puis traduits, embellies de plusieurs figures nécessaires à la connaissance de la médecine et pharmacie et mises en lumière* (Lyons, 1626), p. 433.

48. Louis Guyon, *Les Diverses Leçons divisées en cinq livres contenant plusieurs histoires, discours et faits mémorables, recueillis des auteurs grecs, latins, français, italiens, espagnols* (Lyons, 1625), pp. 22, et seq.

49. Cf., William R. Dawson, "Mummy as a Drug," *Proceedings of the Royal Society of Medicine,* 21 (1928), p. 35.

50. Louis Reutter de Rosemont, op. cit., p. 543.

51. Pierre Belon, *Les Observations de plusieur singularités et choses mémorables trouvées en Grèce, Asie, Judée, Egypte, Arabie et autres pays estranges, rédigées en trois livres* (Paris, 1553), p. 118.

52. Ambroise Paré, "Discourse de la mumie," in *Oeuvres complètes,* Vol. 3 (Paris: J. F. Malgaigne, 1841), pp. 479, et seq.

53. Cf., Louis Guyon, op. cit., pp. 24–25.

54. Jerome Cardan, *Da la subtilité, et subtiles inventions, ensemble les causes occultes et raisons d'icelles,* edition of 1550, translated from Latin into French by Richard le Blanc (Paris, 1556), p. 359.

55. Ambroise Paré, "Discourse de la momie," op. cit., p. 482.

56. Ibid.

57. Ibid., See also the slight variant in the 1579 edition, p. 481, note 2.

58. Louis Reutter de Rosemont, op. cit., p. 575.

59. Cf., La Martinière, *L'Heureux Esclave ou relation des aventures du sieur de la Martinière* (Paris, 1674), p. 119.

60. Louis de Serre, op. cit., p. 433.

61. Ibid., p. 434.

62. Pierre Pomet, *Histoire générale des drogues traitant des plantes et des animaux et des minéraux,* Vol. I (Paris, 1694), p. 7. See also N. Lémery, *Traité universel des drogues* (Paris, 1698), p. 509.

63. Philippus Aureolus Theophrastus Bombastus Paracelsus, *The Fourteen Books of Summaries of Outstanding Secrets,* translated from Latin into French by C. de Sarcilly (Paris, 1631), p. 15.

64. Paracelsus, *La Grande Chirurgie* (1536), translated from Latin into French by Josquin d'Alhem (Lyons, 1953), pp. 147, et seq.

65. Cf., D. Becker, *Medicus Microcosmus* (London, 1660), p. 293.

66. Cf., Louis Pénicher, *Traité des embaumements selon les Anciens et les Modernes avec une description de quelques compositions balsamiques et odorantes* (Paris, 1666), p. 250.

67. Ibid., pp. 252–253.

68. Ibid., p. 263.

69. Louis Pénicher, op. cit., pp. 270–271.

70. Cf., M. de Sevelinges, "Observation sur les effets de la Momie d'Égypte, par M. de Sevelinges, docteur en médecine à S. Étienne en Foretz," *Journal de Médecine, Chirurgie, Pharmacie* (September 1759), pp. 224–227. Cf., M. Mareschal de Rougières, "Lettre de M. Mareschal de Rougères, Maître en chirurgie à Plancoët en Bretagne, contenant quelques observations sur les effets de la Momie," *Journal de Médecine, Chirurgie, Pharmacie* (May 1767), pp. 466–469.

71. Cf., *Dictionnaire raisonné universel de Matière Médicale* (Paris, 1773), p. 161.

72. Cf., Prus, *Rapport à l'Académie Royale de Médecine sur la peste et les quarantaines fait au nom d'une commission, accompagné de pièces et documents et suivi de la discussions dans le sein de l'Académie* (Paris, 1846), pp. 221–222.

73. Articles 614 and 615 of the regulations set forth in Prus, op. cit., p. 221.

74. "Réponse de M. de docteur Clot-Bey aux questions posées par le Ministère anglais en 1839," in Prus, op. cit., p. 388.

75. Cf., L. Aubert-Roche, *De la peste ou typhus d'Orient* (Paris, 1843), p. 37.

76. Ibid.

77. Henri Vincenot, *La Vie quotienne des paysans bourguignons au temps de Lamartine* (Paris, Hachette), 1976, p. 149.

78. François-Vincent Raspail, *Histoire naturelle de la santé et de la maladie chez les végétaux et chez les animaux en général, et en particulier chez l'homme, suivie du formulaire d'une nouvelle méthode de traitement hygiénique et curatif,* Vol. 2 (Paris, 1843), p. 520.

79. Ibid., 1860 edition, Vol. 3, p. 65.

80. Ibid., 1843 edition, Vol. 2, p. 523.

81. Ibid., p. 526.

82. Ibid.

83. Ibid., p. 452.

84. Jean-Jacques Virey, *Histoire naturelle des médicaments, des aliments et des poisons, tirés des trois règnes de la nature* (Paris, 1820), p. 61.

85. Cf., Theophile de Bordeu, *Recherches sur les maladies chroniques* (1775), in *Oeuvres complètes,* preceded by a note on his life and works by M. le Chevalier Richerand (Paris, 1820), p. 979; Brieude, "Mémoire sur les odeurs que nous exhalons, considérées comme signes de la santé et de la maladie," *Histoire de la Société de Médecine et de Physique médicale pour la même année,* Vol. X (Paris, 1789).

86. Ernest Monin, *Les Odeurs du corps humain* (1885), (Paris, 1903), p. 10.

87. Ibid., p. 16.

88. Ibid., p. 8.

PART THREE. BLOOD AND INCENSE: A SEARCH FOR THE SOURCE OF PERFUME'S POWER

1. A. Dechambre, *Dictionnaire encyclopédique des sciences médicales* (Paris, 1878), p. 146. For the origin of perfumes in fables, see supra, pp. 17, et seq.

2. Cf., Albertus Magnus, *Secrets merveilleux de la Magie naturelle et cabalistique du Petit Albert, traduit exactement sur l'Original latin, intitulé: Alberti Parvi Lucii, Lebellus de mirabilibus Naturae Arcanis, Enrichi de figures mystérieuses et la manière de les faire*, new, corrected, and augmented edition (Lyons, 1729), pp. 87–90.

3. Cf., P. V. Piobb, *Formulaire de haute magie* (Paris, 1937), p. 243.

4. Heinrich Cornelius Agrippa, *La Philosphie occulte* (1531), Vol. I (The Hague, 1727), p. 115.

5. James G. Frazer, *The Golden Bough* (1890–1915), abridged edition (New York: The Macmillan Publishing Company, 1922), p. 109.

6. Cf., W. Atallah, "Un rituel de serment chez les Arabes Al-Yamin Al-Gamus," *Arabica*, Vol. 20, No. 1 (1973), p. 70.

Chapter 1. Blood, Incense, and the Sacred

1. Cf., S. Mayassis, *Architecture, Religion, Symbolisme*, Vol. 1 (Athens: B.A.O.A., 1964), p. 115.

2. Cf., William Kaufman, *Le Grand Livre des parfums* (Paris: Minerva Vilo, 1974), p. 35.

3. Cf., A. Erman and H. Ranke, *La Civilisation égyptienne* (1952) (Paris: Payot, 1976), pp. 682–683.

4. Ibid., p. 679.

5. Entry entitled "Parfum," *Grand Dictionnaire du XIXe* (Geneva: Larousse, 1982).

6. Herodotus, *The Histories*, translated by Aubrey de Sélincourt, revised, with an introduction and notes by A. R. Burn (New York: Viking Penguin 1954), p. 145.

7. Cf., Louis Reutter de Rosemont, *Histoire de la pharmacie à travers les âges*, Vol. I (Paris, 1931), p. 23.

8. Cf., Louis Vincent Thomas, *Le Cadavre. De la biologie à l'anthropologie* (Paris: Editions Complexe, 1980), pp. 142–152.

9. A. Erman, *La Religion des Égyptiens* (1907) (Paris: Payot, 1982), p. 210.

10. Cf., Jean-Claude Boyon, *Rituels funéraires de l'ancienne Égypte. Le*

rituel de l'embaumement. Le rituel de l'ouverture de la bouche. Les Livres des respirations (Paris: Editions du Cerf, 1972), p. 43.

11. Cf., L. Dérobert, H. Reichlen, J.-P. Campana, *Le Monde étrange des momies* (Paris: Pygmalion, 1975), p. 23.

12. Cf., Jean-Claude Boyon, op. cit., pp. 45, et seq.

13. Ibid., p. 165.

14. Exodus 30:34–36.

15. Exodus 30:1–11.

16. Exodus 30:23–25.

17. Numbers 16:31–33.

18. Exodus 29:19–21. See also Leviticus 8:1–7.

19. Leviticus 4:5–8.

20. Exodus 29:36–37 and 30:10.

21. Exodus 24:5–8; Mark 14:22–25.

22. Genesis 17:12–13. See also Exodus 4:25–26.

23. Leviticus, 17:11.

24. Cf., Christian Duverger, *La Fleur léthale. Économie du sacrifice aztèque* (Paris: Le Seuil, 1979), p. 165.

25. Cf., Fray Bernardino de Sahagun, *Histoire générale des choses de la Nouvelle Espagne* (1547–1590) (Paris: F. Maspero, 1981), p. 100.

26. Ibid., pp. 106–107.

27. Cf., Christian Duverger, op. cit., p. 134.

28. F. Bernardino de Sahagun, op. cit., p. 103.

29. Cf., Georges Dumas, "L'Odeur de sainteté," *La Revue de Paris* (November 1907), p. 534.

30. Jean Collin de Plancy, *Dictionnaire critique des reliques et des images,* Vol. 2 (Paris, 1821), pp. 358–359.

31. Plutarch, *Opera moralia,* Vol. VII.

32. Lucian, *True History.*

33. Cf., Michel Aubrun, "Caractères et portée religieuse des 'Visiones' en Occident du VIe au XIe siècle," in *Cahiers de civilisation médiévale* (Poitiers, 1980), p. 117.

34. Cf., Jean Goubert and Louis Christiani, *Les Plus Beaux Textes de l'au-delà* (Paris: La Colombe, 1950), p. 316.

35. Cf., Hubert Larcher, *Le Sang peut-il vaincre la mort?* (Paris, Gallimard, 1957), p. 196.

36. Bollandistus, *Acta Sanctorum* (1643), No. 1047. See also Hubert Larcher, op. cit., p. 27.

37. Cf., Hubert Larcher, op. cit., p. 196.

38. M. Charbonnier, *Maladies et facultés des mystiques* (1874), pp. 43–44.

39. Cf., Georges Dumas, op. cit., p. 544.

40. Ibid., p. 205.

41. Ibid., pp. 221–222.

42. Hubert Larcher, op. cit., p. 222.

Chapter 2. Life Principles: Blood and Incense

1. Leviticus 17:11.

2. S. Mayassis, *Le Livre des morts de l'Égypte ancienne est un livre d'initiation* (Athens: BAOA, 1955), p. 325.

3. Empedocles, in *The Presocratics* (Paris: Gallimard, 1968) p. 416.

4. Deuteronomy 12:23.

5. James George Frazer, *The Golden Bough* (1890–1915), abridged edition, (New York: The Macmillan Publishing Company, 1922), p. 266.

6. Cf., J. Chelhold, *Le Sacrifice chez les Arabes* (Paris: P.U.F., 1955), p. 103.

7. Cf., William Robertson Smith, *The Religion of the Semites* (London, 1927), p. 133.

8. Cf., L. E. de Païni, *La Magie et le Mystère de la femme* (Paris, 1928), p. 271.

9. James George Frazer, op. cit., p. 127.

10. Cf., Georges Maspero, "Le Conte des deux frères," in *Les Contes populaires de l'Égypte ancienne* (Paris: Maisonneuve et Larose, 1967), p. 25.

11. Cf., U. Harva, *Les Représentations religieuses des peuples altaïques* (Paris: Gallimard, 1959), p. 99.

12. James George Frazer, op. cit.

13. *La Quête du Graal* (Paris: Le Seuil, 1965), p. 256.
14. Cf., Georges Raynaud, *Le Popul-Vuh, les dieux, les héros et les hommes de l'ancien Guatemala d'après les Livre du Conseil* (Paris: Maisonneuve et Larose, 1980), pp. VIII and IX, et seq.
15. Cf., William Robertson Smith, op. cit., p. 427.

PART FOUR. THE PHILOSOPHICAL NOSE

Passages quoted in this section were taken from the following texts:

Chapter 1. The Ambivalent Status of the Sense of Smell and Odors in Greco-Latin Philosophy

1. Cf., Aristotle, "De Sensu et sensili," in *Parva Naturalia.*
2. Cf., Theophrastus, *Enquiry into Plants and Minor Works on Odours and Weather Signs,* Greek text and English translation by B. Einarson and G.K.K. Link (London: Loeb Classical Library, 1976), p. 331.
3. Cf., Plato, "Timaeus," in *The Collected Dialogues,* edited by Edith Hamilton and Huntington Cairns, Bollingen Series LXXI, (Princeton, N.J.: Princeton University Press, 1961), p. 1190.
4. Cf., Aristotle, *Problemata.*
5. Cf., Plato, op. cit., p. 1190.
6. Cf., Aristotle, *De Anima.*
7. Cf., Aristotle, "De Sensu et sensili."
8. Lucretius, *On the Nature of Things.*
9. Cf., Aristotle, *De Anima.*
10. Plato, op. cit., p. 1191.
11. Aristotle, "De Sensu et sensili."
12. Plato, "The Republic," in *The Collected Dialogues,* op. cit., p. 799.
13. Aristotle, "De Sensu et sensili," op. cit.; see also Aristotle, *Nicomachean Ethics.*
14. Cf., Aristotle, "De Sensu et sensili," op. cit..
15. Aristotle, *Nicomachean Ethics.*

16. Cf., Lucretius, op. cit.
17. Cf., M. Conche, *Epicure, lettres et maximes* (Villers-sur-Mer: Editions de Mégare, 1977), p. 30.

Chapter 2. The Influence of Christianity in the Devaluation of the Sense of Smell and Odors

1. Song of Songs 1:13, et seq.
2. John 12:1–8.
3. Epistle to the Galatians 5:16–19.
4. Peter, First Epistle General 3:3–5.
5. Clément Romain, *Les Deux Épîtres aux vierges* (circa 96 A.D.) (Paris, 1853), p. 141.
6. Ibid., p. 143.
7. Tertullian, *La Toilette des femmes,* translation by M. Turcan (Paris: Editions du Cerf, 1971), pp. 101–103.
8. Ibid., p. 167.
9. Ibid., p. 143.
10. Ibid., p. 101.
11. Ibid., p. 117.
12. John Chrysostom, *Homilies or Sermons.* The subject is also raised by Paul in 2 Corinthians 2:15–17.
13. J. Chrysostom, ibid., p. 362.
14. Saint Bernard of Clairvaux, *Letters.*
15. Saint Thomas Aquinas, (1266–1274). "The Human Soul," in *Summa Theologica.*
16. Cf., Thomas Aquinas, "The Resurrection," ibid.
17. Genesis, 27:27.
18. Cf., Thomas Aquinas, "The Eucharist," ibid.

Chapter 3. Montaigne and Odors

1. Jean-Noël Biraben, *Les Hommes et la Peste en France et dans les pays européens et méditerranéens,* op. cit., p. 48.
2. Cf., Lucien Febvre, *Le Problème de l'incroyance au XVIe siècle* (Paris: Albin Michel, 1962), pp. 461–462.

3. Cf., Michel de Montaigne, "Essays," in *The Complete Works of Montaigne,* translated by Donald M. Frame, (Stanford, California: Stanford University Press, 1957), p. 443.

4. Ibid., p. 228.

5. Pierre Moreau, *Montaigne* (Paris: Hatier, 1966), p. 52.

6. François Dagognet, *La Maîtrise du vivant* (Paris: Hachette, 1988), p. 29.

Chapter 4. The Alliance of Rationalism and Christian Thought in Depreciating the Sense of Smell and Odors in the Seventeenth Century

1. Cf., René Descartes, "Les Principes de la philosophie" (1644), in *Oeuvres et lettres,* edited by A. Bridoux (Paris: Gallimard, 1953), p. 657.

2. René Descartes, "Traité de l'homme" (1664), ibid., p. 827.

3. René Descartes, "Sixièmes réponses" (1641), ibid., p. 562.

4. Emile Bréhier, *Histoire de la philosophie moderne* (Paris: P.U.F., 1960), p. 72.

5. René Descartes, "Deuxième méditation" (1641), op. cit., p. 280–281.

6. René Descartes, "Sixième méditation," op. cit., p. 333.

7. Nicolas Malebranche, *De la recherche de la vérité ou l'traité de la nature de l'esprit et de l'homme et de l'usage qu'il en doit faire pour éviter l'erreur dans les sciences* (1678), edited by G. Rodis-Lewis, Vol. I, Book I, X (Paris: Vrin, 1962), p. 129.

8. Nicolas Malebranche, *Entretiens sur la métaphysique et sur la religion. Entretiens sur la mort* (1696), edited by A. Robinet, Book IV, XV (Paris: Vrin, 1965), p. 100.

9. Cf., Odile Arnold, *Le Corps et l'âme* (Paris: Le Seuil, 1984), p. 139.

10. Jean-Baptiste Bossuet, *Traité de la concupiscence* (1693–1694) (Paris, 1879), p. 8.

11. Ibid., pp. 13–14.

12. Saint Alphonse Marie de Liguori, *A Help in Sorrow.*

13. Alphonse Marie de Liguori, *The True Spouse of Jesus Christ.*

Chapter 5. Rehabilitation of the Sense of Smell in the Age of Enlightenment

1. Julien Offray de La Mettrie, *Histoire naturelle de l'âme* (1745), (Oxford, 1747), p. 349.

2. Claude Adrien Helvétius, *De l'homme, de ses facultés intellectuelles et de son éducation* (1772) (Liège, 1774), p. 135.

3. Etienne Bonnot de Condillac, "Traité des sensations" (1754), in *Oeuvres philosophiques* (Paris: P.U.F., 1947), p. 222.

4. Ibid., p. 239.

5. Ibid., p. 224.

6. François Dagognet, preface to Condillac's *Traité des animaux* (Paris: Vrin, 1987), p. 10.

7. Denis Diderot, "Lettres sur les sourds et muets" (1751), in *Premières oeuvres,* Vol. 2 (Paris: Editions Sociales, 1972), p. 99.

8. Cf., Denis Diderot, "Lettres sur les aveugles à l'usage de ceux qui voient" (1749), in *Oeuvres* (Paris: Gallimard, 1951), p. 819.

9. Denis Diderot, "Lettre à Mademoiselle de la Chaux" (1751) in *Correspondance* (1713–1757), edition established, annotated, and prefaced by G. Roth (Paris: Editions de Minuit, 1955), pp. 118–119.

10. Jean-Jacques Rousseau, "Emile, ou De l'éducation" (1762), in *Oeuvres complètes,* Vol. IV (Paris: Gallimard, 1969), p. 370.

11. Ibid., p. 370.

12. Georges-Louis Leclerc (Comte de Buffon), "Histoire naturelle des animaux" (1753), in *Oeuvres philosophiques,* edited by J. Piveteau (Paris: P.U.F., 1954), p. 331.

13. Ibid., p. 415.

14. Ibid., p. 325.

15. Ibid., p. 326.

16. Jean-Jacques Rousseau, "Discours sur l'origine et les fondements de l'inégalité parmi les hommes" (1754), in *Oeuvres complètes,* Vol. III (Paris: Gallimard, 1969), p. 140.

17. ———, "Emile, ou De l'éducation," ibid., pp. 416–417.

18. ———, "Discours sur l'origine . . . ," ibid., p. 142.

19. ———, "Emile . . . ," ibid., p. 416.
20. ———, "Discours sur l'origine . . . ," ibid., p. 144.
21. ———, "Emile . . . ," ibid., p. 415.
22. ———, "Discours . . . ," ibid., p. 158.
23. ———, "Emile . . . ," ibid., p. 416.
24. Ibid.
25. Cf., Thomas Hobbes, *Elements of Law, Natural and Politic* (1649–1658).
26. Jean-Jacques Rousseau, "Lettre du 15 décembre 1763 au Prince de Wurtenberg," in *Lettres philosophiques* (Paris: Vrin, 1974), p. 123.
27. ———, "Emile . . . ," op. cit., p. 416.
28. Ibid., p. 418.
29. Pierre Jean Georges Cabanis, "Rapports du physique et du moral" (1802), in *Oeuvres complètes* (Paris: P.U.F., 1956), p. 226.
30. Ibid., pp. 228, et seq.
31. ———, op. cit., p. 555.
32. ———, op. cit., pp. 570–571.

Chapter 6. Kant and Hegel: An Antisocial and Unaesthetic Sense

1. Immanuel Kant, *Anthropologie in pragmatischer Hinsicht* (1798), p. 40.
2. Ibid., p. 39.
3. Ibid., p. 37.
4. Ibid., p. 40.
5. Ibid.
6. Immanuel Kant, *Kritik der Urtheilskraft* (1790).
7. Kant, *Anthropologie in pragmatischer Hinsicht,* op. cit., p. 40.
8. Ibid., pp. 40–41.
9. Cf., I. E. Borowski, R. B. Jachmann, E. A. Wasianki, *Kant intíme,* translated from the German by J. Mistler (Paris: Grasset, 1985), p. 52.
10. Jean C. de La Metherie, *De l'homme considéré moralement, de ses moeurs et de celles des animaux,* Vol. 2 (Paris, 1802), p. 294.
11. Cf., supra, pp. 277, et seq.

12. Cf., infra, pp. 260–261, Cabanis's physiological analysis.
13. J. C. de la Metherie, op. cit., p. 294.
14. Cf., Georg Wilhelm Friedrich Hegel, *Aesthetics* (1832), translated S. Jankélévitch, Vol. I. (Paris: Flammarion, 1979), pp. 66–69.
15. Ibid., Vol. III, p. 140.
16. Ibid., p. 139.
17. Ibid., pp. 137–138.
18. Ibid., p. 136.
19. Ibid., p. 140.
20. Ibid., p. 138.
21. Ibid., p. 139.
22. Ibid.
23. Ibid., Vol. I., p. 192.

Chapter 7. Two Philosophers with "Nose": Feuerbach and Nietzsche

1. Ludwig Feuerbach, "Leçóns sur l'essence de la religion dans son rapport à *L'Unique et sa propriété*" (1841), in *La Nouvelle Critique* (April 1955), p. 29.
2. ———, "L'Essence du christianisme dans son rapport à *L'Unique et sa propriété*" (1841), in *Manifestes philosophiques,* translated by L. Althusser (Paris: P.U.F., 1960), p. 207.
3. Friedrich Engels, *Ludwig Feuerbach et la fin de la philosophie classique allemande* (1888) (Paris: Editions Sociales, 1979), p. 41.
4. Ludwig Feuerbach, "Contribution à la critique de la philosophie d'Hegel" (1839), in *Manifestes philosophiques,* op. cit., p. 15.
5. ———, "Principes de la philosophie de l'avenir" (1843), in ibid., p. 159.
6. Ibid., p. 194.
7. Ludwig Feuerbach, "L'Essence du christianisme . . . ," op. cit., p. 208.
8. ———, "Principes de la philosophie . . . ," op. cit., pp. 196, et seq.
9. Friedrich Nietzsche, *The Anti-Christ* (1888).
10. ———, *Zur Genealogie der Moral* (1887).

11. ———, *Twilight of the Idols* (1888).
12. ———, *The Anti-Christ*, op. cit.
13. ———, *Twilight of the Idols*, op. cit.
14. Cf., Arthur Schopenhaueer, *The World as Will and Idea*.
15. Ibid.
16. Ibid.
17. Friedrich Nietzsche, *Zur Genealogie der Moral*.
18. ———, *Ecce Homo*.
19. ———, *Wille zur Macht*.
20. ———, *Twilight of the Idols*.
21. Jean Bollack and Henri Wismann, *Héraclite ou la séparation*, Fragment 7 (Paris: Editions de Minuit, 1972), p. 77.
22. Friedrich Nietzsche, *Ecce Homo*, op. cit.
23. ———, *Twilight of the Idols*.
24. ———, *Beyond Good and Evil*.
25. ———, *Ecce Homo*, op. cit.
26. ———, *Twilight of the Idols*, op. cit.
27. ———, *Ecce Homo*, op. cit.
28. ———, *Zur Genealogie der Moral*, op. cit.
29. ———, *Ecce Homo*, op. cit.
30. ———, *The Anti-Christ*, op. cit.
31. ———, *Zur Genealogie der Moral*, op. cit.
32. Ibid.
33. Friedrich Nietzsche, *Ecce Homo*, op. cit.
34. Ibid.
35. Friedrich Nietzsche, *Twilight of the Idols*.

Chapter 8. Freud and Marcuse: The "Organic Sublimation" and "Surrepression" of the Sense of Smell

1. Sigmund Freud, *The Complete Letters of Sigmund Freud to Wilhelm Fliess* (1887–1907), translated and edited by Jeffrey Moussaieff Masson (Cambridge, Mass., and London, Eng.: The Belknap Press of Harvard University Press, 1985), p. 180.
2. Cf., Charles Darwin, *The Descent of Man, and Selection in Relation to Sex* (1871).

3. Sigmund Freud, op. cit., p. 279.

4. ———, *Civilization and Its Discontents*, translated by James Strachey (New York and London: W.W. Norton & Company, 1961), p. 50.

5. Ibid., p. 48.

6. Jacques Lacan, *L'Identification*, Seminar 1961–1962 (unpublished).

7. Herbert Marcuse, *Eros and Civilization* (New York: Vintage Books, 1962), p. 36.

Chapter 9. From Philosophy to Poetry: Fourier, Bachelard, and Proust

1. Michel Serres, *Les Cinq Sens* (Paris: Grasset, 1985), p. 23.

2. Maurice Pradines, *Traité de psychologie générale* (1943–1950) (Paris: P.U.F., 1958), p. 513.

3. Jean Jaurès, *De la réalité du monde sensible* (Paris, 1891), p. 198.

4. Cf., Suzanne Oleszkiewicz-Debout, *Le Dictionnaire des philosophes*, Vol. 1 (Paris: P.U.F., 1984), p. 948.

5. Gaston Bachelard, *Fragments d'une poétique du feu* (Paris: P.U.F., 1988), p. 75.

6. Claud Pellarin, *Vie de Fourier* (1839), 5th edition (Paris, 1871), pp. 32–33.

7. Charles Fourier, "Théorie des quatre mouvements et des destinées générales" (1808), in *Oeuvres complètes*, Vol. I (Editions Anthropos, 1966–1970), p. 30.

8. ———, "Théorie de l'Unité universelle" (1822), in ibid., Vol. IV, pp. 31, et seq.

9. ———, ibid., Vol. IV, p. 242.

10. ———, ibid., Vol. II, p. 192.

11. Cyrano de Bergerac, "Histoire comique des états et empires de la Lune" (1649), in *Voyages fantastiques aux états et empires de la Lune et du Soleil* (Paris: Editions L.C.L., 1967), p. 29.

12. Gaston Bachelard, *La Formation et l'esprit scientifique: contribution à une psychanalyse de la connaissance objective* (Paris: Vrin, 1938), p. 115.

13. Ibid., p. 102.
14. Ibid., p. 115.
15. Cf., Macquer, *Elements de chymie pratique,* Vol. 2 (Paris: 1751), p. 54.
16. Gaston Bachelard, *La Formation de l'esprit scientifique* . . . , op. cit., p. 116.
17. Cf., Charas, *Nouvelles Expériences sur la vipère* (Paris, 1669), p. 168.
18. Cf., Herman Boerhaave, *Elements de chymie,* translated from Latin by J.N.S. Allamand, Vol. 1 (Leyden, 1752), p. 494.
19. Gaston Bachelard, *La Formation de l'esprit scientifique* . . . , op. cit., p. 117.
20. Ibid., p. 118.
21. Gaston Bachelard, *Le Matérialisme rationnel* (Paris: P.U.F., 1952), p. 220.
22. ———, *L'Eau et les Rêves. Essai sur l'imagination de la matière* (Paris: José Corti, 1940), p. 10.
23. Cf., Gaston Bachelard, *La Poétique de la rêverie* (Paris: P.U.F., 1960), p. 121; Bachelard, *Fragments d'une poétique du feu,* op. cit., p. 75.
24. François Dagognet, *Gaston Bachelard, sa vie, son oeuvre, avec un exposé de sa philosophie* (Paris: P.U.F., 1965), p. 51.
25. Gaston Bachelard, *L'Eau et les Rêves* . . . , op. cit., p. 11.
26. ———, *L'Air et les Songes. Essai sur l'imagination du mouvement* (Paris: José Corti, 1943), p. 158.
27. Marcel Proust, *Remembrance of Things Past,* Vol. I, translated by C. K. Scott Moncrieff and Terence Kilmartin (New York: Random House, 1981), pp. 50–51.
28. Ibid., Vol. III, p. 19.
29. Marcel Proust, *Jean Santeuil,* Vol. II (Paris: Gallimard, 1952), p. 306.
30. ———, *Remembrance of Things Past,* Vol. III, op. cit., p. 906.
31. Gaston Bachelard, *La Poétique de l'espace* (Paris: P.U.F., 1957), p. 33.
32. ———, *La Poétique de la rêverie,* op. cit., p. 122.
33. Marcel Proust, *Remembrance of Things Past,* Vol. I, op. cit., pp. 47–48.

34. Gaston Bachelard, *La Poétique de la rêverie*, op. cit., p. 119.
35. Ibid., p. 118.
36. Ibid., p. 121.
37. Gaston Bachelard, *La Poétique de l'espace*, op. cit., p. 31.
38. ———, *La Poétique de la rêverie*, op. cit., p. 118.
39. ———, *Fragments d'une poétique du feu*, op. cit., p. 64.
40. ———, *La Poétique de la rêverie*, op. cit., p. 123.
41. Pierre Quillet, *La Dictionnaire des philosophes*, Vol. I, p. 187.
42. François Dagognet, op. cit., p. 63.
43. François Verhesen, quoted by M. J. Lefebvre, "De la science des profondeurs à la poésie des cimes," *Critique* (January 1964), p. 28.
44. Gaston Bachelard, *La Poétique de la rêverie*, op. cit., p. 120.

Conclusion

1. Saint Thomas Aquinas, "The Eucharist," in *Summa Theologica*.
2. A. F. de Fourcroy, *L'Art de connaître et d'employer les medicaments dan les maladies qui attaquent le corps humain*, Vol. I (Paris, 1785), pp. 261–262.
3. François Dagognet, *La Raison et les Remèdes. Essai sur l'imaginaire et le réel dans la thérapeutique contemporaine* (Paris: P.U.F., 1952), p. 25.
4. Antonin Artaud, "Le Théâtre et la peste," *La Nouvelle Revue*, No. 253 (October 1934), p. 490.
5. Gaston Bachelard, *La Formation de l'esprit scientifique: contribution à une psychanalyse de la connaissance objective* (Paris: Vrin, 1938), p. 117.
6. Antoine-François de Fourcroy, op. cit., p. 261.
7. Hermann Boerhaave, *Elemens de Chimie* (1732), Vol. I, translated from Latin by J.N.S. Allamand and augmented by P. Tarin (Paris, 1754), p. 156.
8. Cf., Antoine-François de Fourcroy, *Elemens d'histoire naturelle et de chimie* (1782), Vol. IV (Paris, 1786), p. 77.
9. P. J. Macquer, *Dictionnaire de chimie contenant la théorie et la pratique de cette science, son application à la physique, à l'histoire naturelle, à la médecine et à l'économie animale*, Vol. I (Paris, 1766), p. 592.

10. Jean-Jacques Virey, *Histoire naturelle des medicamens, des alimens et des poisons* (Paris, 1829), pp. 49–50.

11. Ambroise Paré, "Discours de la licorne," in *Oeuvres complètes*, Vol. 3 (Paris: J. F. Malgaigne, 1841), p. 509.

12. Philippe Hecquet, *La Médecine, la chirurgie et la pharmacie des pauvres* (Paris, 1740).

13. Nicolas de Locques, *Les Vertus magnétiques du sang. De son usage interne et externe pour la guérison des maladies* (Paris, 1664), p. 45.

14. Henrich C. Agrippa, *La Philosophie occulte* (1531) Vol. I (The Hague, 1727), p. 115.

15. Piero Camporesi, *La Chair impassible* (1983), translated from Italian by Monique Aymard (Paris: Flammarion, 1986), p. 7.

16. Cf., J. Valnet, *Aromathérapie* (1964) (Paris: Maloine, 1984), p. 15.

17. Cf., *Japan Economy Newspaper* (July 25, 1989).

18. Cf., Richard L. Doty, Patricio F. Reyes, and Tom Gregor, "Presence of Both Odor Identification and Detection Deficits in Alzheimer's Disease," *Brain Research Bulletin*, Vol. 18, No. 5 (1987), p. 599. See also, Sandra Blakeslee, "Pinpointing the Pathway of Smell," *The New York Times* (October 4, 1988), p. C6.

19. K. Smith and J. Sines, "Demonstration of a Peculiar Odor in the Sweat of Schizophrenic Patients," *Archives of General Psychiatry*, Vol. 2 (1960), p. 188.

20. Cf., H. S. Posner, R. Culpan, and A. Stewart, "Cause of the Odor of a Schizophrenic Patient," *Archives of General Psychiatry*, Vol. 7 (1962), pp. 108–113. See also, K. Skinner, K. Smith, and E. Rich, "Bacteria and the 'Schizophrenic Odor,' " *American Journal of Psychiatry* (1964), pp. 121, 64. See also Harry Wiener, "External Chemical Messengers—I. Emission and Reception in Man," *New York State Journal of Medicine* (December 15, 1966), pp. 3165–3166.

21. Alain Omont, "Les molécules aromatiques du milieu interstellaire," in *Aux Frontières de la Science, La Recherche* (October 1989), p. XXXVI.

TRANSLATOR'S NOTE

▼

Problems unique to the subject matter of this book led to frequent calls on friends and colleagues for help during the course of its translation. I should particularly like to thank Germaine Amiel, Nicole Ball, and Robert Guertin, who were unfailingly generous with their time and assisted me over many obstacles; Gérard Témin and Serge Dosogne, who always managed to find an elegant solution to my dilemmas; and, lastly, Betty Teslenko, who has stood as "godmother" to this translation since its inception and whose sharp eyes and ears and valuable suggestions have saved me from many errors. I am very grateful to them all.

R.M.

INDEX

▼

ABOUT THE AUTHORS

▼

ANNICK LE GUÉRER was born in Paris and educated at the Sorbonne, where she studied philosophy and received her doctorate in cultural anthropology. She is currently doing research for a book on Mesmer and "magnetism." She lives in Paris and Burgundy.

RICHARD MILLER has translated many works of French literature, criticism, and philosophy, as well as a number of plays, most recently *The Function* and *Marie Hasparren* by Jean-Marie Besset. He lives in Paris.